U.N. JIGSAW

U.N. JIGSAW

Wilfrid Grey

VANTAGE PRESS
New York

U.N. photographs reprinted with permission.

Published by Vantage Press, Inc.
516 West 34th Street, New York, New York 10001

Manufactured in the United States of America
ISBN: 0-533-13079-4

Library of Congress Catalog Card No.: 99-93593

0 9 8 7 6 5 4 3 2

For Rowena

We travel together passengers on a little spaceship dependent on its vulnerable reserves of air and fuel: all committed for our safety to its security and peace, preserved from annihilation only by the care, the work and, I will say the love we give our craft.

We cannot maintain it, half fortunate, half miserable, half confident, half despairing in a liberation of resources undreamed of until this day. No craft, no crew can travel safely with such vast contradictions. On their resolution depends the survival of us all.

—Adlai Stevenson

Contents

List of Photos

Preface

I was just eight years old when I was shocked to find out that my country, England, was on the brink of war. It was 1938, the year of the Munich crisis in Europe. Eventually the crisis was resolved, but the integrity and independence of Czechoslovakia was sacrificed to buy an uneasy peace. The U.N.'s predecessor, the League of Nations, could do nothing. A year later Germany invaded Poland and World War II had begun. At a very young age I had learned that world peace is a precarious business and can never be taken for granted.

There followed six long years of the world at war. My peaceful childhood came abruptly to an end. I was terrified when in 1940 a bomb exploded a few hundred yards from the house where I was living. Then in 1945 I lived through the bombardment of London by pilotless flying bombs and rockets. Flying bombs were especially frightening because you never knew when their fuel would run out, and they would crash to earth and explode.

At first I worried we might lose the war. Then the battles on the Russian front seemed to rage endlessly. I was afraid that at any time a telegram would come to say my father had been killed fighting in the deserts of Libya and Egypt. I did not see him for five years. Fortunately he survived and came home. But for my sister and myself, nothing could make up for his long absence during those childhood years.

Then came the most devastating moment in my experience of the world at war. The atomic bomb was dropped on Japan. I remember I was standing in a country lane on a warm summer evening when I heard the news. In an instant I knew the world would never be the same again. Of course I had no idea what could be done. But there had to be a new way of doing things if peace was to be secured in the new atomic age. A Third World War in which atomic weapons would be used would be too horrible to contemplate.

The Second World War made me conscious that the world is a very dangerous place. So when I heard about the creation of the U.N., I was filled with a new feeling of hope. When I learned that Dag Hammarskjöld, the famous Secretary-General of the U.N., had said, "Let us never forget the creation of the U.N. was the result of a nightmare, not a dream" I knew exactly what he meant.

My first real encounter with the U.N. came in 1962, when I was living in Central Africa. One night the plane carrying Dag Hammarskjöld, then Secretary-General of the U.N. on a peace mission to the former Belgian Congo, crashed in a Zambian forest only a few miles from the Ecumenical Center where I was working. Dag Hammarskjöld and all the crew were killed.

Up to that time I knew very little about the U.N. I was aware it had played a vital role in the Korean War and in preserving peace during the Suez crisis of 1956. I had personally met people who worked in technical assistance in Zambia for the United Nations Development Programme (UNDP) and they had impressed me. But that was about all.

Now the figure of Dag Hammarskjöld began to fascinate me. Suddenly, in death, he had made the whole purpose of the U.N. spring to life for me.

I was impressed with the way he seemed to be a rare mixture of the practical and the idealist. I liked his advice to all managers: "Your position never gives you the right to command. It only imposes on you the duty of so living your life that others can receive your orders without humiliation."

Dag Hammarskjöld, I discovered, was no lofty internationalist. He always believed that love of your own country need not, and should not, conflict with a wider concern for the well-being of humanity as a whole. Every summer he loved to take a holiday in the remote parts of his own native land—Sweden.

At the deepest level Hammarskjöld drew strength from a belief that in the end "all shall be well." In 1961, in his book of reflections entitled *Markings*, not published till after his death, he wrote: "I don't know who—or what—put the question . . . But at some moment I did answer yes to someone—or some-thing—and from that hour I was certain that existence is meaningful and that, therefore, my life, in self surrender, had a goal."

I began to appreciate that, for the U.N. to succeed, all these qualities—the practical, the idealistic, the mystical—must constantly be exercised. Later on I found that these same values that Dag Hammarskjöld lived out, are, in fact, etched deep into the Preamble and the U.N. Charter itself.

So in 1979, when I was asked to direct the work of a Non-Governmental Organization at U.N. Headquarters in New York, I accepted enthusiastically. I joined the U.N. office of the International Defense and Aid Fund for South Africa, a Non-Governmental Organization (NGO) fighting apartheid. The U.N., I soon realized, was no world government; it could only do what the member states wished it to do. Furthermore, non-interference in the domestic affairs of its members was a key article in the charter.

But the U.N. could and did awaken the conscience of its members. I saw how it did this by tirelessly bringing the issue of apartheid to the forefront of international concerns. On matters that were simply too big for any one nation to tackle, for example issues concerning the global environment, the U.N. seemed to be the best hope for finding joint solutions. Above all, the U.N. was, for the first time in world history, giving a voice to so many medium-sized and small nations who up till then had simply had no say in the counsels of nations.

When I left the U.N. in 1983, I made a decision to return and try to write a book, telling the U.N. story as a whole. It seemed to me the subject had been taken hostage by analysts and academics. If this was a venture of "We the Peoples," as the Charter proclaimed, "the People," I felt, did not yet know much about it!

In 1991 I came back to the U.N. again and embarked on what has turned out to be an enormous and lengthy task. I decided I had to be deliberately personal and selective throughout. The whole U.N. system was just too big and complex to cover it all completely.

I have tried to tell the wide-ranging U.N. story through the voices of the many different nationalities who work at U.N. Headquarters. The more I have discovered, the more I have become convinced of the importance and long-term value of what the U.N. is trying to accomplish. If the U.N. can succeed and prosper, then my grandchildren will not, as I did, have most of their childhood ruined by the fearful uncertainties of a world at war.

Acknowledgments

Special thanks to Malcolm Harper, Director-General of the United Nations Association of the United Kingdom, and to Annabelle Wiener, Deputy Director-General of the World Federation of United Nations Associations, who for eight years have patiently waited for my book to appear and who have meanwhile made it possible for me to fly under their distinguished flag at U.N. Headquarters.

Diplomats, members of the Secretariat, and many representatives of the Non-Governmental community at the U.N. too numerous to mention by name have generously given me of their time and attention. I would like to single out a few people who have been especially helpful to me in writing my book: Maria Almeida, Alexandre de Barros, Bettina Corke, Clarence Dias, Bill Epstein, Anne Fosty, Harold Fruchtbaum, Henry Gordan, Richard Jordan, Lelei LeLaulu, Harry Lerner, Hector Mareque, Sue Nichols, Robert Pollard, Avalar de Tavernier, Richard Walker, and Jim Wurst.

Bhaskar (Papa) Menon has given me valuable insights to U.N. politics and processes in his invaluable newsletter *International Documents Digest*.

Ruth Cohen has been a special friend and supporter and has helped me to see how it is possible to make a lively and imaginative link between the work at U.N. Headquarters and her local community in Connecticut.

I owe a special debt of gratitude to John and Diana Collins who first introduced me to the U.N. in 1979 by sending me to New York as a lobbyist for the International Defence and Aid Fund for Southern Africa.

Lastly, I am especially grateful to my oldest friend and brother-in-law Charles who has, right from the start, given me unfailing encouragement and all-around support.

A Note to the Reader

Some of the people who appear in this book may no longer hold the posts they filled at the time they were interviewed. Diplomats, members of the Secretariat, and people from the Non-Governmental Organizations have relatively high rates of turnover. But the art of diplomacy at U.N. Headquarters remains very much the same.

U.N. JIGSAW

Walkabout:

One

Flags of the 188 member states of the United Nations outside the U.N. Secretariat Building in New York. (UN photo: Milton Grant.)

Good Defeats Evil. A statue in the UN garden by Zurab Tseretali from Georgia. The scupture depicts St. George slaying the dragon. The dragon is made from fragments of Soviet SS-20 missles and U.S. Pershing missiles destroyed under the terms of the Intermediate-Range-Forces Treaty of 1987. (UN photo: A. Brizzi.)

Ambassador Owada of Japan, President of the Security Council in January 1997, opens a meeting of the Security Council to discuss sending a peacekeeping verification mission to Guatemala. On his left is Kofi Annan current Secretary-General of the UN. (UN photo: Evan Schneider)

5

Sir Brian Urquhart of Britain was Under-Secretary-General for Special Political Affairs and was one of the main architects of UN peacekeeping operations. (UN photo: Milton Grant.)

The President of the General Assembly, Ambassador Shihabi of Saudi Arabia, introduces Boutros Boutros-Ghali, former Deputy Prime Minister of Egypt, as the new Secretary-General of the UN in 1992. (UN photo: John Isaac.)

Ambassador Richard Butler was head of the Australian Mission to the United Nations during the 50th Anniversary. (UN/DPI photo: Ky Chung.)

Ms. Rhonda Copelon, Women's Caucus for Gender Justice, lobbies Adriaan Bos from the Netherlands, chairman of the UN Preparatory Committee, during the negotiations for the International Criminal Court in 1998. (Photo: Rik Panganiban.)

Secretary-General Kofi Annan and Ambassador Alain Dejammet, Permanent Representative of France to the United Nations. (UN photo: Milton
Grant.)

1.   The Parade of Flags Outside the U.N.

Flags, flags, and more flags—now 188 in all—are the most vivid and colorful symbol of the United Nations in New York. Every day at exactly eight in the morning a team of up to fifteen security guards take the flags of all nations out of the little white boxes with sloping roofs at the base of each flagpole and haul them up the poles with gold globes on their tops. At four in the afternoon they all come down in the same way they went up—except that it takes half the time to take them down. One man walks down the line of 185 boxes and locks up each one for the night.

Behind the long thin line of the flags of the nations stretching away down First Avenue, and marking the boundary of international territory, stands a single large blue U.N. flag. This one has a different schedule: it is put up at dawn and does not come down till dusk. Another even larger light blue U.N. flag flies at the visitor's entrance.

The raising and lowering of flags goes on relentlessly except when bad weather intervenes, which in this location so near the seashore is quite often, especially in winter. If it rains or the temperature dips below 27 degrees, the flags are not raised that day. Even without bad weather the flags flying in this gusty corner of Manhattan Island begin to tatter after a couple of years, and have to be replaced.

Sometimes, in a blizzard, the flags literally freeze to the flagpole and a tall crane has to be called in to get them down. Sometimes the flags can be on the front line of a demonstration. In 1992 Greenpeace demonstrators chained themselves to a flagpole. This created trouble because the nation of the flag to which the demonstrators had by chance attached themselves thought the protest was directly aimed at it! In any event a chainsaw had to be used to cut the demonstrators free. The flags are always in the same order—alphabetical order. This order changes only when a new nation is born, and nowadays there is only space for about ten new nations on the far edge of the U.N. boundary.

It is a moving sight when all the flags are flying at half mast, as they were in 1996 in a tribute to assassinated Prime Minister of Israel Yitzhak Rabin.

When a new nation joins the U.N., a special flag-raising ceremony takes place in front of the main entrance to the General Assembly. All the Security Staff want to participate in this historic event. The Secretary-General appears. The new Ambassador speaks. Everyone stands to attention as the new flag is solemnly raised. Nowadays, this ceremony is happening much more seldom as the U.N. has now become very nearly a truly universal organization.

Flags started out as emblems of kings and armies, and usually were connected with military campaigns and wars. Nowadays, because they are so prominent at the U.N., they are, instead, powerful symbols of peace and collective security. They are also, in their numbers and their variety at the U.N., a dramatic sign that colonial domination has finally come to an end, and that millions who were not heard in the first half of the twentieth century, now have a voice and a vote in the affairs of nations.

2. Building The U.N.

On March 24, 1947, there appeared a headline in the *New York Times:* DOODLE GIVES GLIMPSE OF WORLD CAPITAL. Behind that modest headline lay the inspiring story of how this 'world capital'—the Headquarters of the United Nations—was being designed for New York by a 'world' team of Design Consultants under the Chairmanship of a marvelous American, Wallace Harrison. The story has now been told for the first time from beginning to end by Robert A. Dudley who was an eyewitness and colleague of Wally Harrison, and who made extensive notes about the birth of the building which would house the United Nations.

Once the U.N. had voted to build its headquarters in New York and once it had been agreed to build on Manhattan Island, huge practical problems still had to be overcome. The desired site on the East River was a confined one: the building had to be complimentary to New York City and to relate to its complex building laws; a large sum of money had to be found to buy the disused abattoir and slums at Turtle Bay.

The plot was soon acquired through the acumen of developer Robert Zeckendorf and the generosity of John D. Rockefeller, who wrote a personal check for eight-and-a-half-million dollars. Robert Moses, the famous New York Parks Commissioner, stood alongside Trygvie Lie, the first Secretary-General, and helped the U.N. to steer a way through New York's labyrinthine tax and property laws. But the real strain was on the team of international professionals, who were working against the clock to produce the final design.

Le Corbusier, the world famous Swiss architect who spoke French, soon made his mercurial presence felt. He describes the team as "laying down the plans for world architecture, world, not international, for therein we shall respect the human, natural and cosmic laws . . . There are no names attached to this work . . . there is simply discipline."[1] Dr. Ssu-ch'eng Liang from China put it differently: "This group of buildings should be not only international in character, but un-national—expressing no country's characteristic, but expressive of the world as a whole."[2]

Time and again Le Corbusier came up with a phase that caught the essence of the building that they were all working on together to design. New York, he said, was a city "with the voltage at the crossroads"; the General Assembly, he described as "king"; the Security Council as "vigilance-daily and decisive."[3]

Every architect in the Design Team of forty or more people was a star in his own country, and all made important contributions to the final result. One who stood out was Oscar Niemeyer from Brazil. George Dudley writes of him, "He called himself simply 'a man from the left.' Speaking seldom and to the point, he held the thoughtful attention of others; his love of people and creating beautiful, enjoyable architecture for them, as well as his sense of humour, made him a favorite . . . "[4]

Niemeyer's vision of the U.N. and of our times was freshly minted. "It is an organism to set the nations of the world on a common direction and give the world security. I think it is difficult to get this into steel and stone, but if we make something representing the true spirit of our times, of compression and solidarity, it will by its own strength give the idea that it is the big political effort, too."[5]

At the crucial thirty-fourth meeting of his design team, Harrison summed up the relative importance of these two great architects: "I conclude that the only scheme that gets complete satisfaction is an early idea of Le Corbusier as carried out and drawn up by Oscar Niemeyer."[6]

Wallace Harrison had an "eye" and could be practical too. He saw that a north-south facing secretariat building would look right for New Yorkers, glimpsing the U.N. for the first time. He accepted that putting a dome on the General Assembly was the only way to get the American Congress—because a dome is the stamp of monumentality—to put up the money for it.

But above all he had the tact and wisdom—in spite of, in his own words, "many bitter arguments in the course of planning"[7]—to leave behind the legacy that a great international building was conceived and brought to birth by a truly international group of architects. They set the highest standard of coordination and cooperation. Now it remains for each generation of diplomats to embellish this achievement in their own unique way.

Notes

1. Dudley, George A., A *Workshop for Peace. Designing the United Nations Headquarters.* The Architectural History Foundation, Inc. and the M.I.T. Press. New York and Cambridge, 1994. P. xi.
2. Ibid p. 224.
3. Ibid p. 40.
4. Ibid p. 110.

5. Ibid. p. 224.
6. Ibid. p. 252.
7. Ibid. p. 340.

3.   The First Stop on the U.N. Grand Tour

The number of visitors that daily make a pilgrimage to the U.N. is extraordinary. The largest number seem to be Japanese—and that is appropriate, as Japan is the second largest contributor to the U.N. budget. A large number of visitors are children, some of whom look much too young to understand what it all means. But on they come—more than one thousand every working day!

As they stream across the great piazza outside the visitor's entrance, they view a striking sculpture of a handgun on a plinth by Carl Frederik Reutersberg, a gift from Luxembourg. It is perhaps ten times the size of an ordinary pistol. It could never be fired. The reason is obvious. The barrel of the gun has been twisted grotesquely and tied into a knot. It is as if some person outraged at so much pointless killing in this world had suddenly seized the gun and with brutal strength rendered this instrument of violence useless forever. This gun makes a memorable background for the first photograph that tourists will take on their visit to the U.N.

The visitors pass through Security, and are then assigned to a team of highly trained young guides who can speak a remarkable number of languages, and who receive daily briefings in order to keep them up to date with current events and their impact at the U.N. More lessons about violence—ultimate violence in wartime—are about to begin.

The first stop on the U.N. grand tour is a special exhibition about what happened to people when atom bombs were dropped at Nagasaki and Hiroshima. They see the shocking effects of an explosion brighter than a thousand suns. Coins were fused together by intense heat. Children's clothes were reduced to tatters. Shards of pottery were blasted beyond recognition.

But the most searing images are a series of small drawings by Japanese artists who survived the atomic bomb—eyewitnesses of a day of indescribable horror. Their drawings are in red, yellow, and black. The sky was blotted out in those days. Kenato Terai shows how rescue trains pulled right up to the curtain of fire, but what could they do for so many burnt beyond recognition, desperately scrambling to board the train? Shoichi Furukami paints upturned corpses floating in the irradiated water. Many are children. Misakao Murakami shows people on fire running desperately to escape. There were not hundreds, but tens of thousands of victims.

Visitors fall silent. Nor is this something that happened a long time ago and is finished with forever. On the walls are charts that show that the power of the atom bombs in store today is equal to one million Hiroshima atom bombs. Overkill—they call it.

Through the window overlooking this ghastly exhibit is the Japanese Peace Bell. The Bell is struck at the start of every General Assembly. It is wrought from coins collected from the children of sixty nations. Inscribed upon it is the text LONG LIVE ABSOLUTE PEACE.

At the end of this exhibit is a statue of St. Agnes, patron saint of girls. The face is serene. The statue was found in the ruins of the Catholic Cathedral after the second atomic bomb was dropped by Nagasaki. Visitors walk behind the statue. The whole of the back of St. Agnes is blackened and charred by fire. The statue was found undamaged, face downwards in the ruins.

Visitors are shocked to be reminded so sharply just why the Charter proclaims that the whole purpose of the U.N. is "to save succeeding generations from the scourge of war which twice in our lifetime has brought untold sorrow to mankind." The U.N. was born with a birthmark, and here at this exhibition visitors can almost touch it!

Part One

Security Council, General Assembly, and Its Committees

1. President of the General Assembly from Portugal

Every year the President of the General Assembly changes. Africa provided Amara Essy from Cote D'Ivoire as President for the Forty-ninth Session, and for the Fiftieth Anniversary Session it was Europe's turn to put forward their choice. So the Assembly elected Professor Diego Freitas du Amaral from Portugal.

Professor du Amaral had an unusual background for this post, more academic than diplomatic, though he had been a candidate in the campaign for the Presidency in his country. He was one of those surprising people who, although he is completely white-haired, had the vigor of a man who could be in his forties.

In the middle of the 50th Anniversary year, he talked about his job. He explained that the work of the President can be divided into two parts, the visible and the invisible. The visible component was presiding over the passing of resolutions at the General Assembly Plenary — and there were plenty of them, often more than 200 taking up 600 pages of text! He also had to preside at ceremonial occasions such as Press Freedom Day, and at Anniversaries such as the recent Tenth Anniversary of the Chernobyl disaster. Also if funds permit — and those days mostly they did not — he liked to pay official visits to a selected number of member states. In the Anniversary year, due to the generosity of the Portuguese government, he had been able to visit China and Japan.

The invisible part of his job, he felt, was more demanding and difficult, but that was clearly the part of his work that Professor Amaral found most rewarding. This was the work of trying to reconcile divergent political points of view and to search for consensus. The President of the General Assembly was in effect the conductor of an orchestra made up of 185 players. The only problem was that too many of the players wish to play their own score!

The high point of his work, he believed, was presiding over four out of five of the Assembly's Committees charged with reforming the U.N. These working groups dealt with matters which were absolutely central to the future credibility and effectiveness of the U.N. They covered reform of the Security Council, arrangements for the future financing of the U.N., approving the U.N. budget, and coordination of the whole U.N. system.

The President has to set up the strategy and tactics for getting through the current agenda and, working with his vice-chairmen, act as mediator when a deadlock in the discussions looms up. Eventual agreement would depend largely on how well the pace and process of negotiations was orchestrated and controlled. The President's office is situated just a short walk from the Delegates' Lounge on the second floor, and is the focal point for the resolution of disagreements and disputes. The continued confidence and commitment to the U.N. by the nations and peoples of the world depend on the successful conclusion of usually lengthy and often difficult negotiations.

President du Amaral remarked, "Sometimes countries like to quote me as a reason of reluctantly agreeing to a consensus, 'We can't say no to the President.'"

And almost always they don't! So far during his Presidency, he said he had dealt with thirty international political disputes, and he had been able to resolve them all, except one, successfully.

More than half the resolutions sail through the General Assembly by consensus. They have, after all, already been carefully worked over by one of the main U.N. committees. Others have a more difficult passage and are controversial. For instance, in 1995 one resolution about human rights condemning the Iranians for abusing the freedom of religion of the Bahá'ís, received 78 votes in favor, 27 against with 58 abstentions. The President commented on that result:

"There was a big majority in favour. Nations abstain for all sorts of different reasons: abstention is not the same as a negative vote. I believe this kind of Resolution embarrasses the Government which is under censure. The opposition will be encouraged. Neighboring countries will put on pressure. It will be helpful to NGOs. It will strengthen the work of scholars. The International Press will know where the U.N. stands, and the official opinion of the world will be publicized. The effect of these combined pressures may not be immediate. But there will be a growing movement in the right direction."[1]

The President went on to reflect on the debates in the General Assembly. He felt the opening General Debate every year is a good occasion for everyone to sound off on world affairs, especially what they feel about their neighbors. He thought it would make the debate more lively if the right of reply could be made immediately instead of at the end of all the speeches. He also thought a better way could be found to tie up the avalanche of resolutions which, just before Christmas, finally reaches the Assembly Plenary from its main committees for approval by a vote or by consensus.

The formal business of voting on resolutions by the Assembly is normally concluded by Christmas, but President Amaral felt strongly that if a crisis blew up, as President he had to give nations an immediate opportunity to resume the Plenary of the General Assembly. So far twice during his Presidency he had recalled the General Assembly when there were crises over Cuba and America, and when a clash between Israel and Lebanon had erupted. He commented, "We must debate the difficult problems of the world, or what are we here for."[2]

20

Like everyone in the U.N., the President was feeling the effects of the continuing financial crisis. He has been encouraged to find that all the polls show that the American public supports the U.N. The problem, he believed, was partly caused by the American Congress and partly by the media. He felt very strongly that nations who use a delay in payment as a means to express displeasure or to get their way politically are acting 'against international law and international morality.' He was convinced that most people are simply not aware that expenditure on the U.N. for the U.S. is miniscule, compared with, say, the annual expenditure of New York City.

The President ranged widely in all his thinking. His greatest inspiration came, he said, from the past, from re-reading the classics—from Thucydides, Aristotle, and Aquinas onwards to Locke and Montesquieu. His face brightened as he concluded "They pose the right questions and often have the right answer."[3]

But he was also attuned to the future and he believed that in 50 years or so there will be some kind of People's Assembly that will sit alongside the General Assembly. Meanwhile, showing that his unremitting focus remained on the problems immediately confronting the 50th General Assembly, he recalled the remark of the famous European statesman Jean Monnet, "I am neither optimist nor pessimist. I am determined."

Notes

1. From an interview with Dr. Diego Freitas du Amaral, President of the General Assembly, May 13, 1996.
2. Ibid.
3. Ibid.

2. Ambassador from the United Kingdom

Sir David Hannay was the British Ambassador at the United Nations from 1990 to 1996. One morning in 1995, he spoke about his work at the U.N.

"When I came to the U.N. in 1990 'the seismic shift' in the way the Council had begun to work after the end of the Cold War had already taken place. Since then the veto has only been used three times and then on not very important issues.[1]

"The single most important single resolution during those years was Resolution 678 authorizing the use of force by U.N. allies of Kuwait to restore peace and security in the region. Then, by Resolution 687 commissions were set up to compel Iraq to destroy weapons of mass destruction, to pay compensation to Kuwait and, for the first time, to agree to recognize the border drawn up by a U.N. Border Commission.

"The Presidency of the Security Council changes every month. I was President four times. Basically the object is to see that the trains run on time and that the rules of procedure are followed. The President can be pro-active or passive. I think it is probably best if the President, especially if he is from a Permanent Member nation, is pro-active. And my country is one of those nations. Interestingly, that approach tended to be quite welcome to members at that time when the Council was very action-orientated, and it is still in tune with the way the Council works nowadays.

"The Security Council does from time to time hold meetings in public. This gives non-members a chance to join in a debate. But it is best to follow the Rules of Procedure and to meet often in private, as otherwise members would be tempted to use a public occasion to project rather extreme domestically-orientated points of view. The media, too, would bear down on the proceedings.

"The Security Council and the General Assembly do not have a close relationship. The Charter has arranged it that way. Only on the appointment of judges to the World Court and on the admission of new members to the U.N. do they have a joint role. . . . In recent years it may have looked as if the General Assembly has been doing less. But it is not so. It is just that the Security Council has been doing so much more in new areas of work.

"Our relationship with the Secretary-General is a daily affair. He does not come to the actual meetings as often as he used to. He is simply too busy. But his Under-Secretary-General represents him. The Secretary-General, when he can, sits in on ongoing contact group meetings discussing Bosnia and Iraq. I have met with him individually a great deal.

"During these years the council has been very innovative in establishing the tribunals for Bosnia and Rwanda. It remains to be seen how effective they will be in bringing justice, and in acting as a political deterrent preventing appalling crimes against international criminal law. This innovation may well lead onto the establishment of an International Criminal Court. But it will be a slow procedure, but then no one wants a legal process to be quick. The Court cannot simply be established by a resolution under Chapter 7 of the Charter. There will probably have to be a Convention, and when a sufficient number of nations have ratified it, it could come into being sometime within in the next few years.

"In recent times the Security Council has used sanctions with varying degrees of success. With the benefit of hindsight the sanctions against South Africa were probably more effective than was thought at the time.

"In the '90s there have been some major sanction decisions—Iraq, Libya, against Savimbi in Angola, an arms embargo in Liberia. Often sanctions in themselves do not bring about the changes of policy desired. But with Iraq, and Libya they have brought pressure on those governments and made them weaker, and less inclined to risk further alienating the United Nations. The international community needs as many steps as possible between purely diplomatic action and the use of force. Sanctions is one of the arrows in its quiver, imperfect though it may be.

"The expansion of the Security Council will come before the end of the century. It should not be rushed, but nor should the matter be left to run into the sand or filibustered. There is a case for expansion, but membership should not go much over twenty. There is not much contention over Germany and Japan becoming permanent members.

"But there are great difficulties over permanent members from Asia, Africa, and Latin America. Italy, Pakistan, Egypt, South Africa, Argentina, and Mexico, are countries which are large, but not large enough to aspire to permanent membership. These countries are extremely resistant to the claims of other nations in their region. This is holding things up.

"Those who say that the Security Council these days is undermining Article 2.(7)—no interference in the domestic affairs of other nations—have got it wrong. That principle still stands, though nowadays it is more narrowly defined. It is not these days considered an impenetrable firebreak. If, for instance, a new Idi Amin arose, he would today find the international community breathing down his neck.

"The United States is absolutely crucial to the work of the U.N. They pay between a quarter and a third of its resources. That the rest of the world can steam ahead and ignore the U.S. is a complete fantasy. That lesson was learned when the League of Nations, without American membership, failed. If America does not want to be the world's policeman, then the U.N. is the right way for them to go. It is the way to mobilize a lot of other people to help. Look how the British and French are willing to provide their troops. The U.N. supports policies basically consistent with American foreign policy objectives, and it can be a multiplier of common action. There needs to be a national debate on these positive points as well as the negative points, which would surely result in a firm engagement of the U.S. in the U.N. and support for its activities.

"The Security Council has had bad setbacks in recent years—in Somalia and Rwanda. But it is doubtful if the slaughter there could have been prevented. In Bosnia, although the situation is extremely fraught, in all circumstances, the U.N. has done the right thing. But it has so far not been very successful beyond its bottom line objective of saving a lot of human lives, through humanitarian action, of containing the threat of a wider Balkan war from spreading, and of keeping some kind of peace process going. Like all other human organizations, the U.N. has had its successes and its failures. The U.N. must learn to live with its failures and we must learn from them.

"What matters for the future is patience and perseverance. In the past five years the U.N. has adapted to rapidly changing circumstances, but it has not adapted anything like enough. It must do more about its finances, about the way the Secretariat is managed, about unnecessary duplication in economic and social affairs, and about reform of the Security Council. If these reforms can come out right, then we will create a U.N. which will be fit to play a really important role in a constantly changing Twenty-first century."

Note

1. From an interview with Sir David Hannay, July 15, 1995.

3. Ambassador from China

Ambassador Wang from China first served at the U.N. in the mid-'80s. He recalled that in the days of the Cold War, the Security Council could hardly agree on anything. The breakthrough for a new spirit of cooperation came when the Council, due to the initiative of the Peruvian Secretary-General Perez de Quellar, began negotiating the end of the Iran–Iraq war. Suddenly the permanent veto wielding members of the Security Council, often known as the P5, began to be able to work together on resolutions. And with the end of the Cold War, the Council found it actually could work together on a sustained basis. One of the productive results of this new era was that more peacekeeping operations were launched in the early '90s than in the previous 30 years of the U.N.

But in describing this remarkable sea-change in atmosphere at the U.N., the Ambassador went on to reflect that maybe nowadays the Council was trying to do too much and was even going beyond its precise mandate in the Charter to protect global peace and security.

Ambassador Wang explained that, as the Security Council was heavily weighted to the Western side, China could play a useful balancing role. He went on to explain how China came to associate itself closely and widely with all the other developing countries known at the U.N. as the Group of 77: "It began at Rio when we wanted to show that we too are a developing country, fighting the battle against poverty. Then we used the expression 'Group of 77+ China.' Now we prefer 'Group of 77 and China.' Quite simply we felt the 'Haves' were giving too much attention at Rio to looking after the birds and the flowers. We felt the first priority should be giving people something to eat!

"Of course we want to get more financial resources for the South. But it is not just about money. It's also about trade and technology. And above all it's about creating the right climate for actions to promote global development throughout the entire U.N. system.

"I believe that more generosity with aid really is in the interests of the developed countries. Prosperity creates new jobs and new markets for everyone and the market these days is essentially a global one. We say, 'To help others is to help yourself.'"[1]

On the subject of the role of NGOs in the U.N. system, the Ambassador said that China welcomes NGOs. But he stressed that the U.N. is mainly an inter-governmental body for inter-government communication. He recalled that China had recently hosted the huge Beijing Conference for Women and nowadays both women and young people were increasingly active in NGOs in China. He also wanted to see proper rules and procedures for NGOs so that their increasing participation in the U.N. system could be properly balanced, and also more NGOs from the developing countries needed to come to New York and take part in the ongoing discussions at Headquarters.

Ambassador Wang emphasized the importance of straight thinking on the complex subject of reform of the United Nations. "We want to see reform, not deform. We have a Chinese proverb, 'Ten years east of the river: ten years west of the river.' The U.N. is now a river with its own history and the river has its own momentum. For instance, it took five years to get agreement on raising the Security Council from eleven to fifteen members. Now we expect the Council to be enlarged, because we want to see better representation of developing countries. We want them to sort out for themselves how they wish to be represented. As regards the veto, it is part of the U.N.'s history and it has played a positive role since 1945. Incidentally, China has only used it four times, because we believe in restraint.

"On either side of the river things have gotten out of control. For instance we now have around sixty Committees of the General Assembly and forty of the Economic and Social Council. If we can get the mission of the U.N. clearly defined, then we will get the right size for the right job. I call this practicing U.N. family planning! Nowadays we talk a lot about 'preventive peacekeeping,' so now we ought to think about what we might define as 'preventive development.' We must never diminish the emphasis on development and we must get better co-ordination with the World Bank."

Ambassador Wang concluded: "We have almost finished building a new Permanent Mission for China which will be much closer to the U.N. The U.N.

has a role to play in the life of the world which no one else can take on. I believe that for any diplomat to contribute to that is to do something really worthwhile."

Note

1. From an interview with Ambassador Wang Xuexian, July 3, 1997.

4. Ambassador from Malaysia

Malaysia is one of the leading nations to speak up for the developing countries. Ambassador Razali Ismail has been Malaysia's Ambassador at the U.N. for seven years and has recently served for a year as President of the General Assembly. The Ambassador was the first Chairman of the Commission of Sustainable Development, the follow-up mechanism to Rio. The Ambassador reflected on his time in these key posts: "Being a Chairman at the U.N. requires infinite patience. You have to broker some kind of consensus. The lowest common denominator won't do. It will be too low. You have to create some kind of chemistry. Elevate the consensus. Broaden the parameters of agreement. The Chair is the catalyst. You have to understand 'the eco-system of the U.N.' Then you will make it happen."

The Ambassador thinks it will take another one or two years before Security Council reform actually happens. He would like to see the end of the big powers' veto and an enlargement that would give regional powers, selected by their neighbors, a place on the Council. They already often do get re-elected to non-permanent places on the Council, but he feels that is not enough to satisfy either democracy or equity.

He also believes the method of payment of dues to the U.N. has to be changed. No nation, not even the U.S., should be allowed to decide unilaterally how much they can and will pay. New methods of raising money have to be tried. Overall he expects there will be a slimming-down of the U.N. Peacekeeping, in particular, he thinks, is overstretched. A leaner U.N. may emerge.

Ambassador Razali is disappointed with the way funds have been drying up in the '90s. He considers there is a climate of 'compassion fatigue' in the air. He put his view strongly, "All the talk of 'new and additional sources' since Rio has turned out to be a pipe dream. Development Assistance is supposed to be at .7 percent of Gross National Product (GNP) but actually it is only averaging .35 percent. It is unacceptable to leave all overseas aid to the Bretton Woods organizations, who have a fundamentally undemocratic structure compared with U.N. Headquarters.

"The only additional money is in the Global Environment Facility, which has $2 billion for new projects, but this is money only for schemes with global, not national, implications."

He says Malaysia is not giving up in this unfavorable climate. Far from it. Malaysia's exports to China and Japan are growing all the time. Unlike some of the poorest countries in Africa, Malaysia's economy does not depend on one crop.

The Ambassador outlined his objections to the Treaty to extend the Nuclear Non-Proliferation Treaty: "We do not accept that some nations should be nuclear powers, while the rest are indefinitely excluded. Second, the promises made by the nuclear powers to disarm are not yet time-bound, and even if Salt 2—a bilateral arms treaty between Russia and America—is ratified, the nuclear powers will still have 12,000 nuclear weapons in their arsenals.

"You ask why then did the Treaty get ratified? The answer is arm-twisting—threats of dire consequences on the economic side, on the trade side. We saw the same pressure being used on the French-speaking African countries when they protested about the French nuclear tests in the Pacific.

"Malaysia has joined in the appeal to the World Court to declare nuclear weapons illegal. We shall know the result next year."[1]

Postscript 1997

The World Court stopped just short of declaring nuclear weapons illegal, but their message that their use would be outside the pale of civilized behavior was clear and unequivocal. The U.N. has finally passed a comprehensive ban on nuclear testing. Nuclear disarmament by the five declared nuclear powers is still only proceeding at a snail's pace.

Ambassador Razali has built a formidable reputation for telling things 'as they are.' He has been one of the best friends of the NGO community and of increasing their role in the world of the U.N. Yet he has not been afraid to spell out why many governments still fear the expansion of NGO influence in U.N. affairs. To the 1997 NGO/Department of Public Information Annual Conference he put the situation like this: "NGOs are not necessarily in themselves democratic. While some are organized along the lines of coalitions that network laterally, others are hierarchical and headed by elites, who in their style of decision-making push forward their own personal agenda rather than

those of their constituents, and they may hardly be different from the governments they confront. . . .

"The politics of building partnerships at the U.N. are enormously complex,
fraught with fear, stereotypes, apathy, legal inhibitions, and ambiguities. No
player is immune from the above."[2]

Ambassador Razali has been a creative and frank President of the General
Assembly. Clearly he would have liked to have achieved more of the U.N.
Reform Program than he did. But his remarkable efforts will very probably
make it possible for his successors to walk through doors which, in his time,
were bolted and barred against him.

Notes

1. From an interview with Ambassador Razzali Ismail, December 18, 1995.
2. Ambassador Razzali Ismail at the DPI/NGO 1977 Annual Conference. Press Release. General
   Assembly GA/9290. P. 4.

5. A Bulgarian Interpreter

Interpreters at the U.N. are mysterious people. They sit at the side of a conference room in special booths behind glass panels and no one knows their names.
Yet they are indispensable to the work of diplomacy. When there is a financial
crisis, which is most of the time these days, no funds are available for them to
work overtime, and meetings have to limp along as best they can with only
English. The U.N. can hardly function at all unless its team of highly professional interpreters are in action all the time.

Gabriel Milev has been interpreting at the U.N. for more than ten years.
He is Bulgarian and interprets into French from Russian and English. He
considers being an interpreter is an exacting and exciting profession: "You never
know what is coming next. When I interpreted for the Atomic Energy Authority
(IAEA) I had to learn 200–300 technical words in Russian and English and
that covered most of the business. But interpreting in the world of diplomacy
requires a mastery not just of words, but of the whole of contemporary culture,
in which language is changing and developing all the time."

Interpretation, Gabriel explained, is always a matter of "interpretation,"
never of mere straight translation of words. He gave the example of the difference between a wet and a dry lease, a concept used in procurement of equipment for peacekeeping contingents. For translation, the full legal sense had to

be understood before it can be meaningfully put into French. Another concept, he said, which will not "fly" in French is "gender empowerment," and behind that concept is the whole debate about women's rights that went on at the Beijing Women's Conference.

Gabriel Milev said the high point of being a U.N. interpreter is taking part in the consultations at the Security Council: "These meetings take place in a special consulting room out of sight of the public eye. Unlike at regular negotiating sessions in General Assembly Committees, these negotiations are very informal and a wide range of language—sometimes colloquial language—is employed. The fifteen Ambassadors all strain to persuade their colleagues that they have the best wording for a resolution. Being an interpreter at these meetings is nerve-wracking and a major test of concentration and interpreters, in order to keep at their peak, often work no more than 15 minutes at a stretch before a colleague takes over."

The language of diplomacy has its own rhythms and fine distinctions. Gabriel gave the example of the difference, diplomatically speaking, between "regret, deplore, condemn." Each of these words carry a very different weight and when they are translated into one of the U.N.'s six official languages they all have to carry as nearly as is possible the exact same weight put on them by the first speaker in a discussion.

Gabriel Milev has been on field missions for the U.N. in Haiti, Namibia, and Western Sahara. He has experienced firsthand how people in troubled situations look eagerly for neutrality and integrity from the U.N. He feels that the U.N. does indeed stand for the conscience of the world.

Gabriel recalled just one occasion when empathy for a speaker got the better of him. In 1973, at the height of a crisis in American race relations he was interpreting Angela Davis, a well-known Black American. She was speaking eloquently, emphasizing her points by bringing her fist down on the table in front of her. Suddenly one of his colleagues switched off his microphone, turned to him, and said, "No one can see *you*, so why are *you* moving your arm up and down like that!"

Sometimes he is asked what would happen if the U.N. gave up interpreters and just worked in English. He has no doubt that something important in global discourse would be lost, and he recalled the recent words of Ambassador Yañez-Barnuevo:

> Interpretation in the U.N. is essential. One could conceive of a U.N. where everything took place in English. But that would impoverish the debate. . . . The United Nations is fundamentally multilateral and universal. It cannot impoverish itself to the point of becoming merely the vehicle for a single source of ideas—the Anglo-Saxon source.

Note

1. From an interview with Gabriel Milev, February 27, 1996.

6. Diplomacy by Blocs

Multilateral diplomacy at the U.N. is increasingly done by blocs. Nation states are finding that they need to combine together to count for something. At times it seems as if the world, as seen at the U.N., is made up of regional federations. At debates in the Committees of the General Assembly, Ambassador after Ambassador will speak on behalf of his region and not just for his own country.

One of the most powerful and well-organized blocs is the European Union. Ambassador Alex Reyn of Belgium is one of the members of this bloc. The Ambassador described how this regional approach to diplomacy affected him:

"Thinking for Europe is something young diplomats learn do from the first day in the service. By the time they get posted to the U.N. it is second nature to them. No nation can exist alone in a world of 185 nations. I believe that the European Union, when it agrees on a common position, carries as much weight as the United States, 'If we say No, it's No.' And sometimes, when we take a stance our bloc is extended to include North America as well.

The Ambassador said that doing diplomacy in this way did not mean you lost sight of your national interest. Not at all. But it did make things more complicated. There has to be constant communication with national capitals and with Brussels, the seat of the European Union. Common positions are arrived at by three major players: the political committee made of foreign policy professionals for the different states involved; the Foreign Ministers, who meet once a month or more if necessary; and of course the Ambassadors at the U.N. themselves.

The Ambassador does not think Belgium is swamped by working in this way: "There is flexibility. We can adapt, we can modify. We are rather comfortable in the framework in which we operate. When one country backs away from an agreement, we call in the current President of the European Union to mediate. It works rather well. But we have to recognize that France and Germany are the engine of Europe. The partnership of President Mitterand and Chancellor Kohl was proof of that.

30

"Another important bloc in the U.N. is the Non-Aligned Movement (NAM). It is made up of the countries of the South, mostly developing countries. They are agreed on broad lines only. But often as the discussion proceeds, they find it difficult to hold together on a common point of view. They have not yet reached as deep a level of integration as the European Union.

"Integration of a common position is never easy. The European Union finds it much easier to reach a common view on economic and social matters than on foreign policy. For instance we all agree that it is desirable we should give .7 percent of the Gross National Product (GNP) for aid to poor countries, but only three of our members have actually done it so far."

"The Non-Aligned Movement used to say 'Give us the money and the problems will be solved.' Now it is much more a question of identifying the issues which need funding from aid and, if there is sound government in place in the developing countries to use the funds efficiently, the money will usually follow.

"We have been taking common positions at the recent summit U.N. conferences. These summits on great social and humanitarian issues have added greatly to our understanding. Look at the positive impact of the Vienna Conference on Human Rights. The results are not seen at once, but they will show."

The Ambassador said that the two key issues of the moment were U.N. Reform and the financial situation. The one reacted on the other. On both issues it was proving very hard to achieve consensus: "It was not helpful when any one nation, especially the United States, suddenly announced what it would agree to pay in the future, when all member states were already legally committed to a framework for contributions to the U.N.'s finances, agreed and voted on by the whole General Assembly."

Ambassador Reyn concluded: "I am more and more convinced that the U.N. will be working and voting on the basis of regional linkages in the future."[1]

Note

1. From an interview with Ambassador Reyn of Belgium, March 6, 1996.

7. A Russian Perspective on Managing the General Assembly

The General Assembly is the Town Meeting of the world. But like so much of the work of the U.N., it is seldom in the public eye. Yet 185 nations, supported by the staff in their Missions, have for the 50th session so far produced 600 pages of resolutions!

Thanks to the hard work and procedural expertise of the small staff of the General Assembly Affairs Division, all these resolutions have been processed and eventually voted on by the plenary of the General Assembly.

The member states decide the resolutions. The President of the General Assembly decides the priorities. And the Secretariat of the United Nations orchestrates the procedure, and the conduct of elections.

These resolutions cover every subject imaginable from Disarmament to Human Rights, from Social Development to the creation of International Law. All these are subjects which are too big for any one nation to tackle on its own. But how does the rest of the world get to know about this unique effort to create global opinion and to spell out plans for global action?

Mr. Vadim Perfiliev, Director of the General Assembly and Economic and Social Affairs (ECOSOC) Division from Russia explained that these days General Assembly Resolutions have in fact never been so widely and easily available: "The U.N. Department of Public Information (DPI) is leading the campaign to make the work of the General Assembly better known. The DPI sends texts to a network of depository libraries who work closely with U.N. Information Centers worldwide.

"In addition all the texts of resolutions can now be found on the Internet. On the World Wide Web there is a U.N. home page which announces U.N. developments on a day-to-day basis. Different constituencies around the world have different priorities, and the U.N. through the Internet makes it possible for them to find texts relevant to their own particular needs and aims.

"NGOs also have a new window on General Assembly Affairs. The Global Policy Institute's home page monitors negotiations and sometimes has texts not yet in general distribution."

Mr. Perfiliev went on to describe the work which it is his responsibility to orchestrate: "The work of the General Assembly is becoming more cohesive, and more central to global governance. Thus more and more resolutions are passed by consensus. This does not mean these resolutions are all about subjects that do not matter much to member states. Often hard negotiations—say in the Disarmament and International Security Committee (First Committee) or the Economic and Financial Committee (Second Committee)—about the exact wording of resolutions can go on for three months. Sometimes only the intervention of the President of the Assembly himself can resolve an impasse. So when they reach the Plenary of the General Assembly they often are ready to be passed by consensus.

"The General Assembly is not yet perceived by the global public as the Town Meeting of the World. But there is no complacency about this state of affairs. The U.N. is now engaged in a wide discussion of General Assembly reform. One of the aspects of this discussion is the equation of the more active involvment of the NGOs in its work and that would be a step that would help to generate much wider publicity, interest and involvment by the general public."[1]

In all sorts of ways the building blocks are now in place for the General Assembly to be publicly recognized as the global Town Meeting for the global society of the twenty-first century.

Note

1. From an interview with Mr. V. Perfiliev, Director, General Assembly Affairs, July 6, 1996.

8.   Ambassador from Australia

Ambassador Richard Butler, who presided over the Committee which ran the 50th Anniversary celebrations, has become a major presence at the U.N. He had the immensely difficult and ticklish task of masterminding a Fiftieth Anniversary Declaration to which all 185 nations could agree.

At first, explained the Ambassador, the prospects looked distinctly unpromising. The veto-wielding five wanted only a plaque to mark the occasion and to indicate in saccharine phraseology, a continuing commitment to the Charter. That was all. But that simply would not do for the great number of new nations who did not even exist when the Charter was written.

The Ambassador wanted, and eventually got, a Declaration which would reflect the new insight that it is the human family which matters supremely today: "Nowadays we think first about our common humanity, not about nation states. Security is about human security."

To get a Declaration along these lines approved, the Ambassador had to persuade the non-aligned developing nations that their original draft would not do. The whole negotiation took two years. Only after months of negotiation in slow motion, and a fresh proposal that all should work from a draft put forward by the Ambassador himself, did the two sides, developed and developing nations, eventually reach a compromise. Finally a Declaration emerged, which gave the U.N. a road map for the next fifty years, and which was worthy to stand beside the original Charter, still the basic engine of U.N. progress.

The Ambassador went on to reflect that it is no longer appropriate to speak of a North/South divide at the U.N.: "There are some thirty nations in the South that have among the fastest growing economies in the world. They lead in their commitment to free markets.

33

"Nations that do not like the present post Cold War arrangements are the ones who were non-aligned in the Cold War, and who are now in some disarray—Cuba, Pakistan, India, Syria, and Iran. For them the issue is more about power rather than ideology. For them the matter of seats on the Security Council is very important. They often stand over against the European Union, which is now a major player in all our U.N. negotiations."

Ambassador Butler gave his views on the vital issue of reform of the United Nations: "First, we need reform of the Economic and Social Council. It is too large and too unwieldy. Its commissions have to be amalgamated and its working arrangements made more efficient.

"Second, the relationship of the General Assembly and the Security Council has to be sorted out. The Security Council has to become, and be seen to become, larger and more democratic. Otherwise the smaller nations will just walk away from the U.N.

"The General Assembly has to meet on an entirely different schedule and deal with its business in a much less repetitive way. Meeting from September to Christmas was an idea conceived when people crossed the Atlantic in ocean liners!

"Third, the Secretariat has to be shaken up. The old-fashioned ideas of patronage with sections and posts permanently reserved for particular nations, especially for the permanent five (P5) on the Security Council, privileges inherited from 1945 have to go. These arrangements are in direct contradiction with the charter.

"Lastly we need a wholesale reform of the Department of Public Information. The Department has wonderful stories to tell such as the success story of the vaccination of children against all infectious diseases, but they have completely failed to do the job. The General Assembly's Committee on Information is too politicized. The only hope is to put telling the U.N. story in the hands of professionals and then give the Department some freedom."

The NGOs rate high in the Ambassadors' estimation. He was full of praise for the NGOs all-around contribution to the U.N. Agenda. He recalled taking part in the great demonstration against the atomic arms race in Central Park in 1982: "It was the NGOs, who almost single-handedly got the arms control negotiations going again. They have been invaluable at the recent U.N. Summit Conferences—on Population, and on Women at Beijing. At the Prepcoms for these events they are on the floor in the negotiations, assisting us in formulating policies.

"In our civil society NGOs must and will play an even bigger part in the U.N. But they must not try to become too like governments. They must be there alongside the diplomats, but must never merge with them. They must stick to their own style of doing things."

Ambassador Butler emphasized that the existence of the U.N., unlike its predecessor, the League, is now deeply embedded in people's consciousness. "If someone dropped it in the East River, it would have to be re-invented.

"Now we have to get the division of labor right within our civil society. If the U.N. can get the political consensus right, then the business community, who have the real money, will see that it's in their interests to help with the implementation of the U.N.'s Agenda. It is already happening in the Environment field and will happen over population affairs." The Ambassador concluded: "For the future we have got to get the balance right between the U.N.'s power and its vision. The League of Nations failed because, although it had the right vision, it failed to take account of the realities of power. For this reason the Security Council has to be reformed.

"But what happens to most human beings in the world is not touched upon at all by the Security Council, so the U.N. in the future must have an agenda that is much more centered on the security of people than on the security of nations."[1]

Note

1. From an interview with Ambassador Richard Butler, February 19, 1996. Since 1997 Ambassador Butler has been the Head of UNSCOM, the U.N. Mission responsible for seeing that Iraq destroys its stock of weapons of mass destruction.

9. Ambassador from Botswana

Botswana has been one of the few success stories of post-colonial Africa. It has managed to maintain democratic politics. It has had no periods of military rule. And recently, due to its economic progress, it has been taken off the list of Least Developed Countries.

It has sensibly kept the same Ambassador at the United Nations fifteen years. He is Joe Legwaila, and recently his country has been elected to a two-year term as one of ten non-permanent members of the Security Council. During that time, Ambassador Legwaila served as the Chairman of the Council for the customary one month of duty.

Ambassador Legwaila is not happy about the essentially undemocratic nature of the Council. He considers that this will continue as long as the five permanent members—the possessors of nuclear weapons—have the power of veto. He does not believe that bringing in Germany and Japan and perhaps regional representatives like India and Brazil will improve matters. Only the complete abolition of veto power will make things more democratic.

The Ambassador did not regard being Chairman of the Council as a particularly memorable business. "The Chairman has no power to wage war," he said.

He found that his work was limited to helping out when the other members found that they could not agree on the wording of a resolution and they had decided to put forward a Presidential text based on consensus.

The Chairman also has the task of briefing members of the General Assembly on the latest work of the Security Council. This innovation came about because Ambassador Cárdenas of Argentina thought that since the Gulf War, the Security Council was meeting more and more informally and more and more privately. To save the image of the Security Council, there was a need to make its work more transparent. This new idea had not worked all that well, because attendance by members of the General Assembly had been disappointing, and different Security Council Chairmen have had some disagreement on how frequently to hold these briefings.

But the biggest problem for the non-permanent members, said the Ambassador, had been that since the Gulf War the self-chosen Contact Group of the veto-wielding countries plus Germany had been managing the business of the Security Council their way. Ambassador Legwaila explained: "Suddenly the Council began to meet Monday, Tuesday, Thursday, even on Sunday to consider a stream of resolutions coming from the Contact Group. Some took umbrage. But the Group was inclined to suggest it would be irresponsible for the other members not to accept their proposals. Also there was the pressure of time to move on to the next item. So the rest of us tended to go along.

"Those serving on the Council from the Non-Aligned Movement (NAM)—Nigeria, Rwanda, and Botswana—try to come up with our own Draft Resolutions. But too often while we are still talking, the others suddenly produce their own version for discussion and agreement.

"The Americans try very hard to behave like equals. But when they want something done, they want it done! Intervention in Haiti was one example of this. Another one was the recent bombing of Serb positions outside Sarajevo during the Bosnian civil war."

Ambassador Legwaila is a strong defender of the value of the General Assembly—because it has 188 members whereas the Security Council only has fifteen. He said, "Some people had almost come to believe the Security Council, plus perhaps key Agencies like UNICEF and UNDP were the U.N. and that the General Assembly counted for nothing. But those of us from the developing countries are in charge there. The General Assembly may be a talking shop, but it is a universal and a very necessary one."[1]

The Ambassador takes a thoroughly positive view of the U.N.'s involvement in peacebuilding, especially in the electoral process. He himself took a leading part in the first free elections held in Namibia and South Africa and experienced how people soon saw that the U.N. was an impartial arbiter.

He believes strongly that human rights are universal and that, if necessary, as has been the case over recent executions in Nigeria, African nations will have to endure some 'self-flagellation' to protect the universal standards that the African Members of the U.N. have themselves proclaimed.

Note

1. From an interview with Ambassador Legwaila, November 29, 1995.

10. Ambassador from Andorra

Ambassador Minoves-Triquell from the Principality of Andorra represents a country on the border between France and Spain of only 60,000 people. Yet in the General Assembly, his vote has exactly the same weight as a country of 60 million people or even 600 million! He is not over-awed by the small size of his own country, or by the large size of his neighbors, France and Spain.

He believes that Andorra has a history which positively gives it strength in U.N. negotiations because it is a country that has not fought a war for 700 years. In 1278 it agreed to renounce war and to dismantle all its castles and fortifications. From that time on its people have learned by necessity how to survive in peace and friendship with two vastly more powerful neighbors.

The Ambassador had more to tell about the role of his small country:

"We believe we can bring a moral dimension to bear on world affairs. As a small nation we have less national interest to defend than larger nations.

"We live by our wits. We try to specialize in the subjects at the U.N. in which we can most usefully get involved in. One is youth. Andorra has a very young population. At the Copenhagen Summit we were able to draft a whole paragraph in the Plan for Action. We want to see a deeper understanding of the whole subject. For instance no one has yet come up with a satisfactory definition of 'Who are youth?' We were proud that our youth choir came to the U.N. to sing Mozart's requiem for the 50th Anniversary.

"All the issues of human rights concern us. We are supporting an Italian proposal to get the death penalty abolished by the year 2000. Due to strong opposition from a few countries we could not get this proposal beyond the Third Committee, but we are not giving up. Together with Ireland and Denmark we shall try again next year.

"We work with other small nations. In Europe that means Monaco, Lichtenstein, and San Marino. Lichtenstein is very interested in defining the right of self-determination more closely, and we think that will be an important issue in the future, so we will work alongside them, too.

"This 50th Anniversary has been very productive. We should rejoice that the U.N. exists, and has survived. It is useless to keep on complaining about the U.N. doing things which it has no mandate to do. After all, it can only do what its member states will let it do. I find it wonderful that the nations in spite of all their difficulties with each other can sit down together in the U.N. and talk."

The Ambassador concluded: "Before I came to the U.N. I knew all about its structures. But actually working in it and being a part of its life has made me see how strong the personal factor is in all the U.N. does. Personalities matter. Bureaucracy is not king. The personal touch is vital in all U.N. negotiations."[1]

Note

1. From an interview with Ambassador Juli Minoves-Triquell, November 29, 1995.

11.   American Ambassador to ECOSOC

The work of the Economic and Social Council of the U.N., better known as ECOSOC, is one of the most inspiring things the U.N. is doing. And no one believes that more strongly than the Group of 77 (actually 113 nations; the bloc of mostly underdeveloped nations that come from the South). ECOSOC for them is the key engine of the U.N. to lift them out of poverty. The work and progress of ECOSOC is what they really care about. And they make up the majority in the General Assembly.

Unfortunately, however, to the outside world, the work of ECOSOC does not come across like that. All too often the Council's performance in recent decades has seemed bureaucratic, overlapping, ineffective and just plain dull.

ECOSOC had a better image in the past. Ambassador Victor Marrero of the United States, who has had, for the last four years, the special responsibility for ECOSOC for his government put the case for the defense of ECOSOC as follows: He recalled that after the foundation of the U.N. in the early years of the U.N., in the late 40s, it was ECOSOC which took on the pioneering work of the U.N. in the fields of Human Rights, Narcotics, Women's Rights, and Population issues. Then it was always ECOSOC issues—and finding the additional sums of money to resolve them—that the developing countries cared about the most.

Gradually, however, as the Ambassador explained, work in these important fields was delegated to ECOSOC special commissions. These functional Commissions, for example the Human Rights Commission in Geneva, developed a vitality, strength, and visibility greater even than that of the parent body itself.

ECOSOC simply did not have the capacity to do more than review the ever-expanding amount of work being done at its request, and to pass it on to the Second and Third Committees of the General Assembly. So, the original goal for ECOSOC to set priorities and make policy recommendations to the General Assembly was lost sight of. ECOSOC began to lose its luster.

But, as Ambassador Marrero explained, there has been, in recent years, a renewed attempt to bring the work of ECOSOC back into focus and make ECOSOC once again the indispensable energizer of development worldwide. It will not be easy. ECOSOC today still has so many different faces.

Besides the Commissions for the major issues—Status of Women, Human Rights, Drugs—there are Sub-Commissions and even Working Groups of the Sub-Commissions. Then there are the Regional Commissions, dealing with the concerns of whole continents. Lastly there is a whole slew of Committees and Expert Bodies covering just about anything and everything in the social and economic field. And to complete the bewilderment there are two Commissions with the same acronyms, but with quite different concerns. There is CSD—the Commission on Social Development and there is CSD—the Commission on Sustainable Development. Yes, ECOSOC is indigestible!

So the Americans have deliberately taken a lead in trying to streamline and coordinate ECOSOC's work for development. The key agencies of UNICEF, UNDP, UNFPA, and the World Food Program (WFP) have been brought into a much closer relationship with ECOSOC. Their Boards have been made smaller, more like the Boards of Corporations and less like debating societies. The U.S. would have preferred just 15 members on their Boards, but after negotiations between the interested parties which took two years, a compromise was agreed to reduce the number to 36, down from the original 48.

Then there has also been the streamlining of ECOSOC itself. Shorter meetings, coordinated agendas, and new links with the World Bank have been created. They are all a part of the one system and all are a part of the U.N. family.

Reform is working. ECOSOC can, the Ambassador insisted, get Foreign Ministers and Attorneys General to come to a crisis meeting. It happened recently over the issue of the growing drug menace.

Ambassador Marrero has also played a leading role in getting ECOSOC to prepare a Declaration on Corruption. This declaration creates a norm for acceptable behavior and targets people from one country who try to bribe those from another one. This is an issue much too broad to be dealt with by ECOSOC's Crime Commission or by domestic laws against criminal behavior. This Declaration levels the playing field for everyone in developed and developing countries alike. The Declaration was passed by the General Assembly and countries from now on will have to report to the General Assembly how they are dealing with offenders.

The Ambassador, who is a graduate of Yale Law School, is not a career diplomat by training. He was an Under-Secretary in the Carter Administration. He commented on looking at the work of ECOSOC from an American perspective: "What we do affects people all over the world. ECOSOC works on crucial questions for the world's well-being. I believe most people—and I include Americans in this—know that what the U.N. does for families, for children, and for health is vital, and opinion polls in America show a steady level of support for this work of the U.N. ECOSOC is a place where issues can be discussed and resolved, where definitions of goals can be decided, and where global priorities can be set."[1]

In sum, the role of ECOSOC is vital in giving people food, shelter, and clothing, and to see to it that they get education, health, and job opportunities. Why then does it not catch the public's imagination? The answer is that the work is just too complex, too multi-faceted, too varied. It's a story that the media can never hope to capture in one quick news-bite. But ECOSOC remains the tip of the U.N.'s shining spear, which it continues to hurl again and again against the all-pervasive enemy—global poverty.

Note

1. From an interview with Ambassador Victor Marrero, United States Mission to the U.N., April 23, 1997.

12.   A Member of the Secretariat from Brazil

The vast majority of the nearly 8,000 civil servants at the United Nations are neither seen nor heard by the general public. They probably prefer it that way. They are professionals whose job is to keep the wheels of the administration turning, and the wheels might not turn at all if they were exposed to the public eye. They are international public servants committed to new standards of impartiality and discretion which the world has never seen before.

Consider the job of Alexandre de Barros who joined the international civil service from Brazil and who works in a division of the Secretariat that services the Second and Third Committees of the General Assembly. As a Meetings Secretary, he has a whole caseload of important subjects which have to be moved along. Some of them require reports annually; others again are matters which come before the diplomats every few months. Some require his presence in the Conference Room; others are more a matter of reporting progress on paper. All these subjects require the collecting and assembling of information from offices throughout the whole U.N. system, including those in Geneva and Vienna. And there is a deadline for everything.[1]

Recently Alexandre de Barros has spent time working on the follow-up to the First Conference of the Parties to the Framework Convention on Climate Control. The parties are working towards a set of complex rules and regulations which they can all agree to about harmful carbon dioxide emissions, which are warming up the atmosphere. The whole subject came to a boil in Kyoto, Japan, in 1998 when nations reached an agreement on a common approach towards cutting harmful emissions into the atmosphere.

For developing countries, emissions control promises to be an expensive business and they need help to be able to acquire the latest technology. The new funds required are likely to be substantial. The Secretariat has to keep a meticulous record of the ongoing discussions, so that there will be need to go back on agreements and understandings, often reached after long and difficult negotiations.

Alexandre de Barros is no secretarial automaton. He finds it hard going to keep up his enthusiasm at this time when the U.N. is downsizing, and when it is none too clear how economic issues will be dealt with in the future. He summed up his expectations and increasing feelings of frustration like this.

"As an experienced economist in Brazil and coming from a country with so much at stake in this crucial field of economic development, I had a very focused goal. Unfortunately, due to the organization's rigid structure, the opportunity to achieve my goal so far has not materialized and, given the current trends and priorities, it is with sadness that I realize it probably never will."

But the work must go on. Alexandre de Barros has to prepare and put together reports of bodies such as the Statistical Commission for the consideration of the Economic and Social Council. This Commission has been at work since 1946 encouraging and educating all governments to standardize and improve their statistical methods. Unless this is done, national development plans cannot be compared and aid from the U.N. cannot be distributed fairly to those who need it most.

He also has to present an up-to-date account on the sharing of progress in Science and Technology. This is a sensitive subject, but technology is being slowly shared with the developed countries, and consideration of extra funding is being discussed and made available through this Commission to a number of projects worldwide.

Yet another Commission of the Economic and Social Council which Alexandre has to service is the Commission on Social Development. Among other things, this Commission covers youth, aging, the disabled, and the family. Since the Summit on this theme in Copenhagen in 1995, this Commission has been particularly busy with the agenda of the follow-up Program of Action.

Still more reports on other matters that come before these Committees of the General Assembly are the responsibility of Alexandre de Barros — the work of the Pledging Conference on Development Activities and the World Food Program, for instance.

Without the unremitting efforts of the Secretariat, the diplomats of 185 nations could not hope to complete their work in this huge field of Development and to bring their resolutions before the annual meetings of the General Assembly for approval. This is the way the world community discovers its common mind. In bureaucracy, as in many other worthwhile endeavors, the longest way around is the shortest way home.

Note

1. From an interview with Alexander de Barros, November 25, 1995.

13. Protecting the Tradition of an International Civil Service

Lelei Lelaulu is editor of the U.N. Secretariat News and month by month he is in close touch with the feelings and aspirations of the U.N. staff. He himself is on permanent staff of the U.N. and is proud to call himself an international civil servant. He recalled that when the League of Nations was founded after the First World War, this was the first time in human history that staff were asked, even expected, to have a loyalty above and beyond their own nation state.

Lelei is from Western Samoa. He grew up on a Pacific Island where the work of the U.N. was visible all around him — the World Health Organization

(WHO) was inoculating people; The United Nations Educational, Scientific, and Cultural Organization (UNESCO) was giving scholarships; and he himself was recruited to Headquarters while working in Beirut where he had seen how courageously the staff of United Nations Works and Relief Organization (UNWRRA) staff got on with the difficult and sometimes dangerous job of looking after Palestinian refugees.[1]

Lelei explained that, though the Cold War was over, the idea of serving in an international civil service, of a lifelong career in the U.N., has not become as popular as it ought to be. There were several reasons, troubling reasons, for this state of affairs. To save funds and to be able to get rid of 'dead wood,' service on contract was becoming the way to employ people at the U.N. This often meant that the best people did not and could not offer themselves for long-term service in the U.N. It became clear that people employed on contract were inevitably subject to pressure from their home country which had lent them to the U.N. for only a short time.

Lelei said that another fact which discouraged new recruits was that the U.N. conditions of service relative to similar organizations like the World Bank and OECD had become less attractive. Furthermore, U.N. salaries had now been made comparable to a low level grade in the U.S. Civil Service. In the circumstances, some governments had taken upon themselves to 'top up' the salaries of their own nationals, and naturally that had created a problem with those who have not received this privilege.

If all that was not enough to discourage people, U.N. finances were so stretched that money for travel to important regional meetings was scarce. Valuable cross-fertilization within the U.N. system was therefore no longer taking place.

Finally Lelei explained that serving in the U.N. was a more dangerous business that it used to be. Nowadays many peacekeeping operations had a civilian component recruited by and from the U.N. To try to protect its own people, the U.N. had ratified a Convention to protect peacekeepers. Its terms were closely related to the Convention against terrorism. But Lelei thought that it would probably always be difficult to bring to justice those who deliberately harm U.N. personnel while they are on a mission.

In these times and for all these reasons, it was much more difficult to achieve the kind of full professional career in the U.N. that the Founders had hoped would be possible. And there was even a problem about those who had now served for forty years, and who had to retire at 60. Lelei felt it was regrettable that their wisdom and experience was not made use of. He believed that they should and could provide institutional memory for the staff in present employment. Re-employed on short term with minimal salaries, they could be of so much help but for the most part, they were not being used at all.[1]

Lelei concluded on a sober note, "It is going to be a long battle to get the young generation while still in schools to understand what the U.N. is all about. And those of us inside the U.N. have to keep on fighting to maintain the idea of an international civil service which will inspire young people to join it for a lifetime career."

Note

1. From an interview with Lelei Lelaulu, Chief Editor of the U.N. Secretariat News, December 19, 1995.

14. A Rapporteur from Tunisia on Religious Tolerance

The Human Rights Commission in Geneva has built up a large team of thematic rapporteurs—call them Investigators—on a huge range of subjects, for example mercenaries, torture, and child abuse. Since the end of the Cold War a comparatively new subject had come to the forefront of attention of the Commission—religious intolerance. Its rapporteur is a law professor from Tunisia. He is Professor Abdelfattar Amor, a Moslem fluent in Arabic and French. He works in the U.N.'s Center for Human Rights in Geneva.

Every year Professor Amor visits the General Assembly's Third Committee to introduce his report for the year. As he is constantly inquiring into the domestic affairs of nations, and so going beyond the strict mandate of the U.N. Charter, he has, in his own words "to proceed with independence and discretion." After receiving a complaint from a particular country about religious intolerance, he then investigates it. He regrets that something like 30 percent of all governments fail to respond to his inquiries, but he still makes a report to the Commission. The Commission has no powers to punish wrongdoers, but, in the Professor's words, "the diffusion of information can shame governments into action."[1]

In 1996 Professor Amor made the first visit ever of a rapporteur on Toleration to China. Not surprisingly his special focus was on Tibet. He sees his role in this, as in all other "delicate" investigations, not as a sprinter, but as a marathon runner.

He commented, choosing his words with care: "There is a transformation going on in China. They no longer talk of religion as the opium of the people.

44

But they still insist on rigid separation of religion from the rest of life. In spite of the extreme moderation shown by the Dalai Lama, they refused to accept his choice for the Panchen Lama. This attitude is difficult to deal with as Buddhism does not make, and never has made, a rigid compartmentalism between religion and politics."

Professor Amor is very concerned about the continuing persecution of the Bahá'i International Community in Iran. He would like to report on this subject as fully as possible. But the U.N., for reasons of economy, has issued a directive that his Annual Reports can be no longer than thirty-two pages. So his summary of visits made to trouble spots will necessarily be far too brief. The global public will therefore not get a proper picture of what is going on.

But he hoped at least the NGO community could publicize the results of his inquiries and possibly the Internet could also be used. This, he thought, given the present difficult financial circumstances of the U.N., was the best hope for educating the public worldwide.

In 1981 the U.N. voted for a Declaration on Religious Intolerance. The U.N. has followed up on this, especially since the demise of Communism. But the U.N. has yet to give the Special Rapporteur the right measure of solid support to enable him to complete his marathon assignment and to strike a decisive blow against religious persecution everywhere. The U.N. is unfortunately still a long way from turning this Declaration into a Convention of the General Assembly, which would put religious intolerance under the force of law.

Note

1. From a discussion with Professor Amor arranged by the NGO Committee on Freedom of Religion or Belief, November, 1996.

15. An International Civil Servant from Spain Reflects on the Political Department

"The Department of Political Affairs in this Secretariat," says Francesc Vendrell, a Spaniard from Catalonia, "is rather like a mini–Foreign Office. Our job is to brief the Secretary General, when he meets Ambassadors and when he travels overseas." Francesc Vendrell is Director of the East Asia and Pacific Section of the Political and International Affairs Department in the U.N.

Secretariat. The heart of the work, covering some thirty-five nations in Asia situated "beyond the Kyber Pass" is preventive diplomacy, preventing uneasy peace from degenerating into war. And if conflict has unfortunately occurred, then the job of the U.N. is to broker peace and also nowadays to take matters much further by playing an active role in peacebuilding.

Francesc explains that besides general monitoring of his East Asian Region he is especially concerned with issues where, according to the Charter, the Secretary General has been given a mandate to exercise his good offices. At present the future of East Timor is at stake. Negotiations are taking place between Portugal, the ex-colonial power, Indonesia, the occupying power, and the East Timorese themselves. Recently President Mandela of South Africa has been helping the U.N. to try to find a solution to this thorny issue.

In Cambodia the East Asia office is trying to maintain the liberal pluralism which is the spirit of the Paris Agreement and a troika of nations from the Association of South East Asia Nations (ASEAN) is assisting in this delicate exercise of preventive diplomacy. In Myanmar, currently under military rule, the Secretary General has a mandate from the General Assembly to try and bring about democratization and national reconciliation. Francesc Vendrell spoke about the special difficulties of this negotiation: "Myanmar has many different ethnic groups—eight major ones I believe. In delicate situations like this—and I remember when there was a similar situation in the long drawn-out negotiations over Namibia—it is often the most effective way if the Secretary General exercises his 'inherent powers' more or less independently of mandates he may have been given either by the General Assembly or the Security Council."

A vital part of Francesc Vendrell's service in the Secretariat has been spent away from U.N. Headquarters on overseas missions. He made some 50 trips a year to Central America when he was involved in negotiating peace in Nicaragua, El Salvador, and Guatemala. He described the importance of building up personal contact with the people on the ground: "It is rather like the family doctor paying regular visits to the patient. And it's a two-way relationship. We at the U.N. need to know the people and to get them to realize and to trust that the U.N. is not in the business of interfering in local politics. We on our side also need to become knowledgeable about potential supporters, like churches and NGOs who are working alongside the U.N. to bring about peace and reconciliation in their region."

In all this work for peace Francesc felt sure that being from Catalonia helped him to do his work for the U.N. more effectively: "During the Franco years in Spain I knew what it felt like to belong to a minority culture that was being suppressed. I knew firsthand the importance of culture, language, and ethnicity on the human psyche. So during the Cold War, I could see that countries under Communist rule were not all bad, and nor were those on the side of the West all good. Later on, when taking part in negotiations for peace in Guatemala, my background helped me to understand the perspective of the indigenous people.

"I am glad that since 1975 Spain has changed so much. In Juan Carlos we have a monarch who has actively supported democracy and cultural diversity. And Spanish links with Latin America are now closer and more fruitful than they have ever been."

Francesc Vendrell explained how peacemaking and peacebuilding had worked out in Central America.

"In El Salvador we played a part in reshaping the whole society. The peace agreement enabled the U.N., for the first time in its history, to field U.N. human rights monitors. Entire military units, including death squads, were abolished. The officer corps was purged and a new and independent civilian police force was created. We also helped to establish a Truth Commission. It helped, too, that the leaders in El Salvador and of the other Central American Republics had a special regard for Secretary General Perez de Cuellar both because he was a Latin American and also because he came across to them as a father figure.

"In Guatemala the situation was different. The army was much stronger than the guerrillas and the American involvment was less. Also in Guatemala the majority of the population was indigeneous and that also gave a different imprint to the negotiations."[1]

Francesc Vendrell fondly recalls the occasion when in 1971 the famous cellist Pablo Casals, also a Catalan, came at the age of 95 to the U.N. to conduct the Annual General Assembly Concert. At the interval Casals spoke briefly, reminding the audience that Catalonia's Parliament was the oldest in the world. He went on to play the famous Catalonian song "El Cant dels Ocells," ("The Song of the Birds") which the great musician said made him think of small birds flying away all over the sky and singing a refrain for peace.

Note

1. Interview with Francesc Vendrell, Director of the East Asia and Pacific Division of the Department of Peace and International Security, October 10, 1997.

16. The Rise of Non-Governmental Organizations at the U.N.

One of the great unanswered questions about the U.N. is so simple it hardly seems worth asking. What exactly is meant by that grand-sounding expression at the start of the United Nations Charter, "We the Peoples"?

It all seemed so simple in 1945 when the charter was signed. "We, the Peoples" were the original fifty-one nation states who stood ready to sign the Charter. Then, within these nations, there was a sprinkling of voluntary citizen's organizations who were concerned with social and humanitarian issues. They lobbied successfully to be brought into the U.N. to consult with its Economic and Social Council about help for refugees and more generally about the rehabilitation of all the people who had suffered in the Second World War. The voice of the millions in the colonial dependencies was nowhere to be heard.

Article 71 of the Charter gave the NGOs the right to be consulted in the negotiations on social and humanitarian issues, but many matters were judged by the nation states to be outside the competence of "the peoples." There was nothing in the Charter, for instance, giving the people the right to be consulted on issues of disarmament of law-making or to be involved in any way in the substantive business of the General Assembly or the Security Council.

Fifty years have passed and things look much more encouraging for citizen activists. We now live in a global civil society. People expect less of their governments and expect to do more for themselves. Equally in a world that is threatened by international environmental disasters, governments find that there are many problems they cannot solve by themselves. So where do they turn for help—to non-governmental organizations. Practical experience has been convincing them that often the NGOs know more about a local situation and are willing to work quietly behind the scenes to implement joint projects.

But who are these NGO people? They are an extraordinary mix of citizens from a world constituency and they have all the strength and weaknesses that one might expect from people representing such a huge variety of interests.

Their greatest strength is quite simply that they have vision and a sense of urgency. They care enough about a particular injustice or suffering to get on and do something about it quickly. Often they have vital local knowledge. They reach out easily beyond national boundaries and loyalties. They are less motivated by personal profit. They can identify a serious issue before the rest of the world is hardly aware it exists.

Of course they have weaknesses, too. Often they concentrate on their own particular cause and they find it difficult to unite with others who seek similar goals, but wish to tackle them in different ways. They are perpetually short of resources. They can find it difficult to create the right relationship between their international offices and their national membership. They find it frustrating to relate to the bureaucratic way of doing things, and not least to the lengthy processes they encounter at the U.N.

Now in the nineties an extraordinary mobilization of citizens is taking place. Education is making this possible, especially in the global South which had very few NGOs in the colonial times of 1945. The women's movement—empowering women on a very broad front—is producing new groups of activists, especially in the areas of education, public health, and domestic human rights. There is also a revolution in international communication through the use of faxes and E-mail. This new phenomenon is creating an exhilarating sense of confidence in ordinary people worldwide that they can and will get together, reaching out beyond national boundaries to solve their social and economic problems.

At U.N. Headquarters this new involvement of NGOs takes place in three ways. First, NGOs continue to have a status with the Economic and Social Council (ECOSOC) but in far greater numbers than in 1945. They can speak and submit comments in writing to the Council and its Commissions. These rights are earned by producing reports every three or four years to the Secretariat's NGO Unit which demonstrate they have been making an expert contribution in a particular area of work in which ECOSOC is active. More than one thousand NGOs have now gained this privilege.

In other areas, such as disarmament for example, the NGOs have no legal standing but they have worked out informal arrangements to interact with the delegates. The formal negotiations remain closed to all but the officially accredited diplomats.

Second, NGOs can relate to the U.N. through the Department of Public Information. This, so far, has been much more of a relationship of receiving rather than giving. These NGOs may attend weekly briefings on U.N. progress on all fronts and are asked to relay accounts of these briefings to their constituencies. There are as many as 1500 NGOs in this category.

Third, NGOs have attended the series of government Summit Conferences and the parallel Non-Governmental Fora which have been such an important U.N. activity in the nineties. The Rio Summit on Environment and Development was *the* highlight so far with literally thousands of NGOs accredited. Only the numbers at the Beijing Women's Conference came close to it. At these conferences NGOs have become more and more able to work closely with governments in suggesting new policies and in helping to draft Plans of Action for follow-up. Fourth, there are arrangements for NGOs to be associated with U.N. Specialized agencies.

At no time has the progress of NGOs in their relationship with the U.N. been smooth and steady. There is still a long way to go before many Member States feel at ease with NGOs. Also the U.N. Secretariat is understaffed to cope with the ever-growing number of NGOs coming to participate and to lobby the diplomats who meet every year in New York. In the meantime the Non-Governmental Liaison Service (NGLS) does its best to act as a go-between and is particularly helpful to new NGOs from developing countries. Because the U.N. is nowadays extremely sensitive about security, NGOs are finding that access to the Secretariat is a much more inconvenient business than it used to be. For example, it is almost impossible for them to bring colleagues along for discussions at short notice. It has seemed that for every two steps the NGOs take forward, they have to take one step back as well.

The NGOs have for fifty years had their own coalition—the Conference of NGOs in Consultative Relationship with the U.N. known as CONGO. CONGO does not itself take positions on U.N. issues but it can and does facilitate opportunities for groups of NGOs to make their mark within the U.N. system.

In 1998 Afaf Mahfouz, President of CONGO, reported about the impact of NGOs since the end of the series of Global Conferences of the nineties. "A high official of the World Bank told me how difficult it was for the Bank to cope with demands by NGOs for implementation of the recommendations of United Nations conferences. NGOs do not understand, he noted, that recommendations have no legal binding force. I would submit, however, that NGOs at the doors of his organization, at the doors of governments and in communities, are a potent force for ensuring that many recommendations will in fact be implemented."[1]

This new people's movement is a timely development of those famous first words of the Charter "We the Peoples." So today the U.N. is doing more and more of its work in partnership with NGOs, and their contributions are regularly affirmed and welcomed by the President of the General Assembly and the Secretary-General.

Secretary General Kofi Annan acknowledged the broadening influence of the NGOs in the U.N. system when in 1998 he praised their work during the arduous negotiations for the Treaty to create a permanent International Criminal Court. He said: "I am encouraged that this year, in which we commemorated the Fiftieth Anniversary of the Universal Declaration of Human Rights, has also been the year of the International Criminal Court. As this campaign for ratification of the Rome statute gets under way, I hope NGOs will continue to display the interest and commitment that has helped bring us this far. The conviction of Jean-Paul Akayesu, the ex-Mayor of Taba, Rwanda, of genocide and crimes against humanity, including rape, shows the utility of an international tribunal. It also shows that the U.N. can deliver."[2]

NGOs have come a long way since 1945, but not yet all the way. Until the General Assembly votes for them to have a formal working relationship with the Assembly, its main Committees, and its special Conferences, "We, the Peoples" will not have obtained their rightful place within a U.N. system, appropriately geared for the 21st century.

Notes

1. Afaf Mahfouz, *Congo at Fifty. A Reaffirmation of Commitment.* 50th Anniversary Publication. P. 10.
2. Press Release SG/SM/6697/PI/1079. September 14, 1998.

17. U.S. Senator Pell—U.N. Supporter through Five Decades

How many people in this world care enough about the U.N. to always carry a copy of the U.N. Charter in their back pocket? Probably there is only one: United States Senator Claiborne Pell, who has been doing it every day since 1945—for more than 50 years! And beside the Charter, the Senator keeps always the names of all the original signers of the Charter. Why does he do it? He replies: "I do it to remind myself of the importance of the U.N., and that I must keep on doing all I can to support it."[1]

Senator Pell has been serving as a Congressional Delegate to the 51st Session of the General Assembly. Over the past fifty years he has kept up his unflagging support of the U.N. His independently-minded constituents in Rhode Island have kept on, election after election, voting him back into the United States Senate. He summed up the U.N.'s achievements over these years in these words: "The U.N. has done so much for Health and Education. It has stopped wars and generally the world is a better place because it exits. If the U.N. did not exist we would have to invent it."

Back in 1945 the senator was active at San Francisco in drafting the parts of the Charter that dealt with Security. He worked on Articles 44, 45, and 46, which call for the members of the U.N. to make forces "immediately available" to the U.N. under Chapter 7 of the Charter. This section of the Charter is all about how collective security is designed to work when there are threats to peace or acts of aggression. He regretted that its provisions have still not been acted upon. He acknowledged that the present arrangements for making forces available in a crisis are better than nothing, but they are still not what the makers of the Charter envisioned. Without standing military forces at its disposal, it is not possible for the U.N. to make an immediate response to an act of aggression.

The Senator was present at the Stockholm Conference in 1972, and was particularly pleased with the establishment of the new U.N. organization to deal with issues of the Environment—the United Nations Environment Programme (UNEP). At that time he tried to raise the issue of chemical destruction of trees in Vietnam, but the then-current Nixon administration, he recalled, "quickly shut [him] up."

Disarmament has also been a special concern for the Senator. He was active in formulating the treaty outlawing nuclear weapons on the seabed. And he has always pressed for the control of small arms as well as heavy weapons.

He explained how hard it is to get the Congress to give funds for the U.N.

"There are always Americans who think we are so big and strong we don't have to bother about the rest of the world. Far from us dominating the U.N., the problem is to get the people in Washington to pay enough attention to U.N. matters. In my view, our ambassadors at the U.N. do the best they can."

On being asked what he thought was the greatest achievement of the U.N. so far, he replied, "Preventing a major war from breaking out in the Balkans."

Senator Pell's approach to international politics has consistently been consensual, multi-lateral, and liberal. Down the years the bridge between the U.N. and the American political process has remained a frail and unsteady one, but Senator Pell has made sure, in as much as one man can, that it has been kept in repair and in active use. All believers in the U.N. should be thankful for his rock-solid commitment to the work of the U.N., and never more so than in this decade which so many dignify with the uncomplimentary sobriquet "the lean and mean nineties."

Note

1. From an interview with Senator Claiborne Pell, May 19, 1997.

18.   Options for a People's Assembly

Will there ever be a People's Assembly at the U.N.? Right up to the middle of the nineties the answer would have been "It's just a dream." But not any more. Suddenly the idea has entered the realm of practical politics.

It's always been an idea of exciting possibilities. It would introduce a great breath of democratic fresh air into the debates of the General Assembly. After all, the General Assembly is at present an Assembly where bureaucrats—Ambassadors—speak thoughts that always have to be cleared by other bureaucrats—their bosses in their Ministries of Foreign Affairs back home. A People's Assembly would make the U.N. much more democratic. And if it was made up of the right members, it would match the temper of these times in which people in our global civil society feel wider loyalties than ever before.

More than that. The presence of "We the Peoples" would create a new identity at the heart of the U.N.'s deliberations. Governments cannot realistically renounce war as an instrument of policy, but people can. A United Nations People's Assembly could be a crowning achievement of a global civil society which almost everyone, including nation states, is now trying to bring to birth. A People's Assembly can and should be dedicated to the creation of President Roosevelt's original vision—the establishment of "permanent peace."

There is no need to start from scratch. Way back in 1975 the first World Citizen's Assembly took place and it now has fifty branches worldwide. More recently all the U.N. Summits—on Human Rights, on Population, on Social Development, and most recently on Women—have been preceded by gatherings of citizen's meetings and these have, in effect, been a kind of people's parliaments.

The major independent reports on reforming the U.N. which have been appearing over the Fiftieth Anniversary discuss the subject in some detail. And it will surely come up at the U.N.'s own "Open-Ended Working Group on Reforming the U.N." People are beginning to feel that they are, at one and the same time, both global as well as national citizens. This feeling deserves to be grounded institutionally.

So just how will people be selected for a United Nations People's Assembly? There are all sorts of options and the final solution is likely to be a mix of the best ideas. Would NGOs dominate? Would elections be direct or indirect? Would the Assembly vote, or be essentially advisory? Who would pay for it? Perhaps some new kind of global tax could be created.

Machinery would be required to follow up the Assembly's recommendations for action. This has been a problem with the recent Conferences. Thousands deliberated and decided at the summits, but then only a trickle of people appeared at the U.N., when, later on, follow-up proposals begun to be considered in this or that U.N. Commission.

Perhaps a special commission is needed to sort out all the possibilities. But whatever is decided, a major new idea is now on the wing. A People's Assembly could have a spectacular effect in giving 'the people' a direct voice and a voice of real weight to add to and influence on an annual basis the debates in the General Assembly.

Postscript

In 1998 Secretary General Kofi Annan proposed that there should be a special Millennium Forum to be held before the General Assembly's Millennium Assembly. Already the Conference of Non-Governmental Organizations (CONGO) is working with others to make this unique event a reality. Meanwhile other citizen networks such as the Millennium People's Assembly Network (MPAN) are working to see if, in this age of a global civil society, it is possible to establish the People's Assembly on a regular ongoing basis.

Part Two

Law

1. Congress of Public International Law

When diplomats stroll towards the delegates' lounge down a long wide carpeted corridor, they are usually deep in conversation. On this second floor of the United Nations with its quiet corners, its bar overlooking the East River, and its intimate café, so much of the stuff of real diplomacy gets done.

As delegates of all kinds make their way down the long wide corridor, they often don't even pause to notice a tall gray column by the window with Akkadian hieroglyphics carved into it. It's the Code of Hammurabi—the world's oldest known written legal code—presented to the United Nations by Iraq, and composed by Sumerians from Babylonia as long ago as 1792–1750 B.C.

This column is a silent witness, placed at the heart of U.N. activity, that a code of law is the indispensable foundation of civilization. There can be no world order without world legal order. It is law and the process of law which makes the settlements of disagreements possible before they deteriorate into violent disputes. In fact, one of the Charter's first articles (Article 13) specifically gives the United Nations the authority to make international laws. Now this Babylonian pillar, sixteen centuries after it was created, is "presiding" over the first ever Congress of International Public Law, arranged to coincide with the U.N.'s Fiftieth Anniversary.

In fact the Code of Hammurabi, like all codes of law even today, was incomplete. For instance it apparently had no rules and sanctions for murder, but it dealt at length with rules for fair trading. In a remarkably similar way, the delegates at the Congress are finding the development of law is a very uneven business. For example, laws for the Environment and laws for Outer Space are still in their infancy. Modern international trade law, on the other hand, is reaching a very advanced and sophisticated level of development.

The delegates at the 1995 Congress of International Law gathered to survey the whole state of international law as it has developed over the past fifty years. It was pointed out by Mr. Alexander Yankov of Bulgaria that it was no coincidence that in 1947 both the International Law Commission and the Commission on Human Rights came into existence in the same year. These two United Nations Commissions provide the essential supranational underpinning for peace, security, and relations between nations.

These past fifty years have seen some extraordinary advances in the scope of international law. Mr. Hans Corell, Under-Secretary-General for Legal Affairs, drew special attention to the new Criminal Tribunals for Rwanda and Bosnia; to the Law of the Sea, eleven years in the making; and to the Laws protecting U.N. staff working in areas of conflict.[1]

It might be thought that all proposals coming from the International Law Commission, which is itself a body of experts working on the preparation of

Conventions for the General Assembly, would be ratified by member states and become international law. It does not happen that way. As Mr. Karl Zemanek of Austria explained, some laws, like Conventions on Diplomatic Relations, Consular Relations, and the Law of Treaties, find plenty of support from States. Others like the treaty between States and International Organizations languish for years without sufficient signatures to become law.[2]

Others, again, appear stillborn. For instance, the Vienna Convention on Succession of States in Respect of Property, Archives and Debts has, since 1983, collected only four signatures; it needs fifteen to become law.[3] It seems that states, and especially newly-created states, are nervous of laws which seem to involve commitments relating to the break-up of states. It is one thing to follow the custom about what to do when a new state is created from an old one; it is quite another to sign a Convention and turn custom into law.

Laws are always evolving. Progressive development is always taking place. Thus at the great Rio Conference in 1992, the Convention on Biodiversity says "the financial mechanism shall operate within a democratic and transparent system of governance" (Article 21). This, says Professor Pinto from Sri Lanka, is probably the first time that the term 'democracy' has been applied to inter-state relations.[4]

All delegates at this Congress worried that the general public as yet hardly knows anything about international law. The title of the Conference "Towards the Twenty-First Century: International Law as a *Language* for International Relations," proclaims that International Law is a kind of mother tongue of the modern world. But who outside the professionals in the law knows this language, or even that it exists?

This "language" urgently needs be taught in high schools and be frequently aired on the media.[5] Only if this happens will the public be trained and ready in an emergency to respond to the call of Heraclitus from the sixth century B.C. "The people should fight for their law as they do for their city wall."

Update

In October 1998 Under-Secretary-General Hans Corell addressed Parliamentarians from the Interparliamentary Union. This group with membership in 136 nations was founded in 1889 and is the world's oldest international political organization. They hold an annual meeting at the United Nations.

Under-Secretary-General Corell said that the nineties had seen remarkable progress in creating international law. He cited the new Conventions on Terrorism, on Electronic Commerce, on the Law of the Sea, which has now over 100 ratifications, and most recently the Rome Statute on the International Criminal Court.

58

Notes

1. Corell, Hans. *Under-Secretary-General.* U.N. Secretariat Opening Statement, United Nations Congress. P. 7.
2. Zemanek, Karl. Austria. *Does Codification Lead to Wider Acceptance?* United Nations Congress on Public International Law 13–17 March 1995.
3. Corell. P. 7.
4. Pinto, M.C. Sri Lanka. *Democratization of International Relations and its Implications for Development and Application of International Law.* U.N. Congress. P. 10.
5. Buckingham, Donald E. *Creating World-Class Citizens: International Law as an Essential Ingredient in Secondary School Education.* U.N. Congress. P. 7–11.

2. The Law of the Sea

The Law of the Sea is a colossal piece of international law which has been created by the U.N. to cover a colossal part of the earth's surface–70 percent to be exact! This law affects all of the oceans on the planet and all of the sea-bed which lies beneath. It brings under law what is known as the Global Commons—the huge part of the planet's surface that falls outside the jurisdiction of States.

After fourteen years of hard bargaining, this great omnibus convention finally came into existence in 1982. Its birth will always be associated with the names of the two Presidents of the negotiations, Ambassador Shirley Amarasinghe of Sri Lanka and Ambassador Tommy Koh of Singapore, who tirelessly piloted the tortuous negotiations for the creation of this convention. After ratification by sixty countries, the convention was finally given the backing of international law in November 1994.

At the conclusion of the final Plenary in 1982, Ambassador Koh celebrated the occasion with these words: "It was no exaggeration to say that the majority of the developing countries had not imposed their majority power on the minority, and the minority of powerful states had always tried to accommodate the legitimate interests of the less powerful states."[1]

So what exactly does the Convention do? The U.N. describes its purposes as follows: "The Convention covers almost all ocean space and its uses such as navigation and overflight, resource exploration and exploitation, conservation and pollution, fishing and shipping. Its 320 articles and nine annexes constitute a guide for behavior by States in the world's oceans.

"And then, of course, there has to be ways that the rules and regulations established by the convention can be enforced. So an International Sea-Bed

Authority and an International Tribunal for the Law of the Sea have been set up."

In July 1996, the President of the Fifth Meeting of the States' Parties to the Convention, Ambassador Satya Nandan of Fiji, said that more than 100 states had become parties to the Convention and he felt confident more would soon sign as well. He concluded, "Tremendous progress has been achieved with a very important and significant contribution to the peace and security of the world."[2]

One of the subjects which illustrates the complexities of the subjects which come under the jurisdiction of the Convention is the matter of the continental shelf. Some nations argue that their continental shelf extends beyond the normal 200 miles and therefore the right to exclusive economic exploitation can prevail for up to as much as 350 miles under the ocean. A special commission made up of independent experts has the job of proving, and legally establishing, the precise amount that a continental shelf of coastal countries does in fact jut more than 200 miles into the ocean.

Collecting the necessary geological data can be technically exacting. A recent U.N. report explains:

> Changes in the nature of the seismic source have brought about improvements in the fidelity of the data collected. "Sparkers," in which the pulse is created by the discharge of an electrical pulse in the water, can be used to provide a high-resolution seismic profile, but with limited depth of penetration. "Airguns" powered by compressed air, can be tuned to produce a variety of acoustic pulses appropriate to the depth at which maximum resolution is required. Such systems (unlike explosives) have the added advantage of being more benign.[3]

The coastal state has to satisfy the Commission that it has carried out the survey of the maximum extent of its coastal shelf in the proper scientific manner. The exclusive control of vast resources under the ocean, including oil and gas, may depend on carrying out this geological mapping correctly.

In June 1997, the members of the Commission, with Mr. Yuri Borisovitch Kazmin as their Chairman, were solemnly sworn in at U.N. Headquarters in front of Mr. Hans Corell, Under-Secretary-General for Legal Affairs and the Legal Counsel for the United Nations. The work could now begin.

So institution by institution, the machinery to make the enforcement of the Law of the Sea a reality has now been put in place. Ironically this visionary law, one of the largest the U.N. has ever created, was first proposed way back in 1967 by Ambassador Arvid Pardo from Malta, one of the smallest nations in the world.

Notes

1. 182nd Plenary Meeting of the Third U.N. Conference of the Law of the Sea 1982, P. 167.
2. Ambassador Nandan, Charman of the Fifth Meeting of the States Parties. September 1996. SPLOS/14. P. 12.
3. Study by the Secretariat. SPLOS/CLCS/INF/1. June 1996. P. 9.

3. Creating an International Criminal Court

The count-down to the creation of an International Criminal Court began in the early nineties, but the way ahead was bound to be long and slow. The most positive step forward was that by the mid-nineties the embryo courts or tribunals for Bosnia and Rwanda actually existed and had begun their work by serving some indictments, and in 1998 the Bosnian court made one conviction.

As far back as 1989, President Robinson and the Caribbean Community first brought the possibility of creating an International Criminal Court to the attention of the General Assembly.

Since the Preparatory Committee on the subject met in 1996, states had had an opportunity to submit their reactions to the draft statute created by the International Law Commission. Their constructive criticism could be divided into two halves—the broadly political and the technically legal.

First the political angle. States are hesitant, very hesitant to hand over legal power and responsibility to an international body, however responsible it may be. After all, the first responsibility of a state is to protect its citizens by means of police and a judiciary. To abdicate this basic task of the state to a superior power, especially when it seems the Security Council may be making the crucial decision when to use the new Court is not going to happen easily. Sudan put its reservation like this: "The world's less powerful countries and those of lesser political, military, and economic influence have become wary of the exploitation of global humanitarian principles and objectives to serve the purposes of some parties rather than others."[1]

This kind of reaction makes it essential that the Court shall, broadly speaking, stick to dealing with well-defined war crimes and crimes against humanity. As Cyprus put it: "In our view a code should be comprehensive, but at the same time, lean and defensible, encompassing well-understood and legally definable crimes, in order to ensure the widest possible acceptability and effectiveness."[2]

Then there are the issues where politics and law overlap. The problem is things that can be easy to understand can at the same time be so difficult to define. Take the definition of aggression. The U.N. General Assembly attempted a definition in 1974, but it has not settled the matter. The French even doubt whether it is a crime that can necessarily be pinned on individuals: "The introduction of the concept of 'crime of aggression' raises difficulties. Aggression is a particularly serious violation of public international law, a violation attributable to States, rather than an offense with which an individual may be charged."

The United States was full of reservations about turning over the prosecution of terrorists to an international court. Not the least of their difficulties was the independence of the prosecutor and the cost of prosecution. Thus, they commented that the costs of the tribunal for the former Yugoslavia for two years amount to $49 million. The U.S. made a practical suggestion about court funding which has inevitable political consequences: "In general, one would expect a basic budget to be borne by the states which are parties to the statute. Some formula would be necessary for the apportionment of such costs. We believe an appropriate formula would be that used by the Universal Postal Union, which is also used by the Permanent Court of Arbitration and the Hague Conference on Private International Law.

"Then there is a whole range of technical legal considerations which the committee has to discuss and refine such as the complementarity of national and international law, mechanisms for initiating jurisdiction, rules of evidence and procedure, and so on."

The birth of the International Criminal Court would be almost as great an event as the birth of the United Nations itself and the Founding Fathers of the U.N. would surely not be satisfied until it actually happens.

Update

In July 1998, it actually happened! A statute to bring into existence an International Criminal Court was finally agreed by a gathering of 160 countries in Rome. But it was no easy birth. The conference went on for five weeks and it was itself preceded by four years of preparatory work! It was decided that attacks against international humanitarian aid workers would be classified as a war crime. And for the first time in history, due to the effort of the 300-strong Women's Caucus for Gender Issues, it was recognized in the Statute that rape is a component of crimes against humanity. A particularly encouraging feature was the presence of 250 active NGOs whose members were largely under the age of thirty.

Ben Ferenz, one of the few lawyers still living who had been a prosecutor of Nazi war criminals at the Nuremberg trials was there and summed up his feelings.

"It is a great historic event. It is very gratifying to be here. It's almost the culmination of an idea for which I was mocked and ridiculed for years but we've got to build a world of law. This is what lawyers do."[3]

But a functioning Court is unfortunately still a long way off. Sixty nations have to ratify the statute in their own legislative assemblies before it enters into force. And even then there are still a number of key issues—procedural, financial, and legal—which are unresolved. The Americans, in particular, do not want the Court to be able to do much except prosecute for clear-cut crimes of genocide. An agreement on how to define the crime of aggression—successfully achieved at Nuremberg—has still not been reached.

All the same this agreement in Rome was a defining moment in the search for world order under law. It will give the U.N. teeth as never before, and there is a real hope that the nations which are hanging back will eventually agree to sign and ratify it.

Notes

1. States response to a draft statute for an International Criminal Court prepared by the International Law Commission. July, 1996.
2. Ibid.
3. *War Crimes Court under Fire.* CWRU School of Law P. 2. September, 1998.

4. Creating International Law

The U.N. is about the making of International Law, or it is about nothing. The preservation of peace itself depends on laws in the U.N. Charter. The Charter itself under Article 13 sets in motion all the work that has been done in making these laws since 1945, and also establishes the International Court of Justice, which is based in the Netherlands. The engine of lawmaking is the Sixth Committee of the General Assembly which deals with all legal affairs, including the revision of the Charter itself. In 1947 the General Assembly went further and established the International Law Commission, a committee of experts who advise the Sixth Committee, and who work with a professional team of lawyers in the Secretariat itself.

One of these lawyers in the Secretariat in 1996 was Dr. Roy Lee. He is Chinese, originally from Manchuria, and has degrees from Chinese, Canadian, and British universities. He specialized in space law and laws for nuclear energy. Within the U.N. system he has been involved with Human Rights laws, the creation of the Law of the Sea and, until 1998, he was Director of the Codification Division of the Secretariat.

Dr. Lee worked on a number of fundamental legal principles, affecting subjects which are not well known or understood by the public. One area of concern to him was the Law of Treaties. Another was the laws relating to watercourses and the use and distribution of fresh water taken from them. A third was the principles behind possible new laws for the environment.

The Sixth Committee is working on a wide variety of subjects, some of which are constantly in the news and some of which are unknown to the public. Laws about the safety of diplomats and about terrorism are obvious subjects. Not so obvious is the discussion and creation of the laws which will undergird the possible establishment of an International Criminal Court. Another difficult legal issue is what to do about the Trusteeship Council now that there are fortunately only a very small number of colonies and trust territories under U.N. responsibility.

The Sixth Committee, made up of U.N. diplomats, looks at the creation of law from an essentially political rather than a technical, legal perspective. Neither viewpoint makes for rapid progress!

Roy Lee shares the concern of all those who feel the general public is simply unaware of the amount of international law which exists to make life easier for everyone in the modern world. International laws about the telegraph and post go back as far as the nineteenth century. Nowadays we are dependent on an international legal framework to sort out radio frequencies. We also now have a vast body of international trade law, and arrangements for arbitration in disputes.

"Take the simple business of buying a tin of tuna-fish," says Roy Lee. "Every purchase is only possible because of laws which determine where the fish can be caught and in what quantities; how the fish can be exported and imported; what are the health and safety regulations; and how payments will be made."[1]

To get people to understand about the laws the U.N. is making we are, in fact, in the middle of a Decade of International Law Education. But Roy Lee is disappointed with the progress made so far in educating the general public. He believes this kind of education has to start with civic classes in schools and go on to embrace political science courses and training for lawyers who so often only study domestic law at college. He comments, "All we have at present is the experts discussing the subject with other experts, and that is not good enough."

As long as we live in a world of nation states, the progress of international law will never be easy. States know they cannot do without international law, but at the same time they are aware that the stronger it gets, the weaker will be the authority of their own domestic laws. They are not going to give up the powers that national sovereignty confers without resistance all the way.

Update

The process of creating new international law is always complex and never swift. In August 1998, Dr. Roy Lee was working with the 50th Session of the International Law Commission. This commission, which is made up of more than thirty independent lawyers, was considering such subjects as reservations to treaties, diplomatic protection, and the difficult legal situations when states change their names and sometimes their nature as well. These deliberations will eventually result in the creation of Conventions which, after approval by the General Assembly, will become part of the body of International Law.[2]

Notes

1. Interview with Dr. Roy Lee, Head of the Codification Division of the Secretariat. March, 1996.
2. General Assembly. A/CN.4/1.566 August 10, 1998.

5. An Optional Protocol to Protect Women

When the U.N. gives individuals the right to petition the U.N. over the heads of their governments for a violation of their human rights, that is revolutionary. Yet it is already happening, and many governments have committed themselves to add protocols to Conventions, drawn up by the U.N. A protocol makes it possible for an individual to bring a complaint to the U.N. over the head of his or her national government.

True, before Governments will allow international lawyers to get involved, national legal remedies have to have been exhausted and the U.N. panel of experts, set up to examine complaints from individuals has first to be satisfied that justice may not have been done in the national courts. But governments nowadays are recognizing that when it comes to the rights of their own individual citizens, they sometimes do not have the last word.

Spurred on by the women's conference at Beijing, the Commission on the Status on Women is looking at bringing this same process into action exclusively to protect the rights of women.

Complaints procedures are long, drawn out affairs. The process mainly takes place by correspondence. For obvious reasons this is not a door that governments wish to open too wide. But governments have been getting used to the idea, and they have found that it is not too threatening if these Conventions have a clause—and it is left strictly optional for governments to sign on to it or not—by which individuals and sometimes groups can complain to the U.N. These clauses are called optional protocols.

Protocol processes for individuals to petition to United Nations bodies are already in use for the International Covenant on Civil and Political Rights, for the Convention on Racial Discrimination, and for the Convention on Torture.

In 1995 the Economic and Social Council asked governments and NGOs to give their view to the Secretary-General on having an optional protocol procedure to add to the Convention on the Elimination of all Forms of Discrimination against Women (CEDAW). Both individuals and groups would be able to petition under the new protocol. The experts would also be able to initiate a procedure against a state in which there was good reason to believe there was widespread discrimination against women still continuing.

During 1996 fourteen governments and nineteen NGOs replied with thoughtful answers. Almost all were in favor of a protocol. Finland, the Netherlands, Australia, and New Zealand were strongly positive. Others, like Germany and Japan, saw a number of difficulties ahead. Everyone agreed that it would be some time before there would be a consensus to have a draft protocol to present to the Economic and Social Council.

Almost all have come up with problems of real substance. But none stand in the way of the fundamental point that a protocol would focus uniquely on the violation of the human rights of women. Earlene Horne from St. Vincent and the Grenadines put it like this: "We want this protocol to become established, workable, and well known. Then the complainants will use it with their governments. Then in our national and regional Caribbean NGOs we will see to it that governments, which have signed the convention and the protocol stick to their commitments to protect women."[1]

One of the most difficult issues is the problem enforcing a verdict for a woman who has won her case. Would the complainant be able to claim some kind of financial restitution? If so, from whom? Would the complaints only be in written form? What about visits to talk to the complainants on the spot? From what kind of groups and organizations will complaints be accepted? How much publicity would be given to the offending parties? In Europe the Maastricht protocol stressed the importance of publicity to pressure governments to raise their standards of protecting human rights.

Another potential difficulty is overlapping with procedures in other Conventions. Under many of them women can already bring complaints, but the practical point is that mostly they do not. Too often women victims are poor and illiterate, and they do not know that procedures to help them already exist.

Every new step to be taken would involve time and money, and more work in particular for the Secretariat's Division for the Advancement of Women. And at this time the U.N.'s budget is contracting, not expanding, and Human Rights is notoriously underfunded anyway. Is this really the right time to add yet more procedures to the U.N.'s Human Rights Law?

Whatever the Women's Commission decides will have to go to the parent body, the Economic and Social Council, for approval, and then on to the General Assembly. If and when a new optional protocol is finally established, governments will have to decide individually whether they wish to sign and then to ratify it or not.

Update

In 1999 the General Assembly passed a resolution which will bring this new protocol into existence.

Note

1. From an interview with Earlene Horne, National Council of Women and Caribbean People's Development Agency (CARIPEDA). March 20, 1996.

6. The Indian Founder of "Law in Development"

The foundation of peace is laws that keep the peace. And it is an international framework of law that alone can make the development of international community possible. The problem is to get the spirit of lawmaking to permeate the whole of society from top to bottom.

Clarence Dias, a lawyer from India, saw this way back in 1977 when he was invited to become the first Director of the Center for Law in Development. He has three university law degrees and a doctorate from Cornell University. He grew up in Bombay in an academic family and always spoke English as his first language. His interest was and is how law can be made relevant to protect and enhance the lives of bewildered people who suddenly find themselves on the front line of economic change and development. To help these people Clarence started what he likes to call "Alternative Law."

He began to concentrate on the creating of community-based law. He wanted to create a new framework of laws which would benefit forest dwellers, subsistence fishermen, and the urban poor. People, he insisted, must know their rights when companies move in and attempt to exploit their living space. They must be able to appeal to lawyers who have been trained to understand their predicament. He likes to say about the dedicated people he recruits for his cause, "They must be the best that money cannot buy."

The credo of the Center, said Clarence, was aptly summed up in the words of the Filipino nationalist Jose Rizal; "Those who have less in life should have more in law."

For twenty years now this NGO has been building a network of lawyers in Asia, India, Bangladesh, Thailand, the Phillipines, Nepal, and there are now some thirty-five networks scattered throughout the region. After the Bhopal tragedy in India, companies tried to hire this new kind of people's lawyer to defend them. They were not for sale.

Core support for this work has come from overseas aid departments in Sweden and in Canada. The U.S. government has been excluded because it is often U.S. companies which attempt to ride roughshod over community interests. The American Ford Foundation, however, has recognized the importance of this work and is an active supporter. Time and again the worth of the work is proved by the willingness of local people to pay their full share of the local costs.

Right from its foundation, Law in Development was based at the Church Center, which is so conveniently located alongside the U.N. Clarence spoke enthusiastically about the Center.

"I have always found the Church Center is a place where they take a broad, holistic view of things. In the same building you have the Jacques Cousteau Society and you have an office for the International Indian Treaty Council. I am a Roman Catholic, but we never argue about religion. We concentrate on issues of justice and peace. We are a real community of NGOs. . . . There is no such Center where NGOs can feel at home alongside the U.N. in Geneva and they miss it."[1]

Clarence said he was not comfortable with the slogan "Think global, act local." He felt there was an equal need for "Think local, act global." For this reason he believed it was essential for Law in Development to have an office alongside U.N. Headquarters. He could bring to the counsels of the U.N. the thinking of both community-based and national groups, and demonstrate where international laws to meet their needs were inadequate or simply non-existent.

At the U.N. he explained how he worked within the context of the Conventions on Civil and Political Rights and on the Convention on Economic, Social, and Cultural Rights. And at times he would be in touch with the United Nations Development Programme (UNDP), and sometimes with Human Rights Special Rapporteurs, such as the one on forced evictions.

He spoke vigorously about the importance of the U.N. in all he was trying to do.

"The U.N. sets the standards and keeps on reminding people about the Covenants which flow from the Universal Declaration of Human Rights. The U.N. ensures publicity for issues which national governments often hope will remain covered up. The U.N. is an arena for interaction between governments and civil society. When NGOs raise matters at the Commission on Human Rights there is a pressure on national governments which is greater than any group within a nation can bring to bear by itself."

Besides using the U.N. system to help those who cannot help themselves to receive justice. Clarence explained that his organization acted as an early-warning mechanism to protect rural communities. For example, they needed protection if their local plants were being exploited for genetic material by outside interests or, conversely, if synthetic substitutes were making their locally grown crops uneconomic. And now there was a rising danger that a new wave of consumerism might destroy all the traditional values of local communities.

Over the past twenty years, Clarence Dias said that two things had given him the most satisfaction. First, the Alternative Law movement had really caught on. Even Supreme Court judges and Bar Councils were starting training schemes in their countries to fit in with the need to develop law for the people.

Second, he had noticed a terrific new mobilization of NGO effort around the time of the Vienna U.N. Human Rights Conference. Asians had learned a lot at the Preparatory Meeting in Bangkok to prepare themselves for this great U.N. Summit. The European Union has helped a great deal with finance for this gathering. People were now energized by the Conference Declaration to follow up on the Action Plan and to begin to monitor the results. Whatever business might do for material progress in the future, he was certain that the Human Rights and Environment Agendas which are so vital to village people were now firmly established. Finally Dr. Dias stressed, "Everything in the U.N. Charter with its great themes of peace, development, and human rights is essentially interconnected. At different times, governments for their own purposes suddenly want to prioritize this or that. As we move away from the Cold War mentality, we in civil society must resist the authoritarian tendencies of officialdom with all our strength."[2]

Notes

1. Interview with Dr. Clarence Dias. International Center for Law in Development. November 18, 1996.
2. Ibid.

7. A University Intern from Italy at the U.N.

Where would the U.N. be without interns? Almost all graduates who come to the U.N. in batches of sixty or so from all over the world stay for two months and sometimes a little longer. At a time when the U.N. is slimming down its operations they fill gaps, taking on work which otherwise would not get done. And they are all unpaid.

Most of the time they receive at least as much in terms of education and experience as they give. For them it is a unique chance to get a hands-on feel of working in a major international bureaucracy. They are surprised to discover the size and above all the complexity of the whole U.N. operation at Headquarters! Settling in at the U.N. is not easy either. They have to struggle to find accommodations in New York, and office space in the U.N. is not easy to come by. But most do settle down, and they find they have to learn the ropes as fast they can.

Giovanna Bertoli who had studied at the Catholic University in Milan, Italy was eager to do some work in International Public Law. Since she was a girl, Giovanna had always been very curious about all things international. After completing a study of The European Union at her university, she at least had a limited knowledge of some of the technicalities of international legal systems.

When she was placed in the Office of Legal Affairs, she more than got her wish. She set to work on legal implications of the new Convention of the Safety of United Nations and Associated Personnel. This was not just an academic enquiry. Already some 1,500 men and women from 85 nations have died while serving the U.N. on peacekeeping operations. And recently both in Somalia and Bosnia, the lives of U.N. peacekeepers have been especially in danger. People who risk their lives for the U.N. deserve all the legal protection they can get.

To make sure the law is clear, and then to make sure it is known to all those in an area of conflict is not easy, but it is urgent. There are other Conventions running parallel to the one which is specifically related to the protection of peacekeepers. The General Assembly passed a Convention on the taking of hostages in 1979. Then in 1993 they passed another one on International Protected Persons. This latest Convention now has to be analyzed and compared with the earlier ones.

Giovanna had other responsibilities. She attended and took notes on the Sanctions Committee of the Security Council and assisted her supervisor in discharging his daily work in the Office of Legal Affairs. All the time she felt she was working against the clock to produce some worthwhile work. Giovanna summed up her time at the U.N.

"This experience has made me even more sure than International Public Law is what I want to study more. The framework of laws, which cover all nations, has to be built brick by brick with extreme caution, as it is the bedrock of any kind of relations between states.

"International jurisdiction is a complicated, but fascinating business, partly based on customary rules set up through long practice and partly evolving in a state of flux and continuous evolution. I expect to be busy with it for a long time."[1]

Giovanna completed her work to help to clarify the laws protecting staff who work for the U.N. The Security Council has recently established the Dag Hammarskjöld Medal—named in honor of the only U.N. Secretary-General to die while on a Peacekeeping Mission—to honor the sacrifice made by U.N. peacekeepers, who have died as a result of hostile acts, from disease, from accidents, from landmines, or by the hand of terrorists.[2]

Notes

1. From an interview with Giovanna Bertoli. December 4, 1995.
2. USUN Press Release. July 22, 1997.

8.   The Persistence of Charlie Guetell

People who represent Non-Governmental Organizations (NGOs) at the U.N. are persistent, but some are more persistent than others. Consider the example of Charlie Guetell. He is a small, tough, retired manager of laboratories for alloys development from the United States with a passion for peace, and for the role of the U.N. as a key preserver of it.

Charlie is definitely a long-distance runner! For seventeen years he has pursued his self-chosen task of getting the U.N. to put in place a dispute settlement service offering help, or responding on request with its services of reconciliation early on in disputes. He has always believed that the time to deal with a smouldering fire of conflict is before and not after it bursts into flames. That's called preventive diplomacy!

Charlie explained why it took him so long to get the hand of the U.N. system.

"I was very naive when I started. I simply did not know that people from Non-Governmental Organizations (NGOs) like myself were supposed to stick to covering and reporting on U.N. affairs under the eye of the Department of Public Affairs, and that political activism was out of bounds.

"Anyhow, I thought I had a unique idea and I started looking for an organization who would support my aim. I first worked away under the flag of Global Education Associates and later for the Center of U.N. Reform. They were just the right kind of organizations. They broadly supported what I wanted to do as a non-paid volunteer, but they left me free to get on with it in my own way.

"But it was, and still is, difficult to determine how an idea can be introduced into the U.N. system. I knew that eventually my proposal must be embodied in a U.N. designated working paper submitted by one or more Member State. Could I find a member state to take a lead? It all took time, even years, to get things going. Fortunately during my naive period I made the acquaintance of some quite junior members of diplomatic missions, who actually listened to my proposals. As time passed, they were promoted. One eventually came back to the U.N. as an Ambassador and he agreed to sponsor my proposal.

"The problem with doing business in this manner at the U.N. is that the players on stage are always changing. Just when you get a diplomat to take up your idea and probably improve it, he or she leaves for another posting. Then you have to start all over again—probably with another mission altogether. Then after making real progress the same thing happens all over again!

"Apart from case by case initiatives taken by either the Security Council, the General Assembly or the Secretary-General, there is no permanent subsidary mechanism to deal with the smoldering fires of conflict. My idea was to establish a permanent mechanism which would offer settlement services or provide them on request. The concept I had in mind was a two-tiered operation. The first tier was a board of administrators elected on a regional basis in the U.N.'s Sixth (Legal) Committee and approved by the General Assembly. The second tier would be a roster of settlement experts in conflict resolution provided by the Member States. The settlers with the disputing parties would be the main actors in the process of resolving disputes.

"Member States have been considering, if this scheme were adopted, how much overlap there would be with the Security Council's own mandate under the Charter to maintain and secure peace and security.

"But progress is being made, slowly. Previously one Member State had agreed to sponsor the proposal, but at the last moment had to withdraw due to the new assignment of the Ambassador leading the effort. Then in 1993 two succeeding Ambassadors from another state put the proposal into working paper form. But this effort has received a temporary setback because of an internal crisis in that state."[1]

So Charlie Guettel, now in his eighties, keeps on running nothing less than a marathon in the cause of peace. Until the day comes when NGOs can relate to each other and to the diplomatic community by communication in cyberspace, innovative and imaginative mechanisms like his will depend on loners like Charlie who never give up their vision and their determination—and this is the really hard part—to translate their ideas into institutional reality.

Note

1. Interview with Charlie Guettel. October 14, 1997.

Part Three

Peacekeeping

1. Peacekeeping Founder

Kofi Annan is the first "insider" and the first Ghanaian to be made U.N. Secretary-General. He comes to the top job from successfully running the Department of Peacekeeping Operations. His appointment—the first African to hold the post—is a good moment to recall the name of the Founder of Peacekeeping, Ralph Bunche, who was a Black American. But for Bunche's extraordinary diplomatic achievement, Kofi Annan might never have had the chance to build his own high reputation in this pioneering realm of U.N. operations.

Ralph Bunche won the Nobel Peace Prize for negotiating no less than four armistice agreements in 1950 which brought about seven years of peace between Jew and Arabs. Later, after the Middle East War of 1956, Bunche defused another explosive situation during the Cold War by creating for the first time a U.N. peacekeeping force to take over in the zone of combat around the Suez Canal.

Peacekeeping does not even appear in the U.N. Charter. To make peacekeeping work, member states of the U.N. have to volunteer to lend their forces to the U.N. These troops must involve themselves in a conflict that may well be thousands of miles from their own borders. The interests, even the survival of their own nation state is not at stake. Paradoxically, too, peacekeepers are military personnel but are not allowed to use force, except for the right of self defense.

The success of this first peacekeeping exercise in the Middle East led to other U.N. peacekeeping ventures—in the Congo, Kashmir, Yemen, and Cyprus. Ralph Bunche continued to be the mastermind behind the development and administration of all these peacekeeping operations. His guiding hand was at work in the initial planning, implementation, and control of all these multinational expeditions. Through the years peacekeeping has become more complex and sophisticated in its aims, but the rules about impartiality by which it is governed remain the same as those that Bunche worked so hard to establish back in 1956.[1]

Ralph Bunche had a rare combination of gifts that made him successful on the highest slopes of international diplomacy. No one knew better than he that diplomatic negotiation is always hard work. During the negotiations on Rhodes he wrote to his wife:

> "I talk, argue, coax, and threaten these stubborn people day and night, in the effort to reach agreement. I made a bit of progress here and another bit there, but it is so hard and so arduous. Sometimes I feel that I should just tell them to go home and forget about the armistice . . . this is killing work. I haven't been out of the hotel for two weeks now. . . ."[2]

Fortunately he also knew how to relax and to get the rest of the negotiators to relax with him. At Rhodes in 1949 he arranged games of billiards and ping-pong between Jews, Arabs, and U.N. staff and produced some remarkably "mixed" teams. There was friendly rivalry away from the tension of negotiation, and everyone lightened up.

But when the time came to resume negotiations again, Bunche showed his special qualities. He could always temper toughness with patience. He was exceptionally skilled at transporting verbal discussions into written terms on paper, so much so that when everything was finally concluded, the Jewish delegation gave him a surprise farewell present of—an enormously long pencil![3] Some named him "the new Colossus of Rhodes."[4]

When Ralph Bunche died in 1971, U Thant the U.N. Secretary General from Myanmar, said of him: "He was modest but tough, brilliant but unassuming, tireless but compassionate, strong but understanding; and he gained a position and a reputation in the world which any man might well envy."[5]

And Bunche achieved all this in a land still scarred by outbreaks of racism and still ambivalent about recognizing the talents of its African-American population.

Outside the gates of the U.N. stands a great steel monolith, "Peace Form One," created by a black sculptor Daniel Johnson, and erected in memory of Ralph Bunche. It is regularly used as the gathering-point for speeches and demonstrations by a wide range of oppressed people, who wish to draw the U.N.'s attention to their plight. Bunche would have liked that.

Peacekeeping remains as exacting a discipline as it was under Ralph Bunche's inspiring leadership. In October 1998, Secretary General Kofi Annan unveiled a bust of Count Folke Bernadotte of Sweden, who was assassinated in 1948 while supervising the truce in the Arab-Israeli War. The Secretary General said, "Contrary to popular belief the pursuit of peace will not win you any popularity contests. In many respects it is not only one of the most dangerous pursuits—it is also one of the loneliest in the world."[6]

Notes

1. Urquhart, Brian, and Ralph Bunche. *An American Life.* Norton. P. 22.
2. Ibid. P. 208.
3. Ibid. P. 211.
4. Ibid. P. 215.
5. Ibid. P. 458.
6. U.N. Press Release. DH/2742 October 13, 1998.

2. Taking the Pulse of Peacekeeping

Five large clocks dominate the Situation Room of the Department of Peacekeeping Operations (DPKO). In Guatemala the peacekeepers are two hours ahead of New York time, and in the republic of Georgia they are nine hours ahead. Below each of the clocks are the acronyms of the 16 Peacekeeping Operations for which the U.N. is currently responsible. It is almost impossible to remember what the initials stand for! UNMOGIP—Military Observer Group in India and Pakistan; UNDOF—Disengagement Observer Force on the Golan Heights; MINURSO—Mission for the Referendum for the Western Sahara; UNPREDEP—Preventive Deployment Force in Macedonia; and many others. But to the six duty officers who man the room twenty-four hours a day, it becomes second nature to remember the name and location of every mission. The Situation Room is on global time and never sleeps.

In charge of the day shift one week in 1996 is Major George Thomas who is lent to the U.N. by the Singapore army where he has served in the infantry for 13 years. He is in a cheerful mood this morning because the news from Liberia is good. A ceasefire between rival factions is holding. His job is to get the up-to-the minute facts about the missions. Things have recently been very difficult in Liberia. All the equipment in the Operations Center was looted and the U.N. had to fly in replacements. Telephone contact with the Operations Center of each mission is made twice a day and each mission submits a daily Situation Report.

The staff analyze the facts, decide their political implications, and pass their conclusions and recommendations to the Under-Secretary-General in charge of Peacekeeping and then the information goes on to the Security Council, which authorizes and monitors all U.N. peacekeeping missions. Major Thomas commented on his work: "There is no substitute for peacekeeping. It plays a critical role, and monitoring the U.N. peacekeeping operations on a daily basis reminds one how awful life can get in the world's trouble spots. When the news from these areas of conflict is good, it give me joy to see there is still hope."[1]

Head of the Duty Room of the Situation Center is Francesco Manca, a member of the Secretariat from Italy, who has spent five years on peacekeeping activities in the field in Central America. He explained that the Situation Room essentially has two jobs to do. First, the office provides the key contact with peacekeeping missions all over the world. If there is a report of accidents or casualties from the media, his office can instantly call for the facts, and so ensure that the U.N. is not caught on the wrong foot politically. Nations are naturally very sensitive about the safety and well-being of the troops and police they have volunteered to take part in peacekeeping operations.

Second, his office sends out some fifty copies of its consolidated daily Situation Report. This report goes to other parts of the U.N., such as the Department of Humanitarian Affairs and to agencies such as UNICEF and UNHCR. It is the vital in-house news bulletin about peacekeeping operations.

Peacekeeping these days has often come to embrace "peacebuilding" as well. A recent U.N. budget document puts it like this:

"Some peacekeeping operations have been mandated to include different combinations of the following tasks: monitoring ceasefire and buffer zones, protecting humanitarian convoys, disarming and demobilizing ex-combatants, reforming military establishments, defining and establishing police forces, organizing or monitoring elections, monitoring human rights, promoting electoral and judicial reform, promoting aspects of civil and administration and coordinating economic rehabilitation."[2]

"The level of public expectation," says Francesco, "is often far above what the mandate from the Security Council has commissioned the Peacekeepers to do." He also pointed out that fulfilling the mandate can be very difficult, as when volunteering countries find it administratively difficult to take some of their best police off their regular work at home and lend them to the U.N.

Francesco stressed that the DPKO had been increasingly pro-active since the end of the Cold War. DPKO provides the Secretary General with ideas and recommendations which he may decide to put forward to the Security Council for its consideration.

Other U.N. projects can sometimes wait to be implemented: Peacekeeping and peacebuilding never can.

Update

October 1998 marked the 50th Anniversary of peacekeeping. In 1948 peacekeeping began when thirty-six unarmed men from the U.N. went to Palestine to keep the peace between Israelis and Palestinians. Since then, 750,000 military and civilian personnel have served in forty-nine peacekeeping operations. More than 1,000 peacekeepers have died in U.N. service.

Ambassador Burleigh of the United States, in praising the peacekeepers at the Commemorative Meeting, said: "It is fitting at this time that we remember our peacekeepers—men and women, young and old—who have sacrificed their lives in the service of peace. Dag Hammarskjöld wrote that one should 'seek the road which makes death a fulfilment.' Our peacekeepers have sought the right road, and their efforts and sacrifices have not been in vain, for they have fallen so that others may live in peace. The true memorial to their sacrifice is the peace they helped to create, the lives they helped to preserve, and the promise they helped to sustain in order to 'save succeeding generations from the scourge of war'."[3]

Notes

1. Interview with Francesco Manca and Major George Thomas in the Situation Center of the Department of Peackeeping Operations. May 28, 1996.
2. Proposed Program Budget 1998–1999. Section 3. Peacekeeping operations and special missions. P. 6 May, 1997.
3. USUN Press Release #164–(98) October 6, 1998.

3. Peacekeeper in Mozambique

Take a person who has a Ukrainian father and a Bulgarian mother, who went to school in Belgium, earned a B.A. in America, majoring in Chinese Studies, lived in London, Paris, and Rome, and make her a coordinator for the U.N. team in a remote province of Mozambique before the first free election in that country. What is her attitude when she is suddenly posted to such a place? Tatiana Androsov is just such a person, and her attitude is—not to have "an attitude!" "There is no time for it," she says, "The work on a U.N. mission is simply too absorbing and too urgent."

U.N. staff are by no means all desk-bound. People are constantly being selected to go on missions. Sometimes the missions can last a year or more, as for Western Sahara, and sometimes just for a few weeks, as for the Algerian elections.

Tatiana has worked as a consultant for the U.N. and as a Russian and French interpreter and now holds herself in readiness to go on U.N. missions for peacekeeping and peacebuilding. She has also been on preelection missions to South Africa and Cambodia.

In Mozambique in the Province of Nampula she used to start her day at 5 A.M., going over her notes of all the unsolved problems collected from the previous day. Then a crisis would occur—for example, persuading the Military Hospital, manned by Bangladesh and staffed by Moslems, to swallow hard and not be scared to take in a female member of the U.N. staff who had been in a car crash.

Besides dealing with endless shortages of transport, she had to teach what democracy was all about to a whole host of fledgling political parties. A vigilant outlook for outbreaks of violence was essential. Trouble might develop much more from unemployed ex-soldiers roaming the streets than from political quarrels. She had only twenty people to oversee preparations at the polling stations scattered over hundreds of miles on narrow dusty roads. "Working on a U.N. mission," she reflected, "is like becoming a monk or a nun. The only difference is you know it will not go on for more than a year."[1]

During the build-up to the Election, everything turned on building up the U.N. team. She would drop in on the warehouse which was so crucial to their supplies. On Sundays, with her love of French cooking, she would put on a long lunch for all her colleagues. Her indispensable Portuguese-speaking colleague from Cape Verde, Sagna Augustin, went on a brief holiday to South Africa and brought back excellent wines to make the Sunday gathering even better. A few drinks did wonders in solving apparently unsolveable problems! Yet more visits to the office on Sunday rounded off her "day off" and Tatiana would end it by working into the night on her fluency in speaking Portuguese.

She felt her extraordinarily varied international education and experience helped her on missions: "I reject nothing. From my Belgium background I get my love of food; from America a pragmatic outlook; from Russia my love of literature; from the British, my sense of humor. From the Chinese I learned self-control. The Chinese language also showed me completely fresh ways of looking at words. For instance the Chinese word for peace shows a woman sitting under a roof. The image for a nation state is 'force' coupled with 'law.' Those are unforgettable images."

Tatiana's experience on missions has made her more committed than ever to the U.N.'s involvement in peacebuilding. But she cautions, "For now the U.N. is only able to do what its member states want it to. But it must go further. It must think, not in terms of just nation states, but of humankind as a whole. That is the way it has to be, if we are to make it through the next century."

Note

1. From an interview with Tatiana Androsov. October 10, 1995.

4. Preparing Forces for Peacekeeping

When U.N. peacekeepers began to be taken hostage and even killed, as happened in Bosnia and Somalia, it sounded an alarm around the world. Is peacekeeping becoming impossible?

Ambassadors therefore need to be briefed regularly by the Department of Peacekeeping Operations, better known around the U.N. as DPKO, about the plans for the future of U.N. peacekeeping forces.

The nineties were a difficult, even a precarious time for peacekeeping. On the one hand, peacekeepers have been required more and more frequently to keep the peace in more and more impossible situations. On the other hand, governments, and especially the United States government with its Congress now dominated by Republicans, have not been willing to pay the sort of funds that new and additional forces would cost.

In 1995 Kofi Annan from Ghana, then Under-Secretary-General in charge, and his military staff, explained what he was doing about developing further standby arrangements for peacekeeping forces.

He asked a Canadian staff officer to give a precise briefing on the progress made since the standby scheme for peacekeeping forces was launched in 1993.

Since 1994 some 44 member states had indicated a willingness to provide emergency forces at short notice to keep the peace, and 30 of them had given precise details of the back up they could provide — medical staff, civilian police, mine clearance, ordinance and air services. So far just two states — Jordan and Denmark — had signed legal undertakings to provide the forces on request. Of course nothing can happen until the Security Council is faced with a new crisis, and it mandates that new peacekeepers are required.[1]

All in all, DPKO estimated that these offers would enable the U.N. to put together five fully-equipped brigades, each of four to five thousand men, and five brigades of a similar size, but without equipment as yet. The problem was now to provide these men with armored personnel carriers and a request for six packages of 60 vehicles each has made. Such a force could be made ready in anything from seven to 90 days after the request had been received from the U.N.[2]

It was estimated that a further 40 nations would offer forces in the future. And in the discussion, Australia and Spain said they would make their offers very soon. The general atmosphere at the meeting was one of satisfaction about this excellent response. Undoubtedly more standby forces would be made available soon. There was no feeling that peacekeeping was becoming so complex and costly that the burden on the member states was getting too heavy to be borne.

In 1995 the U.N. was already dealing with the second and third generation of peacekeepers. The days when peacekeepers only went in to a trouble spot only if requested are long passed. For humanitarian reasons, as in Yugoslavia, peacekeeping forces nowadays find themselves trying desperately to keep a peace where there is no peace. For military men to have their hands tied behind their backs in this kind of situation is a thankless task indeed. Dangerous, too. Yet that is precisely what U.N. forces have been asked to do in the Balkans since the Dayton Peace Accords.

Standby arrangements are one thing. For the U.N. to have its own rapid-response force is quite another. Yet such a voluntary force may be what is most needed for quick response and for peace enforcement in the future. The Netherlands have put forward a reasoned proposal in favor of this kind of rapid deployment force.[3] Kofi Annan has aptly said that to write of a rapid-response force is "like telling New York City that you will build a fire-house when the fire occurs."[4] Time alone will tell it the members of the United Nations are prepared to think long-term about a peacekeeping fire brigade, and to pay for it.

Meanwhile Canadians are always particularly active in peacekeeping—planning for it, staffing headquarters, and providing troops for it. Indeed the very concept owes its creation to Canadian Lester Pearson who in 1956 initiated, and with the help of his Prime Minister, pushed through the establishment of a peacekeeping force at the time of the Suez crisis. At a particularly dangerous moment in postwar history the U.N. decisively prevented the Cold War from turning into a hot one.

Update

In 1997 a group of small to medium-sized nations have, with the support of the U.N., banded together to build a rapid deployment force which might be ready within 15 to 30 days instead of up to three months for an ad hoc force. This force now known as SHIRBRIG would be of brigade strength and could be ready much sooner than the already established force because its troops would have have already have met and trained together in all sorts of ways, giving special attention to logistics and communications.[5] This force, which should be trained and ready by 1999, would be an advance tactical arm of the large deployment forces for which nations have already been volunteering to provide troops.

Nations remain adamant that their forces can only be used by the U.N. on a case-by-case basis. And the question of who will be the overall commander of a U.N. force remains a thorny issue. Because each nation state still has a veto on whether or not its troops can take part in a joint operation—even if it is a humanitarian operation—this new scheme, which will have a base in Denmark, is still far from providing the U.N. with a standing army. But at least it gives the Security Council a new option when it is looking for quicker and effective means to begin a peacekeeping operation.

Notes

1. United Nations Standby Arrangements System. Briefing, June 16, 1995. P. 3.
2. Ibid. P. 4.

3. General Assembly. Security Council. A/49/886. April 10, 1995.
4. *New York Times,* Dec 3, 1994. P. A12.
5. Briefing for Ambassadors. October 21, 1997.

5. Reflections of an Italian Peacemaker

Giandominico Picco is one of the few prominent names to emerge from the U.N. bureaucracy in the nineties. He was a crucial figure in negotiating the end of the Iran–Iraq war and courageously allowed himself to be taken as a hostage in order to achieve the release of the hostages in Lebanon who had already been held captive for several years. In fact he is no longer in the U.N., having resigned after 20 years to start his own business. He is now free to talk openly about his views on the workings of the U.N.

He is a tall, imposing Italian and all his sharp reflections on current affairs are mingled with a faint smile and a nice sense of irony about his own ideas on how to do things better. Of one of his latest proposals, he remarked: "It might be one of my imaginative Italian ideas which usually don't work." He may have formally left the U.N., but it certainly doesn't sound like it.

One day in New York in 1995 he spoke about how immediately after the Cold War ended the U.N. had from 1987–1991 its most glorious years thus far.[1] The highlights were the negotiation of peace in the Iran–Iraq war, in Afghanistan, and in El Salvador. Then things started to go wrong. They went wrong, he explained, because the partnership between the Secretary-General and the Security Council ceased to work properly.

Giandominico explained it like this: "For things to go well the Security Council and the Secretary-General must never forget that their roles are complementary, but never the same. The Security Council, because it is made up of nation states, has two things the Secretary-General, because he is not a State, can never have—money and power."

Therefore, Picco said if the Secretary-General tries to act like a state and take control of the means of force, he will fail. This is what had happened in Somalia and it was a disaster. And it could happen again if the Secretary-General gets into the management of peace enforcement as over against peacekeeping.

"The Secretary-General must remain the conscience of the world. He must remain above power politics. His role is to be a persuasive, sensitive mediator. It is never enough for him to say 'I am available.' He must actively seek out the right moment to intervene, and find a way to peace. It is a paradox—as I found out when I was made a prisoner in Lebanon, the Secretary-General has the most power when he is powerless."

85

As always, Picco concluded, when we are trying to think straight about the power and influence of the U.N., the Charter points the way. The Secretary-General leads when "Pacific Settlement of Disputes"—that is Chapter 6 of the Charter—is in question. But when it comes to "Breaches of Peace and Acts of Aggression"—that is Chapter 7—then the business should be handled by the Security Council who alone have the means to act and to enforce their resolutions.

Picco stressed that keeping the power in the hands of the Security Council is what the major powers want. Thus, they arranged for Ambassador Ekeus of Sweden, the man responsible for disarming Iraq after the invasion of Kuwait, to report to them, and not to the Secretary-General. So, Picco believed, if the U.N. is ever to have its own rapid deployment force, only if it were under the direct control of the Security Council would it be acceptable to the members, especially the United States.

Picco spoke about a whole lot more, but it was enough that he made it so clear that evening that the Secretary-General is not and never should be the Chief Executive Officer of the Security Council. The Secretary-General stands, not even at the pinnacle of the political process, but in a realm outside and beyond it. He stands quite literally as the mediator of last resort, and nothing must be allowed to diminish his lonely eminence.

Note

1. From a speech by Giandominico Picco at the 92nd St. YMCA, Fall, 1995.

6. Reflections of a Woman Ambassador from Central Asia

Ambassador Zamira Eshmambetova of Kyrgystan is well known and respected in the U.N. community not only because she is a female Ambassador—there are still only seven women who hold the top post in the missions at the U.N.—but also because previously she filled a difficult and dangerous post as a U.N. peacemaker in the war-torn regions of Bosnia.

She deliberately chooses to give her time and attention to only a limited number of the most pressing subjects on the General Assembly list of over two hundred resolutions. Her priority is peace and security in her region of Central

Asia. Drug trafficking and arms smuggling is rife in the neighboring countries of Afghanistan and Tajikistan, and the interests of Russia and China further complicate a potentially explosive situation.[1]

The second priority for her country is the control of refugees, who number as high as one in one hundred of the total population of over four million. The United Nations High Commission for Refugees (UNHCR) and UNICEF do what they can to help on very small budgets. People are encouraged to stop growing poppies for the drug trade and to cultivate wheat instead.

Since the end of Communism, women especially have been finding it difficult to find employment as the old regime fostered an attitude of passive dependency. Now throughout Kyrgystan there is a new stress on the importance of individual effort and self-sufficiency, but people are finding it difficult to adjust to this drastic change in their whole outlook on life.

Kyrgystan has all the special problems of a country that is overwhelmingly mountainous. Ambassador Eshmambetova explained how mountain dwellers have to face the difficulties of social isolation, of liguistic differences, and often of being without a unifying culture. The physical dangers of living in mountain regions—earthquakes, landslides, and floods—are also ever-present.

Recently Kyrgystan hosted a special meeting in Bishkek, the capital, on mountain research. The conference stressed that it is the economic and social costs of living in mountainous areas, rather than the physical difficulties, that are the ones which urgently require study and action. It was noted that the subject of mountains received attention at the Earth Summit at Rio. The Summit's recommendations in Agenda 21 emphasized the extent of the rich ecological resources, especially water supplies, which depend on mountains. So the conference asked that the U.N. declare the year 2002 as the International Year of Mountains, and the Ambassador has already introduced this proposal at the U.N.

At the U.N. the Ambassadors of the countries of the Commonwealth of Independent States (CIS) meet together as a group to discuss issues like terrorism and refugees. "We become a chorus," says the Ambassador. When the fighting in Afghanistan threatened to engulf the whole region, the five Central Asian States raised the matter of regional peace and security with the Security Council, and then attended its subsequent meetings on that issue as invited observers.

To keep on top of this demanding schedule of work, together with regular reporting back to her capital, would test any mission to the U.N. But for Ambassador Eshmambetova in her very small mission, there are special problems as well: "I don't think being a woman makes the job of being an Ambassador any more difficult or different. But family status—now that does really matter. I am a single mother with a fourteen-year-old son. I have to run a home, do all the shopping, and even drive myself to work. I remember the American Ambassador Madeleine Albright used to say 'I do not have a wife.' "

The Ambassador is a totally convinced supporter of the U.N.'s role in peacekeeping. She recalled her experience as a political officer for UNPROFOR near Tuzla in Bosnia: "When I was with the Serbs I struggled to speak Serbo-Croat and they trusted me because of my knowledge of Russian. When I moved to Sarajevo and worked with the Bosnians they said, 'We like you because to us Zamira is a Moslem name.' Above all a U.N. peacekeeper must strive to be impartial. But being impartial is not the same at all as being indifferent. I saw a lot of suffering there and tried to work with NGOs, like Die Johanniter from Germany, to help where I could.

"I am very pleased that President Akaev is now working on establishing a peacekeeping training school for forces recruited from our part of the world. Peacekeeping is always evolving and we have to have special training to overcome difficulties of language and communications systems. Now, too, the training of police is becoming very important in peacebuilding."[1]

Ambassador Eshmambetova explained that the most famous epic poem in Kyrgystan is "Manas" and even the international airport is named after it. It has existed for one thousand years. She said that in this post-Communist time the value of an epic poem like this to teach tolerance, peace, and unity could not be overestimated. She was delighted that the General Assembly had recently passed a resolution celebrating the Millennium of this ancient Kyrgyz saga.

Note

1. Interview with Ambassador Zamira Eshmambetova. March 21, 1997.

7. The Peacekeeper Rose

Pier 92 used to be famous as the place where the world's great luxury liners set sail from New York. In 1995 it was the home of the New York flower show and a unique horticultural event happened that year—the launching of a specially-created new flower, the Peacekeeper Rose, to mark the 50th Anniversary of the United Nations.

This rose was bred to honor the 700,000 men and women who have worn the Blue Beret of the Peacekeepers since 1948, and even more to honor the 1,000 and more who died on peacekeeping duty in the field.

Launching a new variety of flower is neither easy nor quick. This rose was selected in Britain in 1989 by David Wardrop and Myriel Davies from a huge experimental stock of roses. It was given the secret name 'Harbella,' and sent to different nurseries around the world to test it for hardiness and resistance to disease.

One might have expected that the rose selected would be red or white—the colors for commemoration after wars. In fact, the rose that was chosen is peach—a subtle kind of peach with a hint of pink when the flower opens, and a touch of orange as it matures. Maybe peach was an inspired choice. After all, the dictionary describes a peach as 'a person or thing of exceptional worth or quality.'

The new rose passed all the tests. It did more. In 1993, after being entered anonymously, it won a Gold Medal at the International Rozenconcours at The Hague in the Netherlands. The rose is the floribunda type and will be especially suitable for planting in profusion in public spaces. It stands tall and vigorous and produces a large number of blooms over a long flowering season.

This new rose had to be marketed by its creators, the people from the United Nations Association of the United Kingdom. They nominated the World Federation of United Nations Associations as the beneficiary of all sales. But numbers had still to be multiplied. The bunch of roses on display in New York were grown in South Africa in the height of their midsummer, and especially flown to Pier 92 for display in the North American winter. All nations are not yet rushing to buy it. Some think there are difficulties of botanical quarantine, which is not the case. Namibia, Korea, and Qatar were among the first to order it. So far America has not registered its importance, nor has India, which had lost more soldiers on peacekeeping missions than any other nation.

The work of U.N. peacekeepers was recognized in 1988 by the award of a Nobel Peace Prize. Since then, the number of peacekeeping missions worldwide has doubled. Steve Roswick, an assistant editor of the U.N. Secretariat News, marked their achievement on being awarded this coveted award with this encomium, entitled "The Silent Ones":

> They serve quietly, in order to keep the world quiet. They serve in silence, in order that silence, and the peace that comes with it, can survive. Their silence is sacred to them. They are sworn to it—to live in silent dignity—in a world where the loud rule. They are the exception to that rule. With them, silence rules. It is the source of their strength—what communicates impartiality to those who surround them. Perhaps they have invented a new language—of silence—in which the most important things are not spoken, but sensed; in which impossible things, such as hope, and the possibility of peace between men are transmitted to all men. One day, their new silent language may tell us even more—so much more that spoken languages will be transcended by it. If so, we will have the universal language we have always sought—a language of peace.[1]

89

The Peacekeeper rose symbolizes the silent vigour which the U.N. peacekeepers display as they keep their vigil in the trouble spots of the world.

Note

1. U.N. Secretariat News. Steve Roswick. United Nations, 1988.

8. Volunteer from the Secretariat for Peacekeeping

During the nineties, peacekeeping has taken a great leap forward. It happened suddenly when countries like Namibia and El Salvador asked, even begged, the U.N. to manage their first ever free elections.

For the first time the U.N. force would be made up of much more than soldiers. Civilians would be deplored as policemen and they would monitor the work of local police; they would supervise the registration of voters as well as the election themselves; and through the media they would explain to a repressed and nervous electorate all about the strict impartiality of behavior which is at the heart of U.N. peacebuilding everywhere.

The U.N. began to recruit volunteers from its own Headquarters Staff to take on this new venture. One of these volunteers was Lena Yacoumopoulou, a broadcaster from the Department of Public Information. She recalled, as a young Greek girl, seeing young U.N. peacekeepers from Sweden in Egypt after the Suez crisis in 1956. They planted a seed of admiration in her for the good work they were doing and she determined, one day, to follow in their footsteps. Of course there would be risks, but she determined to do it. But first she made her will.[1]

Together with more than 1,000 other peacekeepers, she was sent to Namibia as a broadcaster. Nothing was easy. The Europeans disliked the whole idea of the U.N. taking over "their country." Outside one restaurant in Windhoek they put up a notice: "No U.N. people allowed." They needed a lot of persuasion that the U.N. was indeed impartial and not the tool of the Namibian African Liberation Movement, SWAPO. Even the Africans after years of colonial domination were cautious and repressed.

But both races got to know Lena as a friend. Both communities came to realize that the U.N., with its major procurement program, was good for local business and local employment. Eventually the Europeans invited her into their homes—"We like your voice even if we don't like your opinions." Changing public opinion quite rapidly was possible, because there was a state broadcasting system in Namibia that had no competition.

Lena talked enthusiastically about the United Nations Special Representative to the Secretary-General Martti Ahtisaari from Finland, who was a figure with whom everyone felt comfortable. People started to name their babies after him. People even stole U.N. license plates as a memento of this historic last stage on the road to freedom.

Lena's next assignment turned out to be in Haiti—at the time Aristide took power and before he was deposed by Colonel Cedras. The problems for the U.N. Mission were similar. Ignorance about what the U.N. stood for was enormous, and the U.N. military observers were even thought to be part of a new wave of American colonization, similar to the occupation of the country in the 1920s.

It was even more difficult and scary in Haiti. The poverty was overwhelming and the crowds would gather and block roads in a frightening and unpredictable way. Though Lena was only broadcasting in two languages, English and French, with Creole adaptions, instead of arranging for translation into seven different languages as in Namibia, the exchange of letters and conversation with the local people was much harder. But slowly the people of Haiti learned to trust the U.N. a little.

By the time Lena went on her third assignment, to Yugoslavia, she knew only too well that she and her colleagues would certainly not be seen as goodwill missionaries from the U.N., bringing the tools of peace. She found herself in Belgrade, and on every side the U.N. was unwelcome. No one really believed that the U.N. was impartial. Cars with U.N. emblems were stolen and placed on tramway tracks and drivers in cars with U.N. number plates were ridiculed. But the Belgrade broadcasters at least gave them time to tell their story, even if they did not think enough was being done for refugees by the U.N.

This is a new and testing era for U.N. peacekeepers. But nowadays peacekeepers in the field, and administrators like Lena, now back again at Headquarters, know firsthand so much more about each other's work than ever before. Both are struggling to explain to a skeptical and often indifferent global public about the U.N.'s mission of strict impartiality in all peacekeeping operations.

Note

1. From an interview with Lena Yacoumopoulou on August 15, 1995.

9. Humanitarian Aid—the View of a Chinese International Civil Servant

As murderous attacks on women and children catch up in civil conflicts increase, so does the importance of the U.N.'s Office of Humanitarian Affairs. The Director of Advocacy for this office is Ed Tsui, a Harvard-educated Chinese from Hong Kong. Ed has served in the U.N. for twenty-six years and he is dedicated to the idea of an international civil service. As he put it himself, "I believe in the way the U.N. is energetically striving for equity, equality, and human rights and especially so for developing countries. I vividly recall when in 1972, shortly after I had joined the U.N., I was sent down to tell the committee dealing with Social and Economic Affairs that the start of their meetings had been postponed for one day. At least six delegations came up to the podium and protested vigorously about this delay 'when there was so much work to do.' I find that sense of urgency is still there in the U.N., though I have learned from experience to be more realistic about what we can and what we cannot do."[1]

Mr. Tsui explained that the department came into existence after the end of the Cold War, when the opportunity for the U.N. to intervene in crisis situations other than natural disasters was suddenly so much greater. And there was a new realization that in conflict situations it was not enough simply to deliver food, shelter, and medicine to those who were suffering. The victims were more often internally displaced persons, not technically refugees and, due to disrespect for international authority, it was often very difficult to reach them. Legally governments were responsible for these people, but often it was governments themselves that has caused their displacement.

Mr. Tsui said that now there is close attention to the human rights of those entangled in the horrors of civil conflicts. The Department of Humanitarian Affairs has to find out and report to the Security Council if there is evidence of torture and arbitrary arrest. Then in countries where sanctions are being applied such as Iraq and Yugoslavia, these sanctions may be hurting innocent and vulnerable people the most.

Mr. Tsui emphasized the difficulties of coordinating help swiftly and efficiently: "The U.N. with all its different agencies is decentralized. When there is an ongoing conflict as recently as in Afghanistan and Liberia we appoint a humanitarian coordinator. Often it remains a formidable challenge to provide protection for those who are returning to devastated homesteads and towns.

"When the conflict has subsided, we arrange for the representative of the United Nations Nations Development Programme (UNDP) to take over the co-ordination and to put the emphasis not on rescue and survival, but on rebuilding local communities and their infrastructures. Our aim is never simply to bandage the wound, but to find out the underlying causes of conflict and get something done to overcome them.

"A number of U.N. activities do not receive anything like sufficient funds from the regular core budget. Humanitarian Affairs is no exception. Two-thirds of their funding has to come from voluntary contributions from governments. And of course Non-Governmental Organizations (NGOs) who play such an important part in all operations, which are coordinated by Humanitarian Affairs, have to raise their own voluntary funds from their own membership.

"Nowadays the Internet plays a crucial role in helping to deal with humanitarian crises. For instance, in Nairobi there is a website for the Great Lakes area of Central Africa which is updated twenty-four hours a day and we have just started one for West Africa, based in the Ivory Coast."[2]

Mr. Tsui concluded by stressing the courage of those who work in Humanitarian Relief. He said that in 1998, for the first time, more civilian relief workers had been killed than those serving in U.N. peacekeeping operations. He said that his office was endlessly urging the General Assembly to create a protocol to the 1994 Convention on the Safety of U.N. Personnel to protect civilians who are working in U.N. operations in places like the Sudan and Afganistan where there are no peacekeeping forces on the ground.

Notes

1. Interview with Ed Tsui, Director for the Policy, Advocacy, and Information Division of the Office for the Coordination of Humanitarian Affairs. October 21, 1998.
2. Ibid.

10.   A Lobbying Couple from Pax Christi

It is rare to find a married couple who work together in the NGO world at the U.N. Vince and Joan Comiskey are just such an American couple. Both have recently retired; Vince from special education, and Joan from nursing. And the well-known Catholic peace organization Pax Christi has found a way to use both their different talents and experience. Working voluntarily, like so many in Non-Governmental Organizations, they find that tackling Pax Christi's huge Agenda on disarmament, social justice, and non-violence is virtually a full-time job.

When he first came to the U.N., Vince imagined that he would be lobbying Ambassadors all the time, but he had quickly learned that working for causes at the U.N. was more complicated than that. He discovered that first he had to join up with other like-minded NGO groups, like the Committee on Disarmament. Then long-term strategies and aims could be worked out together and used to lobby foreign ministries in capitals back home. He remarked; "I found I have become part of a vast conglomerate. Progress at the U.N. on particular issues like disarmament is like the movement of a glacier. You see movement over years. The glacier moves because we all move.

"But, sometimes, yes, I do get to lobby Ambassadors. I did it recently when the Malaysian Ambassador asked NGOs to help win support from other countries for a resolution about a timetable for nuclear disarmament. We all lobbied Ambassadors. The Nuclear Abolition Caucus has more than 100 NGO members. The nuclear powers gave us no encouragement. But the resolution got more than 100 votes in favor and only a handful of votes against it. We don't neglect the home base either. Constant interacting with the members of our Congress makes them aware of our views on disarmament issues."[1]

Joan and Vince said that Pax Christi mostly got on with its work for justice and peace without direct reference to the Observer Mission of the Holy See at the U.N. In fact there are now more than thirty Roman Catholic NGOs active at the U.N. The Comiskeys explained that inside Pax Christi there were many different shades of opinion. They felt that using labels like "liberal" or "radical" was not a helpful way to label either themselves or their colleagues. They themselves were influenced and enlightened by the great body of Papal Encyclicals on issues of social justice which had appeared in the twentieth century. They had found that these Catholic issues were largely the same ones that preoccupied the U.N. as a whole.

Joan had also found that the way to influence things was to work with others in the NGO community with the same aims. For her this meant working with UNICEF. She spoke "chipping away at a rock" rather than trying to move a glacier. She, too, had found that the agenda about child rights was just as formidable and intractable as progress with disarmament. She had also come to realize that child labor, sexual exploitation of children, and safety for children in armed conflict were all thorny subjects on which no quick progress was possible.

Both the Comiskeys put great store by regular contact with their Pax Christi Headquarters in Brussels. In fact, their headquarters were so impressed with the focus on children in the New York chapter that they set up a whole new division in Brussels to deal with the issue of child rights. Vince and Joan were delighted with this news because they believed that Headquarters, through its more than thirty national chapters worldwide, can make an impact on national governments well before that government makes up its mind about its official position.

Both of them expressed dismay about the negative attitude to the U.N. they encounter among their friends. They meet people who think the U.N. means world government. They blame the media for this. But criticism and ignorance from outsiders has not weakened their own enthusiasm for the U.N.

Joan had the last word: "The U.N. speaks with a universal voice. It gives us an inclusive picture of both good and bad. It challenges parochialism. It is a voice for morality and a voice for prophecy."

And on the subject of their working partnership, she added: "At the end of day it is good to talk over our different experiences together, and we both benefit by helping each other to understand better the complexities of the enormous U.N. agenda."

Note

1. Interview with Vince and Joan Comiskey, representatives of Pax Christi at the U.N. December 3, 1996.

11. At Age One Hundred—An Activist for Women

Esther Hymer was impatiently waiting for the Agenda of the Commission on Women which was beginning its 1995 session. Tired of waiting, she got up and walked away briskly down the halls of the U.N., which are so familiar to her. Nothing unusual about that—except that Esther happened to be 97! Is there a secret to her *seventy* years of dedication to peace and women's rights?

She first took part in suffragette marches with Cary Chapman-Catt in 1919. This was in protest against bad political decisions that had resulted in the First World War. At that time there was a new determination by women to be involved in future decision-making in American politics. In the '30s she found her place in the International Federation for Business and Professional Women. She was present at the signing of the Charter in San Francisco and remembers how at that time the war was still going on and it was thought essential to wrap up the negotiations quickly in order to keep the Russians on board. At that vital moment unity was achieved—but only just.[1]

What we could consider obvious to put in the Charter was not so obvious then. For instance Esther remembered the achievement of Virginia Gildersleeve, the only women in the American delegation in getting the preamble of the Charter to begin with the vital words, "We the People," words which were so much more evocative than the formal and coldly impersonal. "The High Contracting Parties" used for the charter of the League of Nations.

The principle of equal opportunity had to be struggled for and Esther remembers the international group of women—among them Dr. Bertha Lutz of Brazil, Miss Minerva Bernadino of San Domingo, and Miss Wu Yi-Fang of China—who lobbied to make sure that the Charter called for fundamental freedoms for all "without distinction as to race, sex, language or religion."[2]

The Commission on Women is one of the earliest Commissions to be established and was soon active in getting the crime of genocide made into a convention. Recent events in Rwanda and Bosnia have shown that their instinct that this was a top priority was all too necessary. Now this Commission has forty-two members and has vastly increased the number of human rights declarations and conventions which affect women.

Esther remembers the work that went on for seven years to achieve the Declaration on the Elimination of Discrimination against Women. She said that at no time was there a feeling against men as such, but a desire to help them to do a better job in all walks of life. And nowadays with the creation of women's banks, she was especially pleased that the emphasis was on opening up *economic* opportunities for women.

This Declaration on the Elimination of Discrimination against Women became a Convention in 1979; by 1981, twenty nations had ratified it and now it has the force of law in 135 countries.

By 1975 the women had overcome both Russian and Brazilian resistance to the establishment of an International Women's Year. The Women's Conference in Mexico was the highlight of that year and three more for women have followed it. At first developing countries were simply not aware of NGOs and were often not comfortable to have them around, but in recent years NGOs have grown spectacularly in numbers and in public recognition all over the world.

As the women's movement gathered strength, Esther felt that the key factor was the changing of *attitudes*. Laws were secondary. She had always taken a keen interest in linking up with national and local chapters of her organization. Thus if governments reported situations in their countries, she always checked through community organizations to see if those governments had been telling the truth. In this way public opinion was nurtured by the U.N. Convention and given both a local and an international grounding.

And, as a centenarian, what is the secret of her extraordinary energy and commitment? Not just the quest for equal opportunity for women. Not just a simple sense of justice. No, above all what drives her most is a determination that the horrors of the two world wars should not be repeated for a third disastrous time. When her husband, having seen his best friend killed in action, came back from the First World War, he said to her, "I'll make a living for us, if you save the world." She was still working at it at 97![3]

Update

In September 1998, Esther Hymer, now 100, was seen active and alert in attendance with some 2000 other delegates at the Department of Public Information's Annual NGO Conference.

Notes

1. Charter of the United Nations. Chapter 1. Article 1. Section 3.
2. Ibid.
3. Interview with Esther Hymer. March, 1995.

12. Raising Consciousness through the Theater

Some of the time the United Nations in New York acts through resolutions and conventions. But all of the time the U.N. is acting to raise consciousness and persuade people to think globally. Indeed, it is only after a long season of raising consciousness and touching consciences that the time becomes ripe for an issue to be crystallized in Resolutions and eventually a Convention. And raising consciousness is not always just a matter of talk.

Occasionally someone introduces new ideas to the U.N. through the theater and brings a play to the U.N. to stimulate minds and stir hearts. The Hellenistic Kyklos Circle brought such a play to the Dag Hammarskjöld Auditorium. This play profoundly demonstrated the power of theater to trigger the process of reconciliation between different ethnic groups who had been living in fear and suspicion of each other.

This play was entitled *Rifts in Silence: How Daring is Taught.* It came about like this: Christiana Lambrinidis from Brandeis University in Boston went to the town of Komotini on the frontier between Greece and Turkey. There she found a place that was a borderland inhabited by women of Muslim, Christian, and Gypsy origins. Conflicts in that town stemmed back over centuries. In this community the women had always been "the silent ones." She persuaded these women from very different backgrounds to tell the stories of

97

their hopes and fears and disappointments to her. She then wove their stories into a dramatic shape, and created a play in which the women surprised themselves by becoming the main actors.

Through a series of monologues, the women gradually revealed who they were. They revealed their feelings by speaking about such intimate themes as "The Story of My Name"; "Mother-Daughter Intimacies"; "Materials My Body is Made Of"; "Not Liked"; and "Hands."

Here is the voice of Popi Philippidou:

I wish I was called:
"Hope"
"Peace"
"Love"
"Life"
Why? Because such is my life.
When I hope I want to be called "Hope."
When I quarrel I want to be called "Peace."
When I love I want to be called "Love."
Perhaps we should have many names for different hours of the day.[1]

Popi says of herself, "I had no contact with writing. Writing these texts I found the secret self we should all be looking for."

This is the voice of Theano Paschalia:

I feel my body is made of a strange mix. My hair, I think often, resembles a pathetic imitation of sea-weed around corals. The tips of my hair especially remind me of bodied beet-stalks. What I am sure of is my lips are little pillows, the ones cats and dogs have on their paws. This is why they are warm and a little dry.

My eyes are made of bath-salts, the round ones, for men only.

Theano writes, "Through this play, I realized that all women are the same, regardless of age and religion. I have a lot to teach my children."

Sophia Terzi remembers her daily work.

The machine works ... it cut bricks. ... I must hurry ... the bricks don't come out well ... mud, they are mud. ... Stergio ... the machine ... it broke ... Stergio ... Finally he heard me.

Sophia says, "I could finally express my feelings. I discovered another language. I learned to see myself differently."

There was nothing obvious about the statements in this play, no easy path to understanding and reconciliation, but more a gradual dawning of how similar are the small joys and pains of daily life. The play jolted us all to remember the myriad links in our common humanity. Perhaps it was enough for all the women who had been silent for so long simply to speak out.

All who saw the play in the U.N., and outside it began to imagine expressing the rifts in their own communities by creating this kind of spontaneous drama. Christiana Lambrinidis said she hoped to take the play to other ethnic borderlands, Cyprus perhaps.

Note

1. *Rifts in Silence*. Text from the play Christian, Muslim, and Gypsy women wrote and performed. Edition Fournos. Athens, 1996.

Walkabout:

Two

A four-year-old boy scavaging on a garbage dump in São Paulo, Brazil. (UN photo: Claudio Edinger.)

UNICEF in action in Rwanda. Purified water is pumped from a UNICEF truck into a collapsible bladder tank to supply 15,000 displaced persons, 1994. (UNICEF photo: Betty Press.)

Mr. Nitin Desai (left), Under-Secretary-General for Policy Coordination and Sustainable Development, and Mr. James Gustave Speth (right), Administrator of the United Nations Development Program (UNDP). (UN photo: UN/ DPI, Milton Grant.)

Dr. Nafis Sadik, Executive Director of the United Nations Population Fund (UNFPA). Dr. Sadik was a former Director General of the Pakistan Central Family Planning Council. (UN photo: Brian Alpert.)

In Indonesia one half of the population does not get to see how the other half lives. (UN photo.)

The United Nations Development Programme (UNDP) provides technical assistance for a new irrigation scheme in Guinea, West Africa. (UNDP photo.)

Mrs. Eleanor Roosevelt, the widow of President Franklin Roosevelt, displays the Universal Declaration of Human Rights. (UN photo.) She chaired more than eighty meetings of the International Preparatory Committee to create this landmark Declaration in 1948.

United Nations Fourth World Conference on Women, Beijing China. (Left to Right) Chen Muhua (China), President of the Conference; Therese Gastaut, Director, United Nations Information Service at Geneva; Gertrude Mongella (Tanzania), Secretary-General of the Conference; Patricia Licuanan (Philippines), Chairwoman of the Main Committee of the Conference. (UN/photo: Zheng Yan Hui.)

1. Portraits of the Secretary-Generals

"They are saying that it is better that I should be hanging on a wall than hanging about." So quipped Javier Perez de Cuellar, the first Peruvian Secretary-General, at the unveiling of his retirement portrait by Swiss artist Hans Erni. All the leaving portraits of the Secretary-Generals are displayed on a long, carefully roped-off wall, situated right at the center of the main entrance to the U.N. Headquarters. No visitor to the Secretariat can possibly fail to notice these paintings of all six of the Secretary-Generals which hang there.

These portraits may seem rather official and formal, but each one tells a different story about the holders of this unique high office. All of them are painted wearing suits and all of them look bureaucratic. This is no surprise as the U.N., after all, is nothing if not a bureaucracy.

Waldheim, the Austrian, a professional diplomat, wears the most expensive suit and the most formal manner. He was painted by Everett Kinstler, also of Austrian birth, and his spectacles in his hand, and the picture appropriately suggest he was a workaholic. Hammarskjöld stands in a casual manner with one hand in his pocket, but it seems like only a moment's pause in the life of a man who was a rare combination of both administrator and visionary. Hammarskjöld, caught in a moment of reflection, was painted from life by his great Swedish friend Bo Beskow.

It might have been expected that the portrait of U Thant from Myanmar would reveal something about his Buddhist allegiance but his picture, painted by the American artist James Fosburgh, shows him first and foremost as a bureaucrat.

Trygvie Lie, the first Secretary-General, painted by fellow Norwegian Harald Dal, is sitting down, but he looks every inch the downright Norwegian trade unionist, that he was. Trigvie Lie gazes out with eyes that are both strong and sad. As Secretary-General during the Cold War, he had to soldier on through the major crises of the Berlin Blockade and the invasion of Czechoslovakia. After the Blockade was over he wrote:

> The electric tension that the Berlin blockade generated between the two non-negotiating worlds was very great. Had there been no United Nations, it might have been so great that the electricity would have shot across the gap, setting both sides afire.[1]

Look now at the portrait of U Thant. The eyes show a man determined to play the diplomatic game with the same tough and unwaveringly polite manners as everyone else in the profession. Look deeper and you can sense a feeling of disdain for the worldliness of diplomacy. He reflected on the strains of his job:

111

"The Secretary-General's world has two poles: at one extreme the idealism and global objectives of the charter, and at the other, if I may say so, the unconcealed selfish nature of national sovereignty."[2]

There is a great deal to be said about Dag Hammarskjöld, because there was a great deal to the man. The eyes show a certain compassion and a certain distance. Indeed he noted that aloneness, if not loneliness, was a perpetual companion for him. One senses, too, that diplomatic maneuvering was never at the heart of right living for him. He said:

"Results are determined, not by superficial ability, but by the consistency of the actors in their efforts and by the validity of their ideals. Contrary to what seems to be popular belief, there is no intellectual activity which more ruthlessly tests the solidity of a man than politics."[3]

Hammarskjöld knew that diplomatic skill needed to be grounded in a bedrock of integrity. To nurture that integrity he created a meditation room at U.N. Headquarters. At the dedication ceremony of this special place within the U.N. House, he said:

"It is a room of quiet where only thoughts should speak. We all have within us a center of peace surrounded by stillness. . . . It has been the aim to create in this small room a place where the doors may be open to the infinite lands of thought and prayer."[4]

Of all the Secretary-Generals in this portrait gallery, Perez de Cuellar looks the most at ease. But actually the tailored suits he wore to work did not look much like the comfortably fitting one complete with casual shoes shown in this portrait. But the painting is an arresting attempt to portray the tortured heart of the world, which he tried hard for ten years to reconcile. Indeed up to literally the very last late-night minute of his tenure of office he was negotiating peace in the El Salvador civil war.

The dominating color in his portrait is red, symbolizing fire, destruction, and the suffering of civilians. Faces of innocent children are drawn in over this grim background. Holding the whole picture together is a gray geometrical mesh, suggesting the complexity of the world in which he struggled to find diplomatic solutions. The artist remarked at the unveiling of this portrait, "I wanted to show his commitment and his happiness in achieving small steps in the right direction."

Notes

1. Lie, Trygvie. *In the Cause of Peace.* The Macmillan Company. 1954. P. 218.
2. Thant, Aye Aye. *Anthology of U Thant.* Private Papers, 1994.
3. Dag Hammarskjöld. Speech at Johns Hopkins University, SG/424, 1955.
4. Speech at Inauguration of the Meditation Room, 1957.

2. A U.N. Memorial to the Victims of Extreme Poverty

Mahatma Gandhi is said to have described poverty as "the worst form of violence." Every year the U.N. makes a special effort to bring the horror of extreme poverty sharply into focus.[1]

In 1996 the French, under the leadership of President Chirac, gave a lead in this pressing area of U.N. unfinished business. In the U.N. garden running along the East River, a wide and handsome space planted with a rose garden and an avenue of locust trees, the French Ambassador, Mr. Alain Dejammet unveiled a commemorative stone in honor of the victims of extreme poverty. This simple monument was inspired by the original one inaugurated in 1987 by Father Joseph Wresinski, a priest who devoted his life to the poor, and placed on the Plaza of Human Rights and Liberties in Paris.

At this open-air gathering on a bright autumn afternoon—it would be indecent to call it a ceremony—a question was posed to the audience on the Order of Service:

"Through our monuments to those who have suffered and died, we remind ourselves of wars, slavery, and genocide. Why, then, are our landscapes not marked by monuments to recall the victims of hunger, ignorance, and violence inflicted on the extremely poor? The poorest of the poor leave no trace on earth. They are buried in potter's fields. Their slums are consistently erased from our maps. Their stories are not told or recorded in our books."[2]

These commemorative stones for the poor can now be found all over the world—not just in Paris and at the U.N. They are also found in Burkina Faso, Germany, Canada, and the Philippines. People gather at them on the 17th of every month throughout the year to remember and to meditate. Practical action for those in extreme poverty is constantly being initiated by the International Movement A. T. D. Fourth World.

Father Joseph Wresinski proclaimed that the wish to eliminate poverty from the face of the earth was not simply a matter of pity or compassion. It was an issue at the very heart of the spirit of human solidarity in the U.N. Charter. His words engraved on the stone of remembrance are:

> Wherever men and women are condemned to live in extreme poverty human rights are violated. To come together to ensure that these rights be respected is our solemn duty.[3]

Earlier on this same day the Administrator of the United Nations Development Programme (UNDP) had spoken of the absolute poor, still numbering

1.3 billion individuals on this earth who are compelled to live on $1 per day. There is not much hope for them when they hear there has been a 25 percent drop in development aid given by U.N. member states in the last 4 years. Alas, they mostly live in countries where unfortunately they can have little expectation that new business investment will come their way.

For the unveiling of a monument in Paris in 1987 to commemorate the endless travail of the poor Father Joseph wrote these verses:

I bear witness to the millions of young people
who have no reason to believe or even to exist
and who vainly search for a future
in this senseless world

I bear witness to you, the poor of all times,
still poor today, forever on the roads,
fleeing from place to place, despised and disgraced.
Laborers without a trade, ever crushed by their toil,
Laborers whose hands, today, are no longer useful.[4]

By this event the U.N. marked the International Day for the Eradication of Poverty. It remains to be seen what the world will do for the rest of the U.N. Decade against Poverty.

Notes

1. Choices. The Human Development Magazine. UNDP. October 1966.
2. The Orders of Commemoration. Permanent Mission of France to the United Nations and International Movement A. T. D. Fourth World.
3. Words of Father Joseph Wresinski inscribed on the stone unveiled on October 17, 1996.
4. The Order of Commemoration.

3. Korea Salutes the Peacekeepers

Just occasionally the ordinary citizen gets a chance to feel what it is like to sit in the General Assembly. It happened during the Fiftieth Anniversary when the Korean Broadcasting System's orchestra gave a concert for the general public in the General Assembly Hall.

The General Assembly Hall has touches of grandeur about it. It is painted blue and gold, a combination which never dates. On television the seats look level, but actually they slope gently down towards the stage. All delegates sit at desks and close behind them, rather too close, are the seats, where their advisers sit ready to lean forward and whisper last-minute advice in the ear of their Ambassador. This is a hall for rhetoric, not a chamber for debate.

Right ahead and almost diminutive in the distance above the stage is a block of highly polished green marble. Behind it sits the President of the General Assembly flanked, when he is needed, by the Secretary-General and his staff. On either side of the podium, high up on the wall, are the eight voting panels which flash For or Against or Abstain as the 188 nation states make up their minds on the resolutions crafted for their final approval by the six main committees of the General Assembly. But in recent years they have been voting less and less, as the Assembly strives to do business by consensus.

High above the President is a great circle in metallic gray. In the center of this emblem is a most unusual map of the globe. It's a strikingly fresh projection which shows all continents in an entirely new perspective. If any-thing, Antarctica dominates. The map is surrounded with bay leaves—a symbol of peace. This is appropriately a map of Planet Earth and not of nation states.

The eye moves on round the hall, past the long lines of windows from which the media and the interpreters stare down on the diplomats. Finally there is the dome. The main impression is of its height. It is very high and impressive; much more impressive than when seen from outside where it seems almost squat. Its soaring strength must do something for the spirits of the diplomats, when they are making last-minute adjustments to their speeches. The American Congress, when giving a loan to complete the building, insisted that a dome be part of the condition of the loan. They have been proved triumphantly right!

Maestro Myung-Whun Chung began this concert by the Korean Broad-casting System Orchestra with a Beethoven concerto, in which he both con-ducted and played the piano, while his sister, Myun-Wha Chung, played the cello. This showed extraordinary virtuosity, but then the orchestra produced another surprise by playing a concerto by Joon-Il Kang in which western instru-ments were complemented by Samulnori—a Korean folk ensemble of four traditional percussion instruments. This unique celebration of musical diversity seemed a perfect prelude to the "rainbow coalition" of all nations who would shortly gather for their 50th Anniversary in this hall to reaffirm their loyalty and dedication to the United Nations.

The highlight of the evening was an eloquent reminder that the concert was in honor of peacekeepers. As the Beethoven concerto concluded, the solo-ists came back on stage to receive flowers. Then three peacekeepers in uniform were invited to join them. They all received a big ovation, which swelled to thunder when the performers suddenly handed their bouquets to the U.N.

soldiers! As they pursue their difficult and thankless work in faraway places, the peacekeepers are inevitably out of sight at Headquarters, but on this night, due to this imaginative Korean initiative, they were suddenly and deservedly center stage.

Part Four

Disarmament

1. A Short History of the U.N. and Disarmament

Countries who would not subscribe to disarmament were simply not permitted to join the old League of Nations. The U.N. Charter, on the other hand, put the emphasis firmly on collective security, and not on disarmament, and in view of the success of the two U.N.-sponsored collective security operations against aggression in Korea and Kuwait, who can say that it was a wrong decision.

Not until Article 26 of the charter is there a firm call to member states of the U.N. to formulate plans for the regulation of arms. The Cold War made these plans unfold desperately slowly, but the will to do something about disarmament was never entirely abandoned.

Bill Epstein is a still-feisty Canadian who has been specializing in disarmament—mostly working in the Secretariat—for more than fifty years! He has lived through the Cold War and beyond it and always been energetically in the thick of U.N. planning in the field of disarmament.

Bill likes to remind people that the very first Resolution of the very First General Assembly of 1946 called for the abolition of nuclear weapons. At that time the U.S. might actually have, under the Baruch plan, handed over the know-how both how to make nuclear weapons and how to control them through an international authority. But the Cold War began, and the plan came to nothing.[1]

Undaunted by the Cold War, in 1954 Prime Minister Nehru of India proposed a ban on nuclear tests, but not until 1963 was a partial test ban negotiated. Even then the treaty did not forbid underground testing, which went ahead more intensely than ever.

Nineteen sixty-five was a highlight in Bill's long and remarkable career. In the aftermath of the Cuban Missile Crisis, the Latin American nations determined never again to be subjected to the threat of nuclear war in their region. So they determined to make their region a nuclear weapon free zone.

Bill was asked by one of the leading disarmers of our time, Ambassador Garcia Robles of Mexico, to write the first draft of a treaty to create a nuclear free area for Latin America. It was to be called the Treaty of Tlatelolco. He worked all through the night to get the draft ready in time for the meeting of the Latin American diplomats by the next morning. He succeeded, and the treaty was signed in Mexico in 1967.

Thirty years later Bill Epstein commented on this enormous step forward, for which Ambassador Robles was awarded the Nobel Peace Prize in 1982.

"The Treaty of Tlatelolco is the most successful anti-nuclear treaty in existence. It is binding not only on all the states of Latin America and the

119

Caribbean, but also on all five nuclear weapon powers who are prohibited from testing, producing, stationing, deploying, using, or threatening to use nuclear weapons against the states in that zone. Tlatelolco has become the model and inspiration for a series of nuclear weapon free zones in other regions of the world."[2]

Not until 1987 when intermediate and short-range nuclear weapons were abolished by the superpowers did the thick ice brought on by the Cold War begin to crack. At last it became possible to look at proposals for disarmament with less fear and suspicion and with more hope.

Then in 1995, the very important Nuclear Non-Proliferation Treaty, first signed in 1968, was renewed indefinitely. The essence of this treaty is that the non-nuclear states have agreed not to develop nuclear weapons themselves on condition that the nuclear powers, over time, take definite tangible steps towards nuclear disarmament and the elimination of nuclear weapons.

The decision to extend the treaty in 1995 was conditioned on a new set of nuclear principles and objectives. These principles in Article 6 of the new treaty call for a closer and more continuous monitoring of what the nuclear powers are actually doing about disarmament than was agreed when the treaty was first negotiated twenty-five years earlier. There are to be review conferences every five years and preparatory commissions leading up to them. This gives the non-nuclear states a measure of political leverage. Indeed, there is the possibility that some of them, if they consider that the nuclear powers are not living up to their obligation to disarm, could give the agreed 3-month notice and leave the Treaty altogether.

Bill Epstein is implacably opposed to all weapons of mass destruction. He welcomes the treaties now in place to ban and to monitor the banning of chemical and biological weapons. He is pleased that more than one hundred nations have signed the Chemical Weapons Convention which now has a verification system in place. He hopes for more progress in the difficult task of establishing a verification system for the challenging business of exposing the manufacture of biological weapons. But he reserves his greatest sense of outrage for the dangers posed by nuclear weapons.

All progress in disarmament will have to be pushed forward by the three main disarmament bodies which are the First Committee of the General Assembly, the Disarmament Commission, and the Conference on Disarmament.

In September 1996, after efforts which went on for forty years, the Comprehensive Nuclear Test Ban Treaty (CTBT) finally came into existence. All five nuclear powers signed it on the first day. It is regarded as the first step on the way to the elimination of nuclear weapons.

In a recent ground-breaking judgement, the World Court has ruled that, except in extreme circumstances of self-defense, the use of nuclear weapons is illegal. And more than sixty generals, including Americans, have publicly announced that they are against the production and use of nuclear weapons and they urge their abolition.

Bill points out that there is still so much more for the nuclear powers to do.

"Some of the actions required are practical, such as taking nuclear weapons off alert status, declaring a moratorium on the production of fissile material for manufacturing nuclear weapons, arranging for more treaties to achieve nuclear weapon free zones in Asia and Eastern Europe. At the same time it is necessary for the bilateral nuclear disarmament negotiations between Russia and America, known as the Strategic Arms Reduction Treaties (START) to gather momentum. Even if the steps called for under START 3 were completed, Russia and the United States would still each be retaining 2,500 nuclear weapons each.

"Among other steps to be taken are for the Conference on Disarmament in Geneva to begin negotiations for conventions on security assurances for non-nuclear weapon states, and on a comprehensive phased program for the total elimination of nuclear weapons."[3] Bill concluded his round-up with a characteristically blunt message:

"Lobbying at the U.N. is useful, but not enough. The key people to reach are the legislators in the capitals of the world and the public at large. Hard work and more hard work is what is required. There is no other way that the threat of nuclear weapons can be ended."

And then came Bill Epstein's climax.

"We must abolish nuclear weapons before they abolish us."[4]

Update

In June 1998, the urgency of Bill Epstein's plea for nuclear disarmament was reinforced by a letter sent to the Secretary-General by the Ambassadors to the U.N. of Brazil, Egypt, Ireland, Mexico, New Zealand, Slovenia, South Africa, and Sweden. The Ambassadors wrote:

> We fully share the conclusion expressed by the commissioners of the Canberra Commission in their statement that "the proposition that nuclear weapons can be retained in perpetuity and never used—accidentally or by decision—defies credibility. The only complete defense is the elimination of nuclear weapons and assurance that they will never be produced again."[5]

In August 1998 the Organization for the Prevention of Chemical Weapons drew attention to Mr. Ichiro Akiyama, the Director of the Inspectorate established by the Convention for the Prevention of Chemical Weapons and located in the Netherlands. Mr. Ichiro Akiyama is a scientist and former Major-General in the Japan Defense Agency. There are 206 inspectors and inspection assistants in the Inspectorate.[6]

Notes

1. From a speech by Bill Epstein at the fifth Seminar of the Campaign for a More Democratic United Nations (CAMDUN). New York October 6, 1995 and at the meeting at the U.N. in January 1996 to commemorate the 50th Anniversary of the adoption of Resolution 1 on January 24, 1946.
2. Interview with Bill Epstein. International Diplomatic Observer. March 11, 1997. P. 11.
3. Ibid.
4. Speech by Bill Epstein.
5. General and Complete Disarmament. Letter Dated June 9th, 1998 addressed to the Secretary-General. A/53/138.4.
6. Newsletter of the Organization for the Prohibition of Chemical Weapons. August, 1998. P. 4.

2. Nobel Laureate Oscar Arias Speaks Out on Arms Sales

Unfortunately the end of the Cold War did not mean the end of the arms race. The U.N. keeps on hammering away at the heart of the problem, which is on, the one hand, fears about national security and, on the other, the large profits being made from arms sales. But the situation is changing all the time, and that is why the U.N. invited Oscar Arias Sanchez, former President of Costa Rica and Nobel Peace Prize winner, to give a Hoffman Lecture at U.N. Headquarters on arms sales.

Paul Hoffmann was a founder of the U.N. development program, so it was absolutely right that this lecture should highlight the point that less money spent on arms means more money available for the battle against poverty. President Eisenhower reached the heart of the matter when he said, "Every gun that is made, every warship launched, every rocket fired, signifies, in the final sense, a theft from those who hunger and are not clothed."

So where are we now seven years after the end of the Cold War? President Arias explained we are still far from out of the woods. True, there has been a substantial drop since 1987 in the value of the world trade in arms. But the bad news is the substantial growth in trade of light and small weapons. 90 percent of arms exports come from the big nations. All these countries subsidize their arms makers, and it is impossible to find out by how much. Arias concluded on a grim note:

"Today arms are cheaper and more uncontrollable than ever before. The consequence is that combatants and groups eager to make war have no difficulty getting the arms they need to prosecute their ends."[1] Dr. Arias continued:

"In a world of nation states there are no magical ways to make the arms bazaar an unattractive and unprofitable place to do business. The only workable way forward is to strengthen the disarmament measures which are already in place and also to create new ones.

"Small arms and munitions ought to be included in the U.N. arms register when it comes up for review in 1997. A global moratorium on all types of land mines ought to be achieved and arms control agreements should be negotiated, directed just now to countries in Africa. In Central America and the Caribbean, Costa Rica, Panama, and Haiti have already abolished their armed forces altogether. Why can't others, also on a regional basis, work out further total abolition?

"It is unconscionable that the developing countries are still spending $150 million on arms annually.[2] Resources have to be found to be directed to human development. Demilitarization, breaking with the absurd traditions of bellicosity, could become the source of these resources."[3]

Oscar Arias keeps returning to New York again and again to press for conventional disarmament. In May 1997, joining together with 15 other Nobel Laureates including Adolfo Perez Esquivel of Argentina and Lech Walesa of Poland, he endorsed an International Code of Conduct on Arms Transfers. At the ceremony he said:

"The international community can no longer ignore the repercussions of irresponsible arms transfers. Indiscriminate weapons sales foster political instability and human rights violations, prolong violent conflicts, and weaken diplomatic efforts to resolve differences peacefully."[4]

He went on to criticize the United States government's lack of control over its arms exports:

"In 1993 the U.S. was responsible for 73 percent of arms sales to the developing world. . . . Over two-thirds of the recipient nations were characterized by the U.S. Department of State as human rights abusers."[5]

Update

In 1997, the U.N. passed a resolution to do something about controlling small arms. A panel of experts under the chairmanship of Ambassador Donowaki of Japan has, after contentious negotiations, come up with recommendations about how to deal with countries that are awash with small arms that kill civilians more often than soldiers and which, unlike mines and rockets, can be recycled for decades to come.

One of the panel's primary goals is the collection and destruction of these weapons, so that they cannot be recycled. An encouraging sign has been that the government of Mali has asked the U.N. to advise and help them with getting rid of small arms. Because Mali called the U.N. and not the other way around, there is a real hope that regional control of smuggling in this part of Africa and the collection and destruction of light weaponry will really begin to happen.

Notes

1. Sanchez, Oscar Arias. 1995 Paul G. Hoffman. October 11, 1995. P. 2.
2. Ibid. P. 6.
3. Ibid. P. 6.
4. *Disarmament Times*. June 1997 P. 4.
5. Ibid.

3. Indefinite Extension of the Nuclear Non-Proliferation Treaty

How was it possible that in 1995 such a controversial subject as the indefinite extension of the Nuclear Non-Proliferation Treaty could pass by consensus and without a vote at the U.N.?

Before the month-long conference in April 1995 began, there was a strong groundswell among the non-nuclear nations—the vast majority of member states, of course—that in the previous twenty-five years the nuclear powers had not done enough to get rid of their own stock of nuclear weapons, nor had they offered sufficient assurances to the non-nuclear states that they would come to their aid in the event of nuclear blackmail. Yet this opposition, passionately felt opposition, previously spelled out by Ambassador Wisnumurti of Indonesia and leader of the Non-Aligned Movement (NAM)—somehow faded or became muted as the moment for the vote about extension drew near. Why was this?

The answer is complicated. Those opposing the treaty, countries like Malaysia, Nigeria, and Syria, did not just fade away. They would have much preferred a treaty, voted on by secret ballot, which would run for twenty-five years only with the opportunity, at the end of that time, to evaluate what progress the nuclear powers had made in reducing their nuclear stockpiles.

But a combination of pressure, including economic pressure, from the nuclear powers, and a feeling that the terms of the new treaty were a definite improvement on those in the old nuclear non-proliferation treaty, persuaded the great majority of non-nuclear nations to sign up for indefinite extension.

The recent accident at Chernobyl in Ukraine was also a fresh reminder to all the delegates of the original gust of fear about atomic weapons and their poisonous aftereffects which circled the world after the first atomic bomb was dropped at Hiroshima.

Besides a feeling that the new deal was one which they could live with, the non-nuclear states found the atmosphere at the conference was more positive, more full of trust, than they had expected. There was, too, a sense of relief that fewer nations than anticipated had acquired nuclear weapons over the past decades. And four nations—Belarus, Kazakhstan, South Africa, and Ukraine—had actually renounced them.

So when South Africa—a new South Africa free from apartheid—came up with proposals for regular monitoring of progress in nuclear disarmament, these ideas carried weight, because South Africa had practiced what they preached and disarmed themselves, and now they were even taking a lead in making Africa a nuclear-free zone.

Further, the President of the conference, Ambassador Jayantha Dhanapala of Sri Lanka had the confidence and respect of all present and his leadership helped to propel the conference to push for a substantial vote in favor of indefinite extension.

What then exactly were the new arrangements which won over the vast majority of delegates to vote for indefinite extension of the treaty? There were a number of them, none of which carried the force of law, but all of which, taken together were felt to be strong enough to advance the prospects for nuclear disarmament.

First, the monitoring process was to be more stringent. Reviews of disarmament progress, which would look both forward and backward, would be held every five years and there would be as many as three preparatory meetings in the years before the final review itself.[1] Second, there was an undertaking to complete a comprehensive nuclear test-ban not later than the end of 1992. Third, there was a commitment to pass a law, sign a convention, banning the production of fissile material for use in atomic weapons.[2] Fourth, there was a declaration to create more regional nuclear-free zones, especially in the Middle East where Israel was still refusing to sign the NPT treaty, while being known to possess nuclear weapons.[3]

And that was not all. The non-nuclear powers wanted and were given more assurances that their access to nuclear energy for peaceful purposes would be improved. It was agreed that the International Atomic Energy Agency would be given more power to facilitate access to technology and also to ensure, by regular inspection, that countries were not making atomic weapons in secret.[4]

In his concluding statement, the President, Ambassador Dhanapala from Sri Lanka praised the role of NGOs over the years for their encouragement and advocacy of all that the Nuclear-Non-Proliferation Treaty had stood for, and, thinking ahead, the proposed greater opportunities for the NGO community in the process of negotiations.

Ambassador Dhanapala summed up the twin purpose of the indefinite extension of the treaty in these words:

"The permanence of the treaty does not represent a permanence of unbalanced obligations, nor does it represent the permanence of nuclear apartheid between nuclear haves and have-nots. What it does represent is our collective dedication to the permanence of an international barrier against nuclear proliferation so that we can forge ahead in our tasks towards a nuclear-free world."[5]

After the agreement some saw no reason for rejoicing. Mr. Agam of Malaysia said:

"Even as we speak today . . . stockpiles of nuclear weapons are far greater than when the NPT was originally signed. Two of the major nuclear-weapon states have a total of 40,000 warheads today, compared with 38,700 in 1970. The explosive power of two tons of TNT for every person on earth remains in the nuclear arsenals to haunt us, even as a billion people live in abject poverty. . . ."[6]

But many others went along with the more optimistic assessment of Mr. Westdal of Canada:

"With our extension decision, we have given our treaty's norms and obligations a powerful, new dimension. Make no mistake. We have thus enshrined new values, a perceptible step forward. The world is a safer place today. And we are a finer bunch."[7]

Time alone will tell who most nearly spoke the truth to a world community which is filled with unquenchable hopes for a totally nuclear weapons-free world. At the end of the conference no less than 208 NGOs signed up as members of an 'Abolition Coalition Caucus': they certainly will not be letting the matter of total abolition of nuclear weapons rest.

Update

The explosion of nuclear weapons by both India and Pakistan in 1998, due to the continuing dispute over Kashmir, has set back the process of non-proliferation and even of nuclear disarmament itself. However, both the Prime Ministers of India and Pakistan have said they are in principle prepared to sign the Nuclear Test Ban Treaty. Global events will undoubtedly determine how quickly this could happen.

Notes

1. NPT/CONF. 1995/L.4 May 10, P. 1.
2. NPT/CONF. 1995/L.5 May 9, P. 2.
3. NPT/CONF 1995/L5 May 9, P. 3.
4. NPT/CONF 1995/L5 May 9, P. 3.
5. NPT/CONF. 1995/32 (Part 111), P. 215.
6. NPT/CONF 1995/PV. 17 May 11, P. 7.
7. NPT/CONF 1995/PV. 17 May 11, P. 21.

4. A Canadian Quaker on the Outlook for Disarmament

Some people believe that even though the Cold War has ended, a new chapter in disarmament has unfortunately not yet begun. David Jackman, a Canadian who works on the problem in the Quaker Office at the U.N., takes a more hopeful view.

He argues that if the Cold War had not ended, it would simply not have been possible to have achieved both the successful renewal of the Nuclear Non-Proliferation Treaty and the Comprehensive Nuclear Test Ban. He also believes that vital arms control agreements about nuclear weapons have opened the gates to new possibilities for conventional disarmament.

David Jackman argues that for governments, the appeal of weapons of mass destruction is slowly fading. Their preparation alone causes enormous long-lasting pollution, and disarming them is enormously expensive. They are grossly indiscriminate and their effects can linger on for centuries. So the major powers have signed conventions on both chemical and biological weapons. A recent opinion by the International Court of Justice that almost all uses of nuclear weapons are clearly illegal has further weakened the value of nuclear weapons in the public consciousness.

David is upbeat about the role of the general public in disarmament.

"NGOs these days may not be able to get people in large numbers into the streets to protest about the arms race, but in the past decade the public had become much more professionally knowledgeable about the complexity of disarmament issues.

"NGOs concerned about disarmament now can and do have constant contact with Ambassadors who meet every year in the First Committee of the General Assembly—the disarmament and arms control committee—and in other related fora. NGOs are permitted to attend most formal sessions of the First Committee and they can informally follow the progress of the negotiating sessions themselves."

David Jackman summed up the reasons for his own commitment to the work of disarmament.

"As a Canadian I always felt that as a medium-sized nation we found ourselves immersed in a world which affected us, but which we could not control on our own. We also can recall what colonial status means. So we are attracted to working with other nations and other people to prevent war. I grew up at a time when the long shadow of the Second World War stretched over us and I also felt the ominous new threat of the nuclear weaponry being developed during the Cold War.

"As a Quaker I believe we all carry 'that of God' directly, so that, in the field of disarmament, listening to other people's ideas and proposals seems to me vitally important and I try to participate in an ongoing dialogue with them. It is only now that we are able to reach out beyond national self-interest and deal with the subject internationally and in the context of human security."[1]

This preoccupation with human security, David explains, has been gradually strengthening over the last twenty-five years. The health of the environment and the economic and social role of women have affected how we think about "security." Even the great powers have had to take notice of this new outlook. Decisions in the Security Council to help the Kurds and, most recently, the Rwandans, are proof that this new emphasis on humanitarian considerations has penetrated to the highest levels of decision-making.

David went on to describe how a whole slew of actions have occurred in conventional disarmament which give cause for hope. In Europe there has been destruction of a wide range of weapons, like, for example, tanks. The U.N. register of the export of conventional arms is working reasonably well and could lead to making a register of the actual holdings of weapons by individual nations. Meanwhile governments are actively trying to cut the continuing illicit trade in weaponry.

David was encouraged that peacekeeping and peacebuilding now usually include measures for disarmament. The warring parties themselves negotiate the terms for handling and destroying their weapons. In Cambodia, in Mozambique, and now in Liberia, this is having a reassuring effect on regional confidence and security building.

David Jackman ended on a positive note:

"In the 1960s many disarmament proposals were impossible: now they are not. True, the euphoria we all felt when the Cold War ended has now vanished.

But in its place there is a less lofty but new realism, which I hope will soon result in further practical steps in disarmament."

1. From an interview with David Jackman. February 25, 1997.

5. The International Atomic Energy Agency Comes to New York

The International Atomic Energy Agency (IAEA) has a mandate from the U.N. to monitor that the atomic energy being used for civilian purposes is not secretly being used to create atomic weapons. The agency, based in Austria, is part of the U.N. family and every year has to come to the General Assembly to get approval for its latest budget. Its work is not a direct part of disarmament, but it is a vital part of arms control.

The IAEA normally wins approval for its annual budget by means of a general assembly resolution. That is not the problem. The problem is that many countries, especially those that are on the brink of becoming nuclear powers themselves, countries like India and Pakistan and Israel which have chosen so far not to sign the Nuclear Non-Proliferation Treaty (NPT), do not like the IAEA's powers of inspection. They believe it is an authority which interferes with their national sovereignty and their national security.

But the IAEA is not just concerned with policing the Nuclear Non-Proliferation Treaty. It has other positive work which is crucial to all the nations which need nuclear power to give them sufficient energy to enable them to industrialize. These countries will have to build nuclear power stations and will therefore be required to accept advice and training from the IAEA.

The IAEA is particularly concerned with nuclear safety. It is a big subject and includes radiological protection and radioactive waste management. In the present biennium the agency will largely complete the preparation or revision of the entire corpus of safety standards—some seventy documents. It is determined to put in place systems and rules to ensure that a nuclear disaster like Chernobyl can never happen again. A further reinforcement of the standards for nuclear safety is the Convention on Nuclear Safety which entered into force in 1996.[1]

Lastly the IAEA has been charged by the Security Council to stop the development of nuclear weapons in Iraq and to check the applications of nuclear power in North Korea.

In November 1998, Dr. Mohamed Elbaredei, the Director-General of the IAEA, reported to the General Assembly on the wide range of work the IAEA is now engaged in:

"In addition to a complete ban on nuclear testing, two actions have always been identified as indispensable to nuclear arms reduction and disarmament: freezing the production of fissile materials for weapons purposes and the gradual reduction of such materials. I am pleased to note that measures are being taken in both areas."[2]

Dr. Elbaredei also reported on the Agency's vigilance in stopping illicit trafficking in nuclear material and that he was glad the lawyers in the General Assembly's Sixth Committee were working to create a convention on the suppression of nuclear terrorism.[3]

IAEA is also increasingly active in supporting the use of radioactive materials in development. The Sterile Insect technique for eradicating agricultural pests has been used in Zanzibar and will be used in Ethiopia. In Zimbabwe nitrogen fixation in the soil has increased the yield of soybean by 100 percent and reduced dependency on chemical fertilizer. And in Morocco environmental isotopes have been used to trace the source of leaks in dams.[4]

Dr. Elbaradei concluded his address with a message to the General Assembly that highlights just how widely the world is now dependent on nuclear technology:

"Today the beneficial appreciations of nuclear science and technology is a global reality. As we seek solutions to the urgent problems of combating climate change, preserving the environment, feeding and improving the health of growing populations, and supplying the energy needs for economic growth and development, there are compelling reasons to increase cooperation for the safe and peaceful use of nuclear technology."[5]

Notes

1. General Assembly Draft Resolution A/53/ L.18 October 29, 1998.
2. Mohamed Elbaradei. Statement to the Fifty-Third Session of the United Nations General Assembly. November 2, 1998.
3. Ibid.
4. Ibid.
5. Ibid.

6. Peacetime Killing Fields

"It is not a crisis; it's a catastrophe," said Ambassador Molander of Sweden in 1996. Even that was an understatement. It is estimated that 2–5 million land-mines are being laid every year and only 100,000 are being cleared.[1] Somalia is said to have access to mines from twenty-eight different sources! At this rate it will take eleven centuries to rid the world of this scourge! Meanwhile one person is maimed or killed by an anti-personnel mine every hour of every day. In countries like Afghanistan and Angola, most people are too poor to afford prostheses and they have to make do with crutches. It is not surprising that landmines have been called 'the atom bomb of the poor.'

Yet to judge from history, the cause of total abolition of anti-personnel landmines is by no means hopeless. In 1863, exploding bullets were banned and the use of poison gas was banned in 1925. In 1995, governments signed a protocol prohibiting the use of blinding lasers.

Ambassador Molander was the chairman of the recent review Conference of the Convention on Certain Conventional Weapons which were deemed to be excessively injurious. In May 1996 the states' parties to this convention added to it a new protocol on anti-personnel mines. All anti-personnel mines must have eight grams of iron in them to make them detectable. Anti-personnel mines must self-destruct within thirty days with 90 percent reliability. These new regulations would apply to internal conflicts but not to "internal distur-bances." There was no verification procedure, not even a voluntary one.

As so often when diplomats are searching for common ground in making and improving treaties, the devil continued to be in the details. For example, the U.S. proposed that mines should self-destruct in 120 days, but Russia had proposed 365 days. Then there were problems of marking minefields and of control of the exports of mines. Inevitably the protocol would continue to be argued over line by line.[2]

Meanwhile at the General Assembly of 1996, 97 nations pressed for action on landmines. The year before it was only 74. This was a reflection of the growing worldwide outrage, as the killing and maiming of civilians by landmines continued relentlessly.

Every year, as nations hesitated to sign and ratify this convention about excessively injurious weapons and its protocols in their own parliaments, more mines — ever more difficult to detect — were manufactured and laid. The United States, at least, gave $47 million for demining. Twenty-five nations agreed to stop exporting landmines. But these were only crumbs of comfort. There was progress, but the fire for total abolition was still only smoldering.

Update

The smoldering fire did in fact burst into flame! NGOs had become fed up that progress to a total ban on the use, manufacture, and export of landmines was moving so slowly that in 1992 they resolved to form a coalition to speed things up. Both the states who wanted total abolition and the NGOs realized that a treaty for a complete ban to landmines would not be accepted by the Conference on Disarmament and that working with the Protocol contained in the convention on excessively injurious weapons would not achieve the complete ban so urgently needed. Therefore the only way forward for the people and nations committed to a total ban was to work for a treaty formally outside the U.N. system. So a unique partnership between the committed states and the new NGO coalition was created. And right from the start the Canadian government took the lead in forwarding the work of this unique partnership.

All those NGOs determined to move ahead formed a coalition, known as the International Campaign to Ban Landmines. This coalition included the Vietnam Veterans of America; Human Rights Watch of New York; Physicians for Human Rights of Boston; Medico International of Germany; Handicap International of France, and the Mines Advisory Group of England. This coalition grew rapidly to include as many to 400 NGOs. Then, for the first time ever in the creation of a U.N.-type treaty, this NGO coalition was invited to take part in the negotiations between the interested states' parties which took place in Ottawa in 1997.[3]

No one knows exactly what speeded things up, but certainly the death of Princess Diana, who had visited mine victims in Angola, coincided with the conference and maybe shamed delegates into a sense of urgency. The treaty was agreed and began to collect signatures in December 1997. Some key nations—notably Russia and the United States—still could not go along with the final negotiated text of the treaty, but they remain under pressure to join the rest of the world in getting behind the treaty. In September 1998 the treaty had received forty ratifications and so was ready to come into force.

This time, unlike in the terms of the protocol of the convention on excessively injurious weapons, there was a verification procedure in place. The Secretary General of the U.N. was invited to take the responsibility of monitoring the treaty. With the right mixture of outrage from civil society and enough political will from many smaller nations, seemingly impossible things can and do get done.

To mark this great step forward—a victory for the growing influence of civil society—the 1998 Nobel Peace prize was awarded both to the International Campaign and to its major spokesperson, Jody Williams from the United States.

And the campaign is by no means over. At the U.N. in October 1998, Jody Williams announced that 1,000 NGOs in seventy-five countries would be monitoring the behavior of the countries that had ratified the treaty and urging those that had not done so to join the majority who had.

Notes

1. Ambassador Molander at the U.N. November 10, 1995.
2. *Disarmament Times*. October 11, 1995, P. 4.
3. *New York Times*. September 20, 1997, P. A5.

Part Five

Human Rights—an Overview

1. A Progress Report on Human Rights

Elissa Stamatopoulou-Robbins first became interested and concerned about
human rights when she was growing up in Greece under the repressive regime
of the Greek colonels. She studied law and international human rights and
began her career in the U.N. in Vienna. In 1995 she was in charge of the
Human Rights office in New York and she offered an update on current progress
to match with the start of the General Assembly that year.

She explained that the Division of Human Rights for the U.N. Secretariat
used to be based in New York, but in 1974 in the middle of the Cold War,
because the subject was so contentious, the office was moved to Geneva. The
Europeans, as a matter of pride, have ensured that the Commission on Human
Rights has met there ever since, and the Center for Human Rights has its
offices there. But the High Commissioner for Human Rights visits New York
every two months or so and the Committee on Civil and Political Rights has
one of its meetings at Headquarters every year. The General Assembly through
its Third Committee takes time on this subject, too. U.N. Headquarters is
never out of the Human Rights picture.

Elissa pointed that the Security Council in a major breakthrough has been
actively involved itself with Human Rights—in Iraq, in Bosnia, in Rwanda, and
elsewhere. But it does so with caution and does not yet have working links with
the main Human Rights bodies.

Since the Universal Declaration of Human Rights was created in 1948,
there has been a dynamic development in the process of developing Human
Rights. Rights that were simply not envisaged at that time—the right to self
determination, the right to development, the rights of women and of children—have since then all been spelled out and incorporated into U.N. conventions.

Elissa explained that U.N. sanctions against governments, who have vio-
lated their international human rights obligations, include public exposure and
criticism. Even dictatorships go to great lengths to avoid this kind of criticism,
because even they recognize that human rights are the mirror of the moral
health of a state. And even more, lack of proper human rights standards can
be a crucial factor when economic aid is under consideration. All member
states who sign human rights covenants can get help with strengthening their
human rights advisory services.

Of course there is still far too much unfinished human rights business.
Elissa said that, for example, the draft declaration on the rights of indigenous
peoples is still being worked on. And implementation of all existing Conventions—more than 70 of them—through the regular reporting of governments
on progress made is still far from satisfactory. As Elissa put it:

"If in fact all human rights legislation were implemented, we would have an angelic world!"

The monitoring and implementation of human rights is a very concrete, practical matter. Fundamental to the process is the work of the special rapporteurs who are assisted by the Center for Human Rights. Sometimes they are overwhelmed with work. For instance, the Working Group on Enforced or Involuntary Disappearances recently had a backlog of 15,000 cases to look into, and sorting out cases is slow, painstaking work, which takes a lot of time. Due to the limited budget there are simply not enough staff or funds to do it.

Sometimes more than one Special Rapporteur will receive a cry for help about the same case. For instance if a man of religion, perhaps a clergyman, is arbitrarily arrested, his case might arrive at the same time before the Rapporteur on Religious Intolerance, the Rapporteur on Arbitrary Detention, and the Rapporteur on Torture. Offending states are rarely so brazen that they can simply ignore the cumulative pressure by public exposure in the reports of more than one rapporteur.

One of the most important breakthroughs at the Vienna Human Rights Conference was that the international community, for the first time, declared that violence against women was more than a social or humanitarian issue—it was, essentially, a human rights issue. That insight gives this crime an edge which it does not have if simply looked at as a private family matter. In the same way health issues of concern to women have become human rights issues, and at the Cairo Conference on Population, this insight was carried a whole lot further.

Since the World Conference on Human Rights in Vienna, there has been a special rapporteur for violence against women. The Lovelace case from Canada was a recent important case for women which was decided by the Human Rights Committee. Because of that case, the Canadian Government had to change a law whereby, if an indigenous woman married a non-indigenous Canadian, she would lose her rights on the reservation, whereas a man who did the same thing, under the old law would not.

Elissa believes that human rights education is vital at all levels of society. Since the end of the Cold War, it has increased greatly and 1995 saw the start of a Decade for Human Rights Education. In any particular country the people on the ground—Human Rights lawyers, the police, the prison officers—need to have a much more thorough knowledge of what U.N. law enables them to do. In civil society throughout the world there has to be more teaching in schools, among trade unionists, and in the media about laws—both national and international—which relate to human rights.[1]

138

Update

Elissa Stamatopoulou-Robbins addressed the NGO Annual Conference at the U.N. in September 1998 and said that in this 50th Anniversary of the Universal Declaration of Human Rights it has been "We the Peoples" who have all along made possible the growth of human rights laws. She noted that in this era of globalization and privatization the focus was increasingly on economic and social rights. And never before had there been so many human rights monitors in the field, and never before had the U.N. provided so much training to judges, police, and all kinds of peacebuilders in the aftermath of conflict.

In October 1998, Mary Robinson, who has recently been the President of Ireland, made her first full report as High Commissioner for Human Rights to the 53rd Session of the General Assembly. She stressed that in this year of the Fiftieth Anniversary of Human Rights there was still a large amount of unfinished business in this field of work. She said:

"We have measured this year the significant increase in world expectations for the real protection and promotion of human rights, in particular economic, social and cultural rights. . . . We have also measured the immense burden of work that responding to those legitimate demands will require.

"All this will require enhanced resources. . . . It is no longer acceptable for member states to tell the people of the world that these human rights are worth less than 2 percent of United Nations resources."[2]

Notes

1. From an interview with Elissa Stamatopoulou-Robbins. September 18, 1995.
2. Report of the United Nations High Commissioner for Human Rights to the fifty-third session of the General Assembly. (A/53/36) P. 11.

2. Battling for Human Rights

Every autumn the Third Committee gets down to passing resolutions about countries with a bad record of Human Rights abuses. This step is not undertaken lightly. The Human Rights Commission in Geneva has appointed a growing team of special rapporteurs who monitor abuses in countries with a persistent record of abuse.

The commission has more than a dozen countries on its list. In 1995, for example, Burma, the former Republic of Yugoslavia, and Iran were on the list. Only if the countries in question, currently more than a dozen, cannot clear their name at the Human Rights Commission Meeting held earlier in the year at Geneva, is their case is brought before the Third Committee of the General Assembly in New York, and then finally before the plenary of the General Assembly itself.

Consider the case of the Sudan, which is has in recent years been on the Commissions List. The picture painted by the special rapporteur for the Sudan was a grim one. The rapporteur, Mr. Gaspar Biro, was not even allowed to visit the country, so the report had to be put together from witnesses in Kenya and Uganda.

"It is reckoned that over a million people have died since the civil war began in 1983. If people refuse to join the government forces, both men and women are summarily executed. Indiscriminate bombing of villages takes place. Most atrocities take place in the Nuba Mountains and in the Ingassema Hills."[1]

"Life in the Sudan is also brutal in the north. There are repeated reports that the abduction of street children and slavery, servitude and forced labor occur all the time. The rapporteur has repeatedly asked the government to bring its 1991 criminal code into line with the various U.N. conventions it has already signed. Under one particular clause in the code, a child of seven can be executed. There has been no response from the Government of the Sudan."[2]

Mr. Gaspar Biro, the special rapporteur, concluded:

"After careful study, comparison and verification of the information received, the special rapporteur concludes . . . that grave and widespread violations of human rights by government agents, as well as by members of parties to the conflict in southern Sudan other than the government of the Sudan, continue to take place in the zones controlled by them. . . ."[3]

The Third Committee under the polite but crisp chairmanship of Ambassador Tshering of the Kingdom of Bhutan listened to a defense of the Sudan's behavior from their government representative. Then a vote was taken whether or not to support the highly critical resolution of the Sudan.

Lights flashed on the voting board which dominated one side of the conference room—green for yes; red for no; and yellow for abstain. The result was 87 in favor, 16 against, and 40 abstentions. The result, as might have been expected, was decisive, but why were there so many abstentions? Governments may have felt that it might be their turn next to be judged on their human rights record. Alternatively they might have believed that a nation fighting to preserve its national unity does not deserve outright condemnation.

The battle for human rights in the Sudan has barely begun. The High Commissioner for Human Rights will surely have to make a visit there personally to try to alleviate so much abuse and suffering.

Notes

1. General Assembly. Situation of Human Rights in the Sudan. A/50/569. October 16, 1995. P. 4.
2. Ibid. P. 16.
3. Ibid. P. 21.

3. Volunteering for Work on the Implementation of Human Rights

Eleanor Roosevelt would surely be pleased by the way that the Universal Declaration of Human Rights, which she played such a great role in bringing to birth in 1948, has been developed down the decades. The general principles of the Universal Declaration have been grounded in more than seventy Conventions and Protocols which ensure that, in theory, all human rights treaties proclaimed by the U.N. will be followed up and put into practice. But is still not clear that implementation is really occurring in an orderly and effective way.

One man who remains doubtful and who has volunteered to clarify and set in better order what he believes is a very uneven tapestry of international lawmaking is American citizen Robert Kaplan.

Robert first became interested when he was looking into the rights of immigrants for the American Civil Liberties Union and he began to wonder whether U.N. laws covered that subject. So he plunged in, and found the whole terrain of U.N. human rights law is far broader, more complicated, and uneven than he had expected.

Working now as a retired volunteer on behalf of the International League of Human Rights, Bob Kaplan commented:

"The U.N. now has an extraordinary network of twenty-five treaties in place to cover every abuse of human rights, from civil rights to torture, from racial discrimination to the rights of the child. But how effective is the way these treaties actually get monitored?"

He explained that when a country ratifies a Human Rights Treaty, it binds itself to implement these treaties domestically and to provide remedies for breaches of these new laws. Furthermore, countries agree to submit themselves at regular intervals to a panel of independent experts nominated by the U.N. who closely question them on their progress reports.

Bob described some of the complexities of the network now in place:

"There is little or no similarity between the procedures laid down for different treaties. Some require reporting every two years: some every four.

141

Some examining committees meet for more than a month each year: others for only two weeks. There is overlapping, say, between civil rights and child rights. Most important, many countries simply fail to live up to their commitment to report regularly, and some fall years behind the schedule to which they have legally bound themselves.

"Individual complaints to, say, the Committee on Civil and Political Rights, are made through a protocol, which permits individuals to complain to the U.N. over the head of their own country, provided that their country has signed it. Unfortunately these complaints are piling up unanswered."

Furthermore, Robert found that nations have ratified these Conventions very unevenly. Thus while 175 nations have ratified the Convention on the Rights of the Child, nearly eighty countries have not ratified the Convention against Torture and fewer than twenty nations have signed the Protocol to allow their nationals to complain individually about torture to the U.N. Of course the whole point is that all these main pillars of human rights have to be ratified by national parliaments before they have the force of law. Universal ratification may come about with regard to the Convention on the Rights of the Child, but there is still a long way to go for national parliaments to ratify most of the other treaties.

Robert is still patiently at work completing his report, but his overall conclusion is a positive one.

"A good foundation is in place and, never forget, it is a foundation of international human rights treaty law. Governments have to report, and regularly report, their progress on incorporating and implementing U.N. human rights standards in their own country. And it is slowly happening. Some countries are even making their third or fourth progress report to the panel of experts.

"But the whole framework of implementation has many inefficiencies and is spread much too thin. Human rights at the U.N. are still grossly underfunded. Much, too, can and should be done to tighten up and simplify the way reports are presented. There is far too much overlapping. Very few people actually use the Protocols that their country has signed, which allows them to take their case to the U.N. Fewer still know a comprehensive human rights system now exists to bring them and their friends justice, should their own nation fail to do it for them.

"Since the signing of the Universal Declaration of Human Rights in 1948, it has taken almost fifty years of hard legal and political work to create the network of human rights laws, which is in place today. Nations are always worrying that a step forward in recognizing international human rights will mean a step backward in their own national authority and sovereignty.

"A great overarching shelter of human rights to prevent abuses to people of all ages is now at last in place. Never before in history have there been

142

international standards available to protect individuals whatever their nationality. Now the challenge for every nation is to make it all universal, efficient, and publicly available for everyone everywhere."[1]

Since the birth of Amnesty International, the pursuit of Human Rights has always depended as much on individual volunteers as much or more than on governments, and volunteers like Bob Kaplan are continuing that fine tradition through their laborious research.

Note

1. From an interview with Robert Kaplan. August, 1995.

4. Individual Appeals to the U.N. about Human Rights Violations

Nothing is more revolutionary in the U.N. than the ability of individuals to appeal to the U.N. over the head of their own government if and when they consider that the system of justice in their country has not been fair to them.

The heart of this work is the painstaking examination of individual cases by the Committee of Human Rights. This committee of eighteen experts hears appeals from individuals who have submitted an apparent case of injustice to them. Individuals can only do this if their nation has signed the Optional Protocol to the Convention on Civil and Political Rights. By no means, do all nations give this individual right of appeal to the U.N. to their citizens, but those who do represent a broad spectrum of nations from north and south. At the latest count 130 nations have signed the covenant, but only 84 are parties to the Optional Protocol.[1]

The report of the findings of the Human Rights Committee of Experts comes to the U.N. long after the actual hearings, and hardly gets any attention, not least, because it is nearly 400 pages of closely reasoned legal arguments. The results of the 1994 hearing have now become available. Here are some typical cases:

Communication No. 322/1988 Hugo Rodriguez v. Uruguay

This case is about the meaning of an amnesty law passed to exempt torturers during the military regime in Uruguay from punishment. Hugo Rodriguez argued that under article 2, paragraph 3A of the Covenant he was entitled to an investigation which would identify his torturer and enable him to receive civil compensation. He further made the point that the Inter-American Commission on Human Rights had failed to take up his case, so that the U.N. was his appeal of last resort.

When a case comes before the committee, the government of the country accused of a breach of international human rights laws has a chance to put forward a written defense of its conduct. The state claimed that its Law No. 15,848 prevented further investigation of individuals, and that Rodriguez could, in fact, have claimed for compensation.

The committee found in favor of Rodriguez and noted that Law 15, 848 created "an atmosphere of impunity which might undermine the democratic order."[2] They decided that Rodriguez was entitled to compensation and requested the Uruguay Government to let them know within 90 days what action they were going to take.

Communication No. 412/1990 Auli Kivenmaa v. Finland

Ms. Kivenmaa accused the Finnish Government of abusing her human rights to make a public protest against a visiting head of state. Her banner of protest was removed and she was subsequently charged, she contended under a law which covered public meetings, but not protest, by individuals in a crowd assembled for an official occasion.[3]

The Finnish Government argued that what she and her friends had done did amount to a demonstration. And Article 19 of the U.N. Covenant did not give an unrestricted right to freedom of speech and assembly.

The committee found that there was no Finnish Law under which Ms. Kivenmaa could in this instance be rightly charged, and they asked that she be provided with "an appropriate remedy," and also that the state of the law be looked into to prevent a similar situation arising in the future.

Communication No. 458/1991 Albert Womah Mukong v. Cameroon

Albert Mukong was a journalist who was arrested for giving an interview on television in which he spoke against the President of his country and in favor of multi-party democracy. He was harshly treated in prison and had to sleep without his clothes on a concrete floor in a badly ventilated cell.[4]

The government of Cameroon argued that the basic amenities in the prison were due to the overall poverty in the country and that the excessive heat was merely normal for that part of Africa. Further, they argued that the freedom laid down under the covenant could not yet come into being in a country with over 200 ethnic groups.

The committee found that Mr. Mukong's human rights had been abused under Articles 7, 9, and 19 of the Covenant and they requested the government to come up with appropriate compensation, and to ensure that no similar arrests and detentions took place in the future.

The committee heard a substantial number of other cases from all over the world. In most of them, notably those from Canada and the Netherlands, they found that the cases in question had been fairly dealt with at the national level and that therefore was no case for them to answer.

These cases take an unconscionable time to be resolved and the number that reaches the committee is still ridiculously small. And of course the U.N. can only recommend; it cannot enforce its judgement. But never before has the individual had the opportunity to take his own nation to a court which is beyond national jurisdiction. Some nations, by refusing to sign and ratify this protocol, will continue to resist this new limitation to their sovereignty. But without doubt this new door will open much wider in the future, and many will be thankful that the U.N. has been empowered to remedy the injustice done to them.

Notes

1. Press Release HR/CT/410—July 6, 1995.
2. General Assembly. Forth-Ninth Session. Report of the Human Rights Committee. Volume Two. 2. P. 10.
3. Ibid. P. 90
4. Ibid. P. 172.

5.   A Japanese View of the Human Rights Committee

Any state which signs and ratifies a U.N. Covenant finds that certain obligations go with signing that treaty. Every few years a state that signs has to appear at the U.N. and give a progress report about what practical steps it has taken to implement that particular covenant.

The Covenant of Civil and Political Rights is one of the oldest of these covenants, stemming directly from the Universal Declaration of Human Rights.

It has now been ratified by more than 130 states. Its Human Rights Committee has been created to regularly examine how states that have ratified the covenant are handling their civil and political rights; it has already held more than fifty sessions in New York and Geneva.

This eighteen-member committee is made up of independent individuals nominated by their home states. Mr. Nisuke Ando, a professor of Law from Kyoto University in Japan, is one of the longest-serving members of the committee and has served as its chairperson for a number of years.

Mr. Nisuke Ando is well aware that many governments, far from welcoming the U.N.'s network of human rights legislation, are uneasy about the relentless increase of U.N. covenants and conventions dealing with human rights. In answer to the question why the U.N. still spends barely 2 percent of its regular budget on human rights, he responded, "Governments fear that human rights can be used as a weapon of diplomacy against them. Indeed we, the members of our committee, always say, 'There is no paradise in the world as far as human rights are concerned.'[1]

Mr. Ando recalled that the "Human Rights" only came in as a concept in the 1940s. Before that time people spoke mainly about the Rights of Man. The Universal Declaration of Human Rights in 1948 greatly enriches the idea of human rights and awareness of this declaration has now spread all over the world, so that now it is difficult for any member government to refuse the tenets of U.N. Human Rights legislation.

Mr. Ando spoke about the roots of human rights legislation at the U.N.

"The Universal Declaration of Human Rights is the foundation of all subsequent human rights conventions. The declaration has two main legs. One leg is the Covenant on Civil and Political Rights. The other is the Covenant on Economic, Social, and Cultural Rights. Some nations have argued these two legs are not of equal importance. Some have doubts about the Covenant on Economic Rights because it deals with collective rights and because it might be difficult to enforce in courts of law. And indeed it is difficult to frame a definition of poverty that fits all states in the world with equal accuracy."

Mr. Nisuke put the continuing tension between the rights expressed in these two covenants as follows:

"During the East and West confrontation the Communists always said that political rights meant nothing unless people first had food, shelter, and clothing. The West argued that of course bread matters, but so does good government and freedom of expression. I believe there must be a balance. The basic standard of living must be raised to make the political rights work properly. But meanwhile the poverty of the many must never be used as an excuse for any government to exercise dictatorship over its people."

Mr. Ando welcomed the recent creation of a High Commissioner for Human Rights by the General Assembly, but he explained that there might be a political agenda behind this appointment, which might make it not such a big step forward as some nations thought it ought to be.

"The Commissioner was certainly given a wide mandate, but unfortunately the General Assembly gave the person no money. So this individual has to work with the Center for Human Rights, which already has its own director. The staff in Geneva is not sure which way to turn. If, for example, the Commissioner takes up the issue of Refugees, there might be a disagreement with the High Commissioner for Refugees, Mrs. Ogata from my country, who is achieving great results on her own. Indeed I have heard it said that the developing countries voted for this appointment because they knew it would create some confusion in the machinery of human rights."

A further important refinement of the Covenant on Civil and Political Rights is its optional protocol. By this protocol states allow individuals who believe they have failed to achieve justice in their own domestic court, to bring their case to the U.N. To hear these cases is an additional task of the Committee on Human Rights.

Mr. Ando commented on the manner in which the committee does its work.

"We work in a very cooperative manner and usually vote by consensus, seldom by majority vote. But for ten years in the Communist era there was only one person who was acceptable to both sides as our Chairman.

"If we uphold a complaint, we usually prescribe a pecuniary remedy or a release from custody. We had one case where there was sex discrimination to do with social security and the government had to pay a considerable sum in compensation. But it will be up to the General Assembly to decide if and when they want us to have the authority of a Court similar to the European Court of Human Rights."

"I thought the U.S. did very well on their first appearance before our committee. I have been on this committee eleven years with three years as Chairman. The worst kinds of government try to evade each and every question, but the U.S. tried to answer each and every question we put to them after we had first had a chance to read their report to us."

Mr. Ando summed up his view of the first 50 years of the U.N.'s existence.

"The biggest success has been the avoidance of a Third World War. In 1945 half the people of the world were not sovereign. Now sovereignty is all over the globe. But this positive step has not brought everything we hoped it would. That puts me in mind of a Chinese proverb: 'If you want something, you will get another.' And so now having helped to secure freedom for most colonial peoples, we are faced with the quite new and unexpected problems of self-determination. It is clearly described as a right in the first article of the Covenant on Civil and Political Rights. No one is clear to which group or to which entity it refers. We see the self-determination issue arising in the case of Yugoslavia, with parts of Africa, and with Russia. It will be a big issue for the next century."

Update

In 1997 the Secretary General Kofi Annan from Ghana appointed Dr. Mary Robinson from Ireland as the first female Commissioner for Human Rights. She will have the responsibility of choosing who will be the Director of the Center of Human Rights in Geneva, and that may make it easier to get unified policies on Human Rights throughout the whole U.N. system.

Note

1. Interview with Mr. Nisuke Ando, April 1995.

6. The United States Is Called before the Human Rights Committee

This was an historic day in the story of human rights in the United Nations. For the first time ever the United States appeared before a United Nations tribunal to give an account of its record on human rights since Congress ratified the Covenant on Civil and Political Rights.

By signing the Covenant, the United States voluntarily made itself accountable to the world community. Never before was the gallery so full of citizens, mostly American citizens, who came to see the U.S. explaining its laws on human rights before the international independent experts—lawyers all with a global reputation—on the Human Rights Committee.

Why did the Americans wait till 1995 to make their first appearance before this committee? After all, the Covenant on Civil and Political Rights which deals with individual rights and freedoms came into force as long ago as 1966 when thirty-five nations had already ratified it. But the U.S. did not sign the covenant until 1992! Why was there such a long delay, when the U.S. under the inspired leadership of Eleanor Roosevelt, had been one of the main architects of the Universal Declaration of Human Rights way back in 1948?

In fact the U.S. has been very slow to sign a whole clutch of other human rights Covenants. The Covenant against Genocide was not approved by Congress until 1988 and only in 1995 has the Covenant on the Rights of the Child finally been ratified. The important Covenant on Economic, Social, and Cultural Rights has still not been ratified by the U.S.

There are several reasons for these long delays. The relationship between the federal and state governments is complicated. On some important issues like the death penalty there are different incompatible positions. Congress felt, and perhaps some of its members still feel, even after the end of the cold war, that no international body can ever be quite good enough to sit in judgement on a country which has always been both a pioneer and a leader in the recognition and protection of individual human rights.

But now at last it happened! And the U.S. took the challenge very seriously, submitting a detailed report of two hundred pages on the state of American Human Rights in 1995 and sending five Senior Federal Officials to introduce the report, including John Shattuck, Assistant Secretary of State for Human Rights.

But the U.S. felt it had to make some written "reservations, understandings and declarations." For instance, Article 20 of the Covenant prohibits "propaganda for war." The U.S. stated that to accept that clause to would go against the principle of free speech — laid down by the First Amendment to the American Constitution — and America could not agree to accept that article.

John Shattuck said it was a "signal honor" to appear before the committee. Perhaps he felt some reassurance from the fact that, for the first time, there was now in 1995 a distinguished American lawyer, Mr. Thomas Buergenthal, sitting on the other side of the fence, as one of the independent panel of experts.

This first appearance of the United States came, in fact, not a moment too soon. Amnesty International has recently published a report with detailed chapter and verse of areas where the United States falls short of the standards set in the U.N. Covenant. In its summary the Amnesty Report reads, "The issues covered include the death penalty, where the resumption and increase in executions in recent years is incompatible with human rights standards; police brutality and use of excessive force, including deaths in custody and unjustified shootings; and torture and ill-treatment in prisons."[1]

The experts on the committee, however, elected to begin their inquiries by looking at some of the more technical legal issues involved in the U.S. finally signing the covenant. Mrs. Evatt from Australia, having praised the report overall, asked if the individual states of the union were consulted by the federal government in this process. Mr. Julio Vallejo from Ecuador wanted to know how Article 1 of the Covenant, about self-determination, related to American domestic law. Mr. Ando from Japan asked about when deportation was in question (Article 13), whether the case would come before someone from the Judiciary or only before someone from the Executive?

And so the experts began a wide-ranging survey of many points where they felt American human rights law was probably not in harmony with the International Covenant. Later in the week the Americans would get their chance to answer all the questions and criticisms. Perhaps the United Nations on this day was saying to the Americans that even they should be glad to have found an answer to the ancient Roman question, "Who will guard the guardians?" And perhaps the Americans agreed with them.

Note

1. United States human rights violations: a summary of Amnesty International's concerns. Amnesty International. March 1995.

7. The Fight Against Torture

Every working day the Press Corps at the U.N. gather for a briefing by the Secretary-General's spokesman and sometimes to hear a visiting diplomat, who has come to the U.N. to address the Security Council. Sometimes a U.N. Mission will arrange for an advocate of a special cause to speak to the press in the hope of sounding a worldwide alarm. Dr. Inge Genefke, with the help of the Danish Ambassador Mr. Jorgen Hansen Bojer, came to the U.N. in 1997 to advance her passionately-held view that member countries are giving far too low a priority to the fight against torture.

Dr. Genefke, who is Secretary-General of the International Rehabilitation Council for Torture Victims, summed up the current situation as follows.

"Even though the Convention against Torture was open for signature in 1987, there are still no less than 81 member states that have not yet ratified the Convention against Torture. Countries that have not ratified in their Parliaments include Belgium, Indonesia, Japan, South Africa, and the Syrian Arab Republic. And many of those that have ratified have not yet put into operation the educational and financial compensation procedures which the Convention requires.

"Even more worrying in 1997 is the sum volunteered by member states to help rehabilitate victims of torture is pitifully small. Only three million dollars has been pledged from just thirty-two states when at least seven million dollars is needed to keep going some one hundred and sixty rehabilitation centers worldwide."[1]

Dr. Inge Genefke emphasized how much there is still to be done to conscientize the world about torture and its victims: "Torturers do not get punished. Victims are too afraid and ashamed to speak up. And the victims are usually trade unionists, teachers, or members of ethnic minorities—people in the front line in the struggle to establish democracy. Torture is an instrument of power used against democracy. Let me stress that there is no case in history where the use of torture has solved a political problem. We rely on the press to break the silence that surrounds the subject."[2]

So what can the press do to spread this news? Among the press correspondents at this meeting was American Sally Swing Shelley, well known in the U.N. as an administrator and now a journalist, who is on Special Assignment for the Associated Press. She will now broadcast to 400 radio stations about this crisis and also reach out through the Maryknoll Brothers to more than fifty universities.

Most people abhor torture, but, as Dr. Genefke said on an earlier occasion at the Human Rights Commission in Geneva, they need to take to heart the words of Albert Camus, "Turn words into moral actions—then you will become a human being."

Stop Press

On August 20, 1998, the Secretary-General reported to the General Assembly that the Fund for Victims of Torture had topped four million dollars and had been ratified by more than 100 nations. In 1997, the Fund had helped 59,000 victims of torture. In Copenhagen on June 26, on the International Day in Support of Victims of Torture, the Secretary-General said: "The torture of one human being torments the consciences of all human beings. Action, not indifference, must be the motto to eradicate torture and support in the rehabilitation of its victims."[3]

Notes

1. Press briefing at the U.N. by Dr. Inge Genefke, Secretary-General, The International Rehabilitation Council for Torture Victims. November 10, 1997.
2. Dr. Inge Genefke at the U.N. Commission on Human Rights in Geneva. March–April 1997.
3. General Assembly. United Nations Voluntary Fund for Victims of Torture. Report of the Secretary General. A/53/283 August 20, 1998.

8.   A Sacred Pipe Ceremony for Indigenous Peoples

Issues raised at the U.N. filter slowly into the consciousness of nations and the worldwide public. Often they are issues which are not even proclaimed in the Charter, yet gradually they assume greater and greater importance on the U.N. Agenda. Peacekeeping has proved to be one such issue. That was not even mentioned in the Charter. Another is the environment, which first came onto the U.N. Agenda at Stockholm in 1972. At Rio in 1972 the whole subject almost spiralled out of control when nations were asked to digest a huge program of action contained in Agenda 21—more than 1,000 recommendations to digest and to act upon!

So what issue will be next to impinge on the world's conscience? It should now be the turn of indigenous peoples. These are people who inhabited ancestral lands centuries before invaders, usually from overseas, came to conquer and to settle their lands, and to take away their freedom. They are estimated to number over three hundred million people. They are distributed over all continents, especially in Latin America and parts of Asia. Almost all of them have yet to receive from governments the justice and autonomy which is their due. For the first time in 1990 a U.N. Decade for Indigenous People to draw attention to them was established.

In 1996, for the first time, a Day for Indigenous Peoples was celebrated at the United Nations. Due to the inspiration and effort of Avalar de Tavernier, representing the Gayap tradition of Trinidad, a World Peace Pipe Ceremony was arranged on the wide sunlit piazza outside the north entrance to the U.N.

A pipe of peace was smoked by a circle of Native Americans and indigenous friends from the Caribbean—people of Arawak decent. Then in traditional feathered dress they danced to the sound of singing and drumming. Their dancing was intense and concentrated, but hardly joyful. It was dancing that seemed to celebrate survival more than victory. Everyone felt that all who were taking part were honoring their ancestors by this ceremony.

Melissa Fawcett, a Mohegan Tribal historian from Connecticut, told the assembled crowd that the Mohegans were thought to have become extinct after the publication of the famous book "The Last of the Mohicans" by James Fennimore Cooper. But the famous writer got it wrong! Somehow the Mohegans did survive to the present day. Some can even trace their ancestry back for thirteen generations.

This was much more than a gathering of Native Americans. There were Buddhist speakers from Myanmar, where forty percent of the nation is made up of indigenous people. The Tainos were there from Costa Rica. There was a Shuar Delegation from Ecuador. The Chiapas of Mexico, and Rigoberto Menchu for the Mayan people sent messages. Valery Markov spoke for the Finno-Ugric People. Nana Apeadu from Ghana included children in a prayer of blessing.

Attendance by diplomats and members of the Secretariat at this ceremony was sparse and disappointing. This was not so surprising. Member states of the U.N. have always been ambivalent about indigenous peoples, fearing they may break up national solidarity. The U.N. working party on the subject is still known only as "The Working Group for Indigenous *Populations.*"

Besides arranging ceremonies, is the U.N. Decade for Indigenous People achieving anything? Most important in the long term is going to be a draft Declaration on the Rights of Indigenous Peoples, which may be ready for adoption in 1998.

All sorts of gatherings worldwide are increasing attention to the subject. In Canada in 1966 the Center for Human Rights helped produce a Seminar on Land Rights and Claims. And the Arctic Council is bringing together the Inuits of Canada and the Saami of the Siberian Region of the Russian Federation. In Fiji a group assembled drawn from all over the South Pacific. Indigenous People from America met in Copenhagen to define their aims.[1]

Progress on the Rights of Indigenous Peoples is not explosive. It is never likely to be. Human rights issues, and especially this one, are too threatening to governments for that. After all, vital issues of territorial integrity and national sovereignty are being brought to the table for negotiation. Nudging governments along gradually to give more freedom and equity to indigenous peoples is the best hope for this special decade which aims to be a beacon on behalf of so many voiceless peoples.

Note

1. Program of Activities for the International Decade of the World's Indigenous People. Secretary General's Report. A/51/499. October 15, 1996.

9. The Disappearance of a U.N. Civil Servant

As staff who work at the U.N. hurry along to the U.N. Cafeteria, they have been confronted with a mysterious photograph of a U.N. civil servant. It is the only photograph constantly on display in the lobby of the U.N. This person must be important because the U.N. Press Club has made him their Honorary President. He is Alec Collett, a U.N. "disappeared person," and a day in March, 1995 was the Tenth Anniversary of his disappearance in the Middle East.

Who is Alec Collett and why is the whole Press Corps and the Head of the U.N. Staff Council gathering in his honor? He was never a soldier or even a policeman—just an ordinary civil servant doing his job. But the Universal Declaration of Human Rights (Article 9) gives him, as it does to all U.N. personnel, protection against arbitrary arrest and detention.

Alec Collett first worked as a journalist for the U.N. in Ghana and was then given a special assignment in 1985 to go to Lebanon to work for the United Nations Relief and Works Agency for Palestinian Refugees (UNRWA). His job was to publicize the plight of Palestinian refugees in Lebanon. He was excited about this new assignment, but had hardly been there three months when he was abducted. He was not been heard of since.

Many expeditions have been launched to find out what has happened to him. The Secretary-General's special representative Giandominico Picco was in Lebanon for a long time and helped to arrange the release of other hostages like Terry Anderson and Terry Waite. The tragedy of the situation is that it is most likely that it was some group of Palestinians who took him prisoner.

Alec Collett is not the only U.N. international civil servant to disappear or to lose his life while on duty. In fact in the latest list of staff members whose basic rights have not been respected by member states, more than 1,000 have died on duty, especially in Afganistan, Rwanda, and Cambodia, while serving the U.N.

Because he was both a journalist and an international civil servant, Alec Collett has been chosen by the U.N. Press Corps as the one to be remembered, and to keep on searching for. Mr. Mahomed Oummih, President of the Staff Committee said of him today, "Alec Collett is for us the symbol of what has to be done to free all U.N. staff members held against their will. Alec Collett must not die."[1]

The journalists have done more than just publicize the plight of Alec and his wife Elaine. They have funded the education of his son Karim and the staff unions in Vienna and New York are getting together to fund a scholarship for a child whose parent has disappeared or been killed while working for the U.N.

Mr. Oummih said a humanitarian mission will soon go to Lebanon to make yet another attempt to solve the mystery of Alec's disappearance. There is always the hope that, as the peace process in the Middle East goes forward, the truth about Alec Collett will finally emerge.

Meanwhile Elaine Collett, his wife who is from Ghana, and who works at U.N. Headquarters made a heartfelt appeal to all present "Remember those in prison as though you are with them."

154

10.   Colonies Still Exist!

The age of colonialism is over, but unfortunately colonies still exist! It is cold comfort to those who are still not free to be told that since the end of World War Two some eight hundred million people have achieved their political freedom. According to the U.N. there are still 17 territories which are, still, in some way colonial dependencies. And every year the U.N.'s Decolonization Committee of Twenty-Four considers how much progress these often forgotten territories have made towards independence in the past year.

Some people argue that these territories are so small—Gibraltar, for example, has only 2000 people—that they do not need a body in the U.N. to help them. It is argued that they are mostly too small to cast themselves off from a larger power which claims it is giving the people under its protection a better life and a good measure of freedom anyway.

The Chairman for the 1996 session of the Committees of Twenty-Four was Ambassador Alimany Bangura of Sierra Leone and he had other views. Wearing his traditional dress in the Trusteeship Council Chamber, he declared:

"We are halfway in this Decade for the Independence of all Colonial Peoples. This committee exists to make known their wishes and interests. Those of us from Africa can identify with their deprivation. They must be free to meet their own challenges and make their own mistakes. It would be premature to abolish this committee, even if many here in the U.N. no longer take an active interest in what we try to do.

"True independence has still to come to even those who today are nominally free and independent: many still labor under the 'conditionalities' of outside economic interests."[1]

But who exactly are these colonial territories who seek their liberty? Two of the biggest under the microscope of the Committee are East Timor with 750,000 and New Caledonia with a population of 170,000. Both are islands in East Asia and both have very different histories.

The people of East Timor, formerly a Portuguese colony, have been vigorously protesting against the invasion and takeover of their country by Indonesia—a people of different ethnic origin—20 years ago. The Indonesians claim that by the Balibo Declaration they were invited in to stop a civil war and have stayed on ever since to preserve law and order.

All over the world NGOs have been established to proclaim the cause of the people of East Timor. Mr. Akhisa Matsuno of the Free East Timor Coalition has done a scholarly analysis to show that the Balibo Declaration has, in translation, been distorted and that it is not any longer a statement that can be taken to represent the independent views of the majority of the people of East Timor.[2]

From Canada, the East Timor Alert Network quoted Isabel Galhos from East Timor:

"Indonesian soldiers come to our home at any time, use anything they want, eat and drink everything and never pay anything, everything's free. They really like to be adopted by a family that has a daughter. So they can also have sex without any responsibility. . . . We are not free in East Timor, not even in our own home."[3]

It is estimated that large number of people have died—maybe up to 200,000—resisting the invaders, though the Indonesians now claims soldiers who break laws by maltreating civilians are brought to justice.

The bottom line in all colonial disputes is that the victims justly ask that there should a referendum to find out what the majority want. But the colonial power often delays or refuse this crucial test.

In New Caledonia there is a certain openness between the local inhabitants and the French settlers, but in Western Sahara the question of the referendum is still complicated by the difficulty of taking a census of a people who are scattered across great expanses of desert.

Ambassador Bangura said he was not interested in the hearings being just talk. He would take the resolutions from the committee to the Economic and Social Council, currently meeting in Geneva. He was confident that the cases they had examined would come before the General Assembly later in the year. The voice of the voiceless had to be heard. The cause of these mostly forgotten victims of colonialism, said the Ambassador, would be recognized as greater than the political and business interests of their alien rulers who continued to insist that they were dealing with a few agitators and not whole peoples who were fighting for their freedom.

Update: In 1999, the people of East Timor voted decisively for independence from Indonesia. A peacekeeping force, led by Australia, moved in and the U.N. took on the responsibility of managing the transition to independence.

Notes

1. Interview with Ambassador Bangura. July 14, 1995.
2. Statement to Special Committee on Decolonization. Akihisa Matsuno. July 11, 1995.
3. Statement of Special Committee by David Webster. East Timor Alert Network, Canada, July 13, 1995.

Part Six

Human Rights—
Women and Children

1. A Mexican View of Women's Rights

Progress at the U.N. can often be like the flow of an avalanche. Very slowly cracks develop as snow unfreezes and then quite suddenly a huge mass breaks free and rushes downhill, sweeping all resistance before it. The Women's Movement at the U.N. is proving to be very like this.

It all started in a small way in 1946, when the U.N. established a Sub-Commission on Women, which in the following year became the Commission on the Status of Women (CSW). Down the decades this commission has remained the bedrock of progress for women at the U.N.

Ambassador Aida Gonzalez Martinez of Mexico tells the full story. She remembers that it was not until 1975 that there was "an explosion of consciousness" about women's rights. In that year Ambassador Martinez organized the first Women's Summit in Mexico City. That was the beginning of a U.N. Decade for Women from 1975 to 1985.[1]

She remembers that at Mexico City the emphasis was on ensuring there was no discrimination in the legal structure of states, above all in their constitutions. Then in 1981 the General Assembly at the U.N. went on to ratify the Convention against All Forms of Discrimination against Women and that Convention was the highlight of the Decade for Women. Nations who had ratified this Convention committed themselves to appear before a committee of independent experts meeting at the U.N. to give account of their progress in making women equal partners in every aspect of the life of their nation. And that cross-questioning relating to domestic policies has been going on at regular intervals ever since.

But this is to rush ahead. The second Women's Conference took place in Copenhagen in 1980. The main themes continued to be what they were and still are today—Equality, Development, and Peace. At Copenhagen the attention shifted to the subject of Women's Health and its protection throughout the entire lives of women, especially during the child-bearing years.

Then as the decade came to an end the women met again in Nairobi. Whereas in Mexico 8,000 women had gathered in Africa the number rose to fifteen thousand. In Africa, appropriately, the emphasis was on all the hidden undervalued work that women do in the home and in the fields which is outside the cash economy. A plea was made that all kinds of the "hidden" work of women's should find a proper place in national statistics and national accounting.

But, as Ambassador Martinez explained, progress for fairness to women depends on so much more than the U.N. putting machinery in place to help women get a fair deal. In so many countries their whole culture was still against equal opportunity for women. Unfortunately, as the Ambassador noted, even mothers continue to bring up their sons so that they continue with the old ways of looking at the status of women.

Nevertheless, said the Ambassador, who has been a leader in the advance of women's rights for twenty years, women have never looked stronger than they do today. They are now a truly universal constituency. For the first time the women of the former Soviet Union and Eastern Europe are able to speak out. The number of women's NGOs represented at summits has grown tremendously and an increasing number of women are members of official government delegations.

Since the Ambassador told this story of how the movement for justice for women got started, women have celebrated their growing strength at the Beijing Women's Conference in 1996, attended by 25,000 women. And at the U.N. a woman has, for the first time, been appointed the Commissioner for Human Rights. She is Mary Robinson, former President of Ireland. But the avalanche still has a long way to travel and the U.N. is determined to remain in the vanguard of progress for all women everywhere.

Note

1. From an interview with Ambassador Aida Gonzalez Martinez of Mexico. April 1995.

2.   Bella Abzug at San Francisco

Who better to invite to give the women's assessment of the Fiftieth Anniversary than Bella Abzug? Bella is an ex-member of Congress and a well-known American activist. So one evening in June 1995 the women of the Golden Gate City arranged a special evening down in the old docks of Fort Mason to hear Dr. Engoshega of Cameroon, Lily Lim from San Francisco, and Bella Abzug from New York City at the new Cowell Theatre.

Bella is the undisputed Queen of the Women's Movement at the U.N. Wearing one of her famous broad-brimmed hats, ignoring a heart bypass operation, she clambered up onto the stage and rallied the audience like the veteran campaigner she is.

Bella spoke vigorously about the long campaign of women to win their rights in the counsels of the U.N.

"There have always been pioneers who were determined that women should have their share of at least half of the U.N. decision-making. There was Jane Adams who used to say women were 'the cosmic peace activists,' and there was Alva Myrdal from Sweden who did so much to press for disarmament at the height of the Cold War.

"Nothing had come easy in the promotion of women's interests. At first Women had only their 'Day' in the U.N. calendar, then it became a year and finally we won a decade.

"In the old days men were cautiously prepared to go along with us—'provided we behaved.' We did not, and that is why we are making progress![1]

"In the '90s there has been a virtual explosion of women's Non-Governmental Organizations. Rio Conference on Development and Environment triggered a whole new vision on the role of women in the modern world.

"At Rio women really got down to the details of drafting the Program of Action. They did a line by line analysis of what has come to be known as Agenda 21. The women saw that raw concepts of economic development by themselves were no good. So they added a whole new section—Chapter 24—to the final report in which as many as 120 provisions were inserted referring specifically to the concerns of women.

"All this was in line with the central concern of the U.N. for 'Action for Equality, Development, and Peace' in every part of its Agenda. I always say, 'The music is the action!'

"After Rio women began to feel their strength. They prepared their case lobbying governments equally hard at Prepcoms as at Summit Conferences. At the Cairo Conference on Women, 80 percent of the NGO were women. At the Beijing Women's Conference, scheduled for September, women will turn up in greater numbers than ever before. I give you a slogan: 'Half the world: half the pot.'

"Women remain a majority of the poor and the illiterate. The good advice for women used to be 'Speak softly and carry lipstick.' Now women must carry a big stick, and not only for the good of themselves."

Bella had by no means finished all she had to say at San Francisco. In 1997 at the Environment Summit to mark the fifth anniversary of Rio, Bella was again speaking out on the unfinished business of fair shares for women. Giving a rallying cry from a wheelchair, she said:

"In the old days all we NGOs could do was to circulate documents at the Economic and Social Council. Now we want access to all the main U.N. committees and to the General Assembly. We do not wish to beg. And we do not wish to be invited in when governments have made all the decisions. We ought to be in on the planning stage, in on the governing councils of the U.N. and its Agencies, and in on Reform Working Groups about the future of the U.N."

Update

Sadly, Bella Abzug died in 1998, but on the first anniversary of her death Dianne Dillon-Ridgley told us how Bella is far from forgotten: "One woman from Poland came to Budapest in December solely because she wanted to touch, meet, and work with the women from WEDO (Women's Environment and Development Organization) who knew 'the Bella.' On the last day of the Prepcom for Beijing⁺5, Oidov Enhtuya, member of Parliament, came up to me and introduced herself as the 'Bella Abzug of Mongolia.' And on International Womens Day (March 8) several women came to WEDO's Linkage Caucus wearing their hats."[2]

Note

1. From a speech by Bella Abzug. San Francisco. June 1995.
2. Dillon-Ridgley, Dianne, "Bella, a Year Later." *Earth Times*. March 1999. P. 6.

3. Beijing Women's Summit

For months the Beijing Summit for Women loomed over the U.N. as the biggest event of the 1995 calendar. Finally it happened. But it took place, like all summits in recent years, thousands of miles away from the U.N. in Beijing. It was a unique event. Its ripple effects are already being felt in Headquarters itself, where all the women who work at the U.N. have already met to discuss the Beijing conclusions. Women in the U.N. Secretariat are more determined than ever to press their case for equal representation in the staffing of the U.N. at all levels.

When the Conference was all over, Gertrude Mongella, the Secretary General of the Conference from Tanzania exclaimed, "I cannot describe the happiness I feel. I think we have achieved a very strong document for women. It is a launching pad for action for women's rights and for action for peace."[1]

She had good reason to rejoice. Rarely has there been a conference which was so painstakingly prepared. In the years leading up to it there had been five regional group meetings, four expert group meetings, and three preparatory meetings. The women of the world were so well alerted that in the end some 30,000 women attended the two parallel conferences—the official government and one for the Non-Governmental Community.

In spite of the lengthy preparation, the text for agreement that finally was presented at the governmental conference was disturbingly far from being a consensus document. Everything at Summit Conference turns on the context, the weight, and the meaning given to key words. At this conference the controversial words were all too numerous: words like gender, health, resources, employment, and even equal.

Disagreements at conferences become clear because the Secretariat gave delegates "bracketed" texts to consider. The brackets show where consensus has not yet been reached on wording. At Beijing someone calculated that when the conference began there were 438 brackets around 171 paragraphs! The heaviest bracketed sections were in the areas of health and the girl child.

After long negotiations late into the night, the brackets were finally removed because a consensus on compromise wording was eventually reached. Some governments, however, insisted on tabling reservations on the wording which they still could not accept.

But somehow after long negotiations, dragging on far into the night, brackets did get removed. Even so, as too often happens, a number of governments tabled "reservations" to the final official text.

In a huge and comprehensive Programme for Action it is hard to single out the greatest gains for the future. But among them would surely be ending discrimination against the girl child—right from the moment of conception; the equal right of women to loans and to inheritance; and, following on from what had already been highlighted in the Population Conference in Cairo, a fresh understanding that all specifically "women's rights," especially in the realm of health and of domestic violence, are essentially human rights, too.

In the final Declaration and Programme of Action not everyone got everything they wanted. Mary Ann Glendon, who led the Holy See Delegation, put it this way: "The voluminous Program of Action that emerged from the Beijing Conference on women is a field sown by many planters, a place where nutritious grains are competing with ornamental flowers and opportunistic weeds."[2]

She felt that while the special claims of families and mothers for protection, the central role of religion in the lives of many women, and parental rights and duties found a place in the text that was finally agreed, these pillars of progress for women could be elbowed aside by some of the expressly feminist concerns which are also in the document.[3]

Others felt that on issues of war and peace, especially armaments, sustainable development, and the environment, not enough progress was made. And hardly anyone felt that the commitment of governments to additional funding was going to be sufficient to do the wide range of work necessary to empower women that still lies ahead.

As usual, the eloquent American advocate Bella Abzug, co-Chair of the Women's Environment and Development Organization, now well known as

WEDO, put her finger on what really matters for the future. At a meeting back in New York she said:

"The focal point for immediate action is paragraph 297 of the platform of action: 'As soon as possible, preferably by the end of 1995, governments, in consultation with relevant institutions and Non-Governmental Organizations, should begin to develop implementation strategies for the platform and, preferably by the end of 1996, should have developed their strategies or plans of action.' As always, it's up to the women to make this happen. But it's also up to the U.N. and each member nation."

Notes

1. *Earth Times.* September 28, 1995.
2. Mary Ann Glendon. *Wall Street Journal.* September 12, 1995. P.A. 22.
3. Ibid.

4. A Namibian Advocate in Action

Women in Africa were always active in the struggle for liberation from colonialism. So it is no surprise that their political involvement has continued after independence. Indeed Africa was well represented in all the preparatory meetings for the Beijing Women's Conference. The Chairperson of the Conference in China, the Fourth Women's World Conference, Gertrude Mongella, was from Tanzania. She summed up the arduous process of preparing a U.N. document for this big conference like this:

"This process can be compared to a sponge which first has to absorb all possible inputs and then has to be squeezed into a prioritized and compressed text."[1]

There were also present at this preparatory committee a number of people from Africa who had never been to the U.N. before. Just how bewildering did they find this U.N. workshop?

One such person was Emma Kambangula from Namibia, one of the last countries to win its independence from colonialism, and one in which the U.N. was involved at every stage in its long and difficult birth.

Emma found she managed the first meeting at the U.N. with surprising ease. But this was because she had been well prepared. The U.N. had arranged for her to fly to West Africa for a briefing which included African women who had been at the earlier women's conferences at Nairobi, and even at the first women's conferences at Nairobi, and even at the first women's gathering in Mexico in 1975. She found out that these conferences had subjects on the agenda which never go out of date and never get completed. These subjects, she already knew firsthand from her own life as a woman in Namibia were and still are equality, development, and peace.[2]

She said, too, she had had a lot of help from her own government. The Department of Women's Affairs in Namibia which is part of the President's Office guided her and they also made her part of their official delegation going to China.

She did say that, though her English seemed excellent, she found the bureaucratic language in use in the U.N. "bewildering." But she was philosophic about it and said if others could get used to it, so could she.

She was surprised by the religious element that came into the debate about "the family." She saw, for the first time, Christians in confrontation with each other, and she found the Moslem attitude to women perplexing. But as a committed Lutheran, she was determined to be tolerant.

She was especially pleased to learn all about the emphasis on the empowerment of women in jobs, and particularly about the role of women's banks. She felt women in Namibia need that kind of help badly.

With more and more women building up a global network of mutual support, and keeping in touch through E-mail and the Internet, the women's movement has a potential international strength which would simply not have been possible a few years ago. And the women of Africa are determined not to be left behind.

Notes

1. Ashali Varma. Interview with Gertrude Mongella. *Earth Times.* March 31–April 14, 1995.
2. From an interview with Emma Kambangula. April 2, 1995.

5. A Moroccan Ambassador on Religious Intolerance

If the United Nations passes declarations to protect people against religious intolerance, does it do any good? Does the U.N. have any teeth on this issue?

One good example where the U.N. has tried to tackle religious bigotry is the creation of the 1981 Declaration on the Elimination of All Forms of Intolerance and of Discrimination based on Religion or Belief. This resolution has raised consciousness about religious intolerance, but it has also, on a more practical note, resulted in the creation of regular monitoring of abuses.

In 1996 Ambassador Halima Warzazi of Morocco came to the NGO Committee on Religious Toleration to talk about the U.N.'s work in human rights, and more. She graphically told how for more than thirty years she has always found the gap between rhetoric and reality in the pursuit of human rights hard to bear:

"When I first came to the United Nations in 1959, after just being graduated from the university, my eyes were full of readings and my heart was full of illusions.

"I have to confess, it was a shock for me because as months and years passed I had to remove the thick and sad veil hiding the countless violations of human rights affecting all countries and religions of the world without exception."[1]

Acting on behalf of Morocco, she was herself a major force in getting the Declaration on Religious Intolerance passed in 1981 at a time when the Cold War was still raging. She explained how it would never have passed if the words "Or Belief" had not been added to the title. The Communist bloc was maintaining that religion was the opium of the people and they wanted to protect tolerance for those who professed no belief. Moslems, too, were doubtful about its provisions and thought it only favored Jews, but she finally convinced them that its provisions could benefit Moslem minorities, too, in places like the Philippines.[2]

She said that when the demise of Communism came in 1989, there were great hopes for a global outbreak of toleration and peace, but instead it was not long before a new wave of ethnic hatred and religious bigotry broke out. Its effects were seen in countries as far apart as France and Afghanistan, and Ireland and Algeria. She added that ways to combat religious intolerance were never more needed than they were today.

She reminded everyone that all defenses of human rights can be traced right back to the Charter itself and to the Universal Declaration of Human Rights.

One kind of teeth to deal with intolerant behaviour, she explained, existed even before the Declaration on Religious Toleration was passed.

This was the 1501 Procedure which arose from a Sub-Commission of the Commission of Human Rights, based in Geneva. This enables groups, but not individuals, to report persecution to the Sub-Commission. Everything is dealt with confidentially, but if the Commission finds a complaint is justified, it can take it up with the offending country.

But other stronger teeth came into action a few years after the Declaration was passed. In 1986 the Human Rights Commission took things a stage further by appointing a special rapporteur to investigate cases of religious intolerance. This time individuals could write to the rapporteur with their complaints. In fact, special rapporteurs had already been appointed to investigate all sorts of subjects—racism, mercenaries, torture, and to check on complaints from particular countries—Iran, Cuba, and Zaire, for instance.

This special rapporteur for religious intolerance, Professor Amor of Tunisia, now comes every year to the Third Committee of the General Assembly to report his findings.

Then there is a third set of teeth that confront states guilty of intolerant behavior. The Committee of Experts of the Covenant on Civil and Political Rights, founded in 1976, meets several times a year to hear regular progress reports from governments on a wide range of human rights abuses, including the institution by the state of laws of religious intolerance.

These experts also, under a protocol, can hear complaints from individuals, who have not received satisfaction in their home countries and under Article 18 of the Covenant on Civil and Political Rights can and do hear cases that deal specifically with religious intolerance.

Lastly, there is a twenty-four hour hotline to the Center for Human Rights in Geneva. Cries for help cannot wait for U.N. processes to get under way.

Ambassador Warzazi stressed her conviction that governments will do a lot to avoid being condemned in a U.N. forum for religious intolerance, and the U.N. has to keep on pressing offenders to do better.

The U.N. can indeed keep gnawing away at proven abuses, but correction of most human rights abuses is still a matter of raising public consciousness rather than judicial correction. Recently, however, a campaign has begun to establish an international criminal court, so the desire for the U.N.to be able to convict and to punish the most serious abuses of human rights is beginning to receive general acceptance.

Ambassador Warzazi concluded by reminding the group that the Koran itself speaks up for tolerance:

"If God had wanted, he would have made you a single religious community. He thought to enlighten you by your differences. So, do good, help each other, and God, one day, will enlighten you on your differences" (Sourate, 11–256).[3]

Notes

1. Address by Ambassador Halima Warzazi of Morocco to the NGO Committee on Freedom of Religion or Belief. December 11, 1996.
2. Ibid.
3. Ibid.

6. The Covenant against All Forms of Discrimination against Women

Throughout the modern world, women and girls continue to suffer vast discrimination of all kinds:

- Of the world's 1.3 billion poor people, nearly 70 percent are women.
- Of the world's nearly one billion illiterate adults, two-thirds are women.
- Approximately 585,000 women die every year from causes relating to pregnancy and childbirth.[1]

The U.N. has determined to give priority to changing the situation of women for the better. One of its most useful pieces of human rights machinery is the Committee for the Elimination of Discrimination against Women, established in 1981. This independent committee of experts, which meets regularly in New York to evaluate and monitor the treatment of women, is supported by the 159 nations which have now signed the Convention on the Elimination of All Forms of Discrimination against Women (CEDAW), which came into existence in 1979.

That so many nations have ratified this convention is an achievement, surpassed only by the number who have ratified the Rights of the Child Convention. Unfortunately more than fifty nations have ratified the treaty with substantial reservations on the grounds of tradition, religion, or culture. For example, they have reservations when their own domestic laws on divorce or inheritance conflict with the U.N. Convention. This makes it much more difficult to make a comprehensive examination of a country's record when, every two years, its turn comes around to appear before the convention's twenty-three experts to give an account of progress made in living up to the Convention.

For the past four years Ms. Ivanka Corti, a lawyer from Italy, has been the Chairperson of the Committee of Experts. She has made the committee much better known and she has greatly strengthened its work by linking it up with other U.N. agencies like UNICEF and the United Nations Development Fund for Women (UNIFEM). For the first time members of the Committee took part in a field visit—to Egypt.

In the sixties, Ms. Conti was involved in the famous Italian Referendum campaign about divorce. She was also active in helping to create major changes in the family courts and in equal rights for women. She therefore felt ready to accept when the Italian government nominated her to join the U.N. committee of independent experts.

She summed up her four years in the Chair of CEDAW.

"This is a remarkable committee. After all, it is dealing with the human rights of half the people in the world! It can do still more with good U.N. coordination and I have been glad to chair a meeting of all the human rights treaty body committees which concern themselves with women. We discussed the vital issue of reproductive health."

She felt that the recent string of People's Conferences had helped the cause of women a great deal. She singled out the Vienna Conference on Human Rights:

"That was a special occasion. For the first time people came to realize that women's rights are human rights, and, as a result of that insight so much progress has been made. Also at Vienna, for the first time, the official government conference and the NGO forum were held in the same building, one floor above each other. Consequently there was a unique interchange of views and opinions between governmental and non-governmental bodies."

As she retires from the Chair, Ms. Conti feels that the continuous dialogue which the committee is developing with so many countries is now producing positive results. She believes that governments do pay attention to the committee's findings, and that no government likes to read unfavorable publicity from CEDAW in its annual reports to the General Assembly.

But she feels that there is still a long way to go. At home so many women still fear they will be beaten if they report violent abuse. At work, besides sexual harassment, there is still discrimination in jobs. She concluded with regret that nowadays women were unexpectedly confronting a whole new set of problems.

"On the one hand these days women are much more aware of their rights. There are laws to protect them and a growing public opinion is on their side. On the other hand, these are hard times for women, caused by economic structural adjustment. We are seeing the end of welfare. And there seems to be a new climate of pervasive violence."[2]

The committee of twenty-three independent experts, now chaired by Ms. Salma Khan of Bangladesh, will continue its regular cross-examinations of nations. Some countries, like Morocco and Slovenia, will be defending their record for the first time; others, like Canada, and Turkey, will be giving third and fourth progress reports.

In breakthrough, unprecedented in world history, nation states are suspending their national authority and allowing themselves to be judged by the standards of new and universal human rights legislation.

Update

In March 1998, Patricia Flor, Chairperson of the Forty-Second Session of the Commission on the Status of Women—a commission which is now 50 years old—gave some concrete examples of how the U.N. Convention (CEDAW) was helping women all over the world. She cited the example of countries in Southern Africa where a whole set of new laws and new ministries had recently been created to help women.

Patricia Flor, from Germany, explained that the Commission is the main U.N. body in the area of human rights and it had nurtured both the convention and the Programme of Action to follow up the Fourth World Conference for Women held in Beijing.

She concluded her remarks by saying to her interviewer: "If ever you come to the Commission when it is in session, you will see a sea of women and some men, and we need men to be involved in that. We can't only change half the equation."[3]

Notes

1. Women at a Glance. Development and Human Rights Section, Department of Public Information. December, 1996. P. 1.
2. From an interview with Ms. Ivanka Corti, Chair, Committee for the Elimination of Discrimination against Women. January 15, 1997.
3. World Chronicle. Status of Women. Programme No 702, recorded March 11th, 1998. Moderator: Michael Littlejohns.

7.   Uniting for UNICEF

Everybody loves and respects UNICEF and the work it does for children. That's obvious. But it is not so obvious that governments love children enough to make all of UNICEF's work possible. They have other pressing priorities, such as military expenditure. So when Jim Grant, Director of UNICEF at the time, decided to put on a World Summit for Children in 1990, it was by no means certain anyone would turn up. Bets were exchanged on just how many Heads of State would come. Jim Grant, always the optimist, bet 32. In fact, 71 turned up!

"Jim," said Mary Cahill from Ireland, who worked as Jim's Personal Assistant, "always said the children were the 'Trojan Horse' of the UN."[1]

He was proved triumphally right. The World Summit made some great breakthroughs. Heads of State who came for the first time even agreed to a time-bound Plan of Action with clear goals, such as the reduction of child mortality and increase in clean water—by fixed percentages and definite dates. And the Convention on the Rights of the Child has now been ratified by a record 180 nations and should soon achieve universal ratification, another record for a U.N. Convention.

Mary Cahill explained how Jim Grant always had a whole armory of things he knew must be done to get nations to pay attention to the needs of children. He always went right to the top—to get the political commitment. He went round the world to speak to influential people personally. He would, for example, go to Uganda or Indonesia and then build coalitions of goodwill. When civil war raged he would be on the spot and arrange "days of tranquility" so that children could be immunized. He made it happen in El Salvador in 1982 and, even more difficult, in the midst of the hostilities in the Sudan in 1988. The roads he got opened were still open in 1995.

But Jim, recalled Mary, always felt it was the "silent emergencies" which were the hardest for which to get public attention—tragedies like child mortality and the number of children that drop out of school—especially worrying in Latin America. He arranged for members of his Board—a large one with thirty-four members—to visit and see for themselves how the needs for help for the children were urgent.

When a country made extraordinary progress in its work for children, Jim would make sure leaders in neighboring countries and even other continents knew about it. Mexico worked out a great follow-up to the summit for children, with the Minister of Health involving local grassroots leaders and local mayors. The same kind of flying visits were arranged to see progress being made for children in Zimbabwe and then in Bangladesh. Jim Grant called it "constructive competition." It worked and it still works.

In 1994, within just one week of leaving UNICEF, Jim Grant died. In honor of his work Hillary Clinton got the U.S. Government to speed up the signing of the Convention on the Rights of the Child.

Does that mean that all is now smooth sailing for UNICEF? Certainly not! The new Director of UNICEF, Carol Bellamy, explained the plight of children at her very first board meeting.

"In a world in which more than 12 million children will die this year, largely of preventable causes related to poverty, we must constantly ask ourselves what *more* we can do, what more we can do *better*, what do we need to do differently in order to help end, once and for all, this unconscionable, obscene, waste of human potential."[2]

Notes

1. From an interview with Mary Cahill, Senior Communications Officer UNICEF. 1996.
2. Carol Bellamy, Executive Director of UNICEF, 1995 UNICEF. Executive Board. May 22, 1995.

8. First Secretary from the Sudan

Most diplomats wear Western dress most of the time at the U.N., but a notable exception to this custom has been Shahira Wahbi, First Secretary at the Mission of the Sudan. In the conference rooms where resolutions are being painstakingly crafted she moves around in her *tobe*, a white dress and shawl which Sudanese women wear at official occasions. "People think I'm a fundamentalist and they are a bit scared to approach me." She laughs and goes on, "Well, I'm not."

Besides her work with the Third Committee of the General Assembly, Shahira has to monitor what is going on at the Security Council, and she is also responsible for the candidature policy of the mission for many posts, such as who the Sudan will nominate to sit on the Economic and Social Council and whose names will be put forward to be new judges on the International Court of Justice.

During the fall she attends the meetings of the Third Committee where more than half the resolutions are about human rights. She comments on this work, which can be contentious.

"Since the Vienna Conference on Human Rights this whole subject has been gathering momentum. In Africa, ordinary people don't have, until now, had a very high consciousness on this matter. We are now discovering the subject is very flexible, very double-edged. It can be all about dealing with a serious humanitarian issue, or it can be used as a tool to bring political pressure on a nation.

"Too often the approach is confrontational. If you come at a person with a sword, his reaction will be to extend himself by getting out a sword. The Commission on Human Rights sends out special rapporteurs. It is like a foreigner coming into your home and then passing judgment on how you live. The rapporteur, being a human being, can be easily influenced either way. In any case it is rather embarrassing to enter into a foreign home trying to find out what is really going on!"

In fact, in 1996 the committee passed a resolution about the situation of Human Rights in the Sudan, of which Shahira Wahbi commented:

"I would like to see a more positive approach to human rights through cooperation and not condemnation. How would it be if we had resolutions on the human rights situations of all 188 member states of the U.N.?" Shahira remains on 'good terms' with the other members of the committee:

"I find that the Third Committee is one of the most distinguished, lively, and hardest-working committees of the General Assembly. There is a club atmosphere. People are nice to each other, regardless of political differences.

I have found the U.N. gives us all an education in different cultural perspectives. This leads to tolerance. I believe the U.N. enriches human culture."

Shahira Wahbi explained how the geographical position of the Sudan, Africa's largest county, meant that it was in her country's interest to belong to a wide range of different groups, as a part of "Africa, of the Arab world, and of the developing world, and of Islam." Therefore the Sudan has joined the Organization of African Unity, the Arab League, the Group of 77—the economic arm of the developing countries and the Non-Aligned Movement (NAM)—the political arm of the developing countries, and the Organization of the Islamic Conference. She stressed that in these groups the Sudan belonged to no particular party or alliance and judged issues on their merits.

She also spoke about her role in covering issues handled by the Security Council:

"This is the body charged with the responsibility of maintaining peace and security. We have to follow it closely. I linger around the waiting room and when the meeting ends, I see one of the permanent members, grab him and I squeeze him for information!"[1]

Shahira enthuses about the good order of things in the U.N. She admires the way the Secretariat staff prepare a massive amount of documents in time for the work of the next day. And she thinks the cleaners and technicians deserve more credit than they get to for tirelessly tidying up so many long corridors and large rooms in the Secretariat late in the evening when everyone else has gone home.

Shahira Wahbi is living proof that it is never wise to judge the policies and attitudes of diplomats by the clothes they choose to wear when appearing at public occasions. Shahira believes that wearing the national dress is mark of her own self-respect and that it will help others to respect her, too.

Note

1. Interview with Shahira Wahbi. Sudan Mission to the U.N. December 5, 1996.

9. A Panamanian Advocate for Indigenous People

There are more than three hundred million indigenous peoples on our planet and for most of them relating to the modern world in a painful experience. The pressure of Non-Governmental Organizations (NGOs) on governments to help indigenous peoples make full use of the U.N. system is now building up from every continent. People from Latin America are among the leaders of this movement.

One of these leaders is Esmeralda Brown from Panama. She is the Chair of the NGO Committee for the U.N. Decade for Indigenous Peoples and she works out of the Church Center which is very conveniently located alongside U.N. Headquarters.

Rigoberto Menchu, the Nobel Peace Prize winner from Guatemala, has summed up the urgency of the plight of indigenous people like this:

"Freedom for indigenous peoples wherever they are—that is my cause. It was not born of something good: it was born out of wretchedness and bitterness. It has been radicalized by the poverty of my people, the malnutrition that I as an Indian have seen and experienced, the exploitation I have felt in my own flesh and the oppression that prevents us from performing our sacred ceremonies, showing the respect for the way we are."[1]

For Esmeralda the issue of the suffering of indigenous people is part of the wider issue of justice for all the people who live in developing countries. Esmeralda's ancestors came to Panama from Jamaica and Martinique and now she lives most of the time in New York. She feels that everyone who lives in the South—and that includes all of Latin America—still has a battle ahead of them to get their share of the world's resources. She puts it like this:

"I want to see not Free Trade but Fair Trade. For us in the South, globalization can easily mean dumping of surplus goods on our domestic market and tariffs against our attempts to develop our export market. If this goes on unchecked we will never overcome our debt crisis and our poverty."[2]

Esmeralda is now concentrating on ways to help the world's three hundred million indigenous peoples. In Brazil, Guatemala, and Peru, for example, they need an enormous amount of help with education and health. In the past they have been treated as children and not permitted legal rights to own land. By creating a new partnership with them during the decade, the U.N. is seeing that their diversity is respected, and that they are listened to at last.

This NGO Committee for Indigenous Peoples is active in all sorts of ways. The U.N. itself is moving towards a Draft Declaration for Indigenous Peoples and her Committee is meeting with Ambassadors at the U.N. to press them to support the idea. In Panama they have already set up an office for indigenous affairs. Esmeralda described the growth of the network she has been building up to make sure what the U.N. is doing and planning to do is known at the grassroots.

"In Venezuela in Puerto Ayacucho I have a friend who is a teacher, Santiago Obispo. Every month I send him a package of the latest U.N. materials on the decade. He climbs into his canoe and makes an expedition up the remote rivers of Amazonia to explain to the indigenous peoples in the forests what the U.N. is trying to do. And he has links with indigenous groups in Brazil and Colombia."[3]

The committee is also in constant touch with Human Rights Watch and with the Center of Human Rights in Geneva. Esmeralda Brown and her committee also work through the Commission on Sustainable Development, which since the great Conference on Environment and Development in Rio in 1992 has carried the flag for Indigenous Peoples.

Her appointment as Resource Specialist in Economic and Environmental Justice for the Global Ministries of the United Methodist Church enables Esmeralda to build up networks over a wide range of issues of justice and peace. She explained the importance of the Church Center as a focal point for her campaign:

"It was visionary of the Women's Division of the Methodist Church to build this Center. It has helped the churches — Presbyterians, Quakers, Baptists. It has proved a base where people without freedom to speak out in their own country, and who have nowhere else to go when they arrive at the U.N., can find a space to write their petitions. It has been a great help to liberation movements. Only recently the leaders of the struggling people of East Timor spoke at the Center about their continuing persecution. And Indigenous People constantly come here to our Church Center and talk about the aims of the decade."[4]

Over her sixteen years at the U.N. she has seen NGOs make great advances:

"Since Rio, governments have stopped seeing us NGOs as a threat. We have been doing our most important business with them at Prepcoms and not so much at the official Summit Conferences which are much more celebratory in nature. We are getting more skillful at tactics and better at forming coalitions."

Esmeralda's views on the key influence of the United States on the U.N. are mixed:

"Since the end of the Cold War the U.S. has become more influential, not less. It has been very friendly to NGOs and helped them a lot at the recent summits. It pursues its interests in a very sophisticated way. Pressure is exerted quietly. Loans and visas can get denied if countries, like Cuba, for example, go against the U.S. Together with the other nuclear powers it supports undemocratic aspects of the U.N. such as the veto in the Security Council. But we keep lobbying for U.N. reform that will make the words of the Charter 'We the Peoples' more of a reality."

Stop Press

In August 1998 Dr. Arvol Looking Horse of the Lakota People, 19th Generation Keeper of the Sacred Buffalo Calf Pipe, led the Sacred Pipe Ceremony outside the U.N. He asked people to face in turn north, south, east, and west in prayerful remembrance of all the nations on Mother Earth.

Issues of land, natural resources, and health remain a top priority for the International Decade for the World's Indigenous People (1995–2004).[5]

Notes

1. *Endangered Peoples.* Davidson, Art. Sierra Club Books. 1994. P. ix.
2. From an interview with Esmeralda Brown at the Church Center. February, 1997.
3. Ibid.
4. Ibid.
5. International Day of the World's Indigenous People. Department of Public Information. DPI/ 1993–July 1998.

10. The Abuse of Human Rights in Mauritania

When Bakary Tandia and a friend from Mauritania—a country bordering the Sahara desert—came to U.N. Headquarters to tell the story of the abuse of human rights in their country, they did not know where to begin. From across the street the windowless General Assembly building looks like a fortress. The Secretariat Building, a skyscraper of thirty-eight stories, looks equally unassailable. Further, they heard that the U.N. would only admit visitors with a special pass. To the ordinary petitioner, entrance to any part of the U.N. seems impossible.

Fortunately these Mauritanians met up with Jerry Herman, one of the Quakers' most seasoned human rights campaigners. On one of his visits to Africa, he had visited Mauritania and heard firsthand how in Mauritania the dominating Arab minority was trying to weaken and destroy the African Fulani and Wolof culture of the majority. And even more disturbing, he had discovered that, in spite of government assurances, indentured labor and even slavery of Africans were still going on in this country.

Jerry advised his Mauritanian friends that, before their case could be publicized at the diplomatic level and in the committees of the General Assembly, they must first meet with NGOs who specialized in human rights. It would be these NGOs in coalition who could speak about Mauritania at meetings of the U.N. Human Rights Commission in Geneva and then their story would then be officially on the U.N. record. At this point, he felt sure, Ambassadors and the whole U.N. would suddenly begin to take account of the persecution of their people seriously.

Jerry picked two human rights organizations to help publicize the Mauretanians' plight. First he took the Mauritanians to see the Anglican Office at the U.N., where the Rev. Johncy Itty listened carefully to their story. The Anglicans have specialized in bringing human rights issues before the Human Rights Commission in Geneva and have been particularly strong in exposing abuses in East Timor.

Next, he took the men to meet with Techeste Ahderom, the main representative of the Bahá'i religious community at the U.N., who is the current Chairman of the NGO Human Rights Committee in New York, and who is from Eritrea. Techeste explained how abuses had first to be raised at a low level in the U.N. Human Rights system and then, as the facts became clearer, they would be taken up at higher levels until eventually they would be brought to the notice of the whole world at a plenary session of the General Assembly.

Techeste told the story of how abuses of human rights in the Sudan eventually were condemned by a resolution in the General Assembly. But first accounts of those abuses had to come before the Sub-Commission on Discrimination and the Protection of Minorities. At this point the Commission appointed a special rapporteur or investigator to go and make an assessment on behalf of the Committee. When his report appeared on the Sudan, the Sudanese government was outraged. Confidential messages then passed to and fro between the U.N. and the offending government. No effort was spared by the U.N. to make the case of abuse of human rights in the Sudan watertight.

Techeste explained that after further work by the Center of Human Rights in Geneva, the case of the Sudan was then raised at the Economic and Social Council and next at the General Assembly's Third Committee, which deals with human rights. By this time more than a year had gone by. But without this long process of gradual exposure, the issue could not hope to come before the plenary of the General Assembly. The U.N. does not lightly decide to investigate and then to criticize the internal affairs of one of its own member governments.

After hearing how things worked out with the Sudan, the Mauretanians realized that presenting their case would inevitably be a long and tortuous process. But there was at least a clear road to follow. Later, they were pleased to hear that Bishop Ottley, the Head of the Anglican Observer Office at the U.N., had taken the initiative of writing to an American Congressman, pointing out that future American aid to Mauretania should be tied to improving the human rights record of that country.

Recently Elinor Burkett, an investigator of women's rights in Mauretania, underlined why there is no time to lose in confronting the situation in Mauretania:

"The Government claims to have abolished human bondage, making Mauritania the last nation on the planet to have done so. But in the endless expanses of wind-swept nothingness between Senegal and Morocco, an estimated 90,000 slaves labor as they have done for more than 500 years—serving their masters by tending their herds, bleeding the acacia trees for gum arabic, picking their dates, and bearing the next generation of human property."[1]

Note

1. Burkett, Elinor, "God Created Me To Be A Slave." *The New York Times Magazine*. October 12, 1997. p. 57.

11.   Day of the African Child

One day in 1995 the entire United Nations was mobilized to take special notice that throughout Africa today so many thousands of needless deaths of young children are occurring. This year there was a special emphasis on victims of war. In the morning the World Conference on Religion and Peace held a multifaith service. In the afternoon UNICEF opened a new exhibition, and in the evening the Secretary-General addressed the diplomats in the General Assembly.

Edward Luttwak has described the civil war situation in Sierra Leone in these words:

> "The chaotic violence that now engulfs that country cannot be described as a civil war, inasmuch as the contending forces—notably including the government—represent nobody but themselves; nor can it be described as a guerilla war, for no side seriously pretends to be fighting for a cause; and it is not in anyone else's war being fought by local surrogates in the familiar Cold War manner, for no greater power from without seems to care a fig what happens in Sierra Leone."[1]

This passage vividly describes the bleak and dangerous world of the parts of Africa in which so many children they have to live out their childhood. The scale of disadvantage that the African child has suffered in the past decade is overpowering.

UNICEF has reported that 1.5 million children have been killed in armed conflict in the past decade. In addition, more than 4.5 million children have been permanently disabled—mainly by land mines. In Angola alone there are an average of 24 land mine casualties every day. It is reported that in Angola 10 million land mines have been laid—that means one landmine for every child.[2]

178

Even for those who escape the ravages of civil strife, in the poorest African countries—known as the LDCs or Least Developed Countries—the amount spend on each child in school is $2 per head, whereas in the rich countries it is $6,000 per head.[3]

The poorest countries are doing something to help themselves. For instance, in Guinea the village community has stopped waiting for the central government to help them and they are helping themselves.[3] In Bamako, Mali, African Ministers of Health resolved in 1987 to establish essential affordable health centers in their West African countries. And by last year, 295 of these new centers, the result of local initiative, covered 80 percent of the population in Guinea.

Fortunately almost all African countries have now signed the Convention on the Rights of the Child. This means their governments have to report regularly to the U.N. what they are doing to protect children in law, health, and education. They cannot get away with a whitewash report, because their own NGOs will be checking up on what they are doing.

In 1984, shortly before he died, Nils Thedin, a former head of Rada Barnen, the Swedish Save the Children, had an inspiration. Everyone should start to think of children as "a conflict-free zone in human relations." This idea of making children a Zone of Peace caught on with Jim Grant, Director of UNICEF, and it was tried out in the fierce civil war raging at that time in El Salvador in Central America.[4]

Now in 1995 fortunately there is peace in El Salvador, but the children of Africa need Zones of Peace—and plenty of them—especially in Liberia, Rwanda, and the Sudan. The Zone of Peace is more than a slogan, more than even an imaginative idea   to rescue children in acute danger of death in a civil war. It is a protest against every instance in which modern war strikes indiscriminately against children everywhere.

Notes

1. Edward Luttwak. Great-powerless days. Times Literary Supplement. June 16, 1995. P. 9.
2. War and Disability, UNICEF 1995.
3. The Bamako Initiative, UNICEF 1995.
4. Varindra Tarzie Vittachi. *Between The Guns*. Hodder and Stoughton. London, 1993.

12.   Adding Life to Years

The U.N. has not so far devoted much close attention to the vast and growing population of old people in the world. Only occasionally have there been gatherings to consider how the lives of old people can be made more productive for their countries and fulfilling for themselves.

Recently an imaginative meeting was arranged by Dr. Dianne Davis, President of the International Council of Caring Communities, bringing together young social workers, sociologists, and architects to talk about the needs of old people in the communities of the future.

Ambassador Julia Alvarez, from the Dominican Republic, addressed the gathering. Dressed in a bright red suit, she radiated a rare combination of energy and experience. She is one of only seven female Ambassadors at the U.N. and is famous in U.N. circles for her tenacity in trying to keep the Research Center for Women's Training in her own Caribbean country. She gave another fighting speech at this meeting and changed the outlook of all who heard her.

She said that by now everyone knew the world had an aging population. That was not new. Indeed by 2025, grandparents would outnumber babies by two to one. But, said the Ambassador, hardly anyone realizes that the great majority would be in developing countries—three-quarters of all the old people in the world. Indeed the very old—over 80—in the poorer parts of the world were expected to number 64 million! An "Agequake" was just around the corner!

And as their children would probably be earning their living in the new megacities, they would have no room to take care of them. What then? The new societies will hardly have the money to build and maintain homes for old people with the costs amounting to millions.

The solution, Ambassador Alvarez said, was that was that there had to be an entirely new attitude to old people in employment. They could be trained to join the high-tech world. Why should they be stuck with traditional crafts and traditional gardening? In her country she noted that hydrophonic gardening on rooftop gardens was proving enjoyable and profitable. There was a whole world of work on computers which could be done by old people without physical strain. Productive ageing was not just an option; it was going to be a necessity. Then characteristically the Ambassador went on:

"You may be wondering, 'What is she getting at? We are meeting to discuss strengthening and enriching communities and she wants to put eighty-year-olds in factories on the production line.' Be assured I have no such thing in mind. But there is no question that given known social and economic conditions, at least those in their 60s and 70s will have to be integrated more effectively into national economies as well as society in general."

This striking new vision of the place of old people in the twenty-first century would now travel for discussion to Preparatory Committees in Chile and Kenya and then go on to the Habitat II Conference in Ankara in 1996. The vision would be refined. The vision would be more closely related to the special situations of different countries. At the end of the day who could deny the force of Ambassador Alvarez's warning: "In demographics is our destiny"?

Once again the U.N. was raising people's consciousness on an issue just over the horizon and making sure it would radiate out on a global network to the whole world.

Update

At the start of October 1998, Ambassador Alvarez launched the U.N. Year of Older Person at U.N. Headquarters. She said it was crucial to get across the message that older people can be and usually are "useful and active citizens." It was vital to understand just how many older people there now were in developing countries and, as yet "social security for them was just a fantasy."

13. Children in Wars

The Security Council Chamber is dominated by the famous painting of "Peace" by the Norwegian artist Per Krogh. The painting is realistic about human nature. The top part of the picture shows loving parents with their new baby, surrounded by a peaceful world, furnished with all the arts and devices of modern civilization. But the bottom of the painting shows a dark dungeon filled with snakes with men and women desperately trying to pull themselves up with ropes into the civilized world of law and order. Peace has to be earned and history—and this picture—show how again and again mankind keeps on slipping back into barbarism. Now in June 1998, the shadow of this grim lower part of this mural loomed over this first meeting of the Council on the pressing issue of Children in Conflict.

Ambassador Monteiro of Portugal, President of the Council for June, initiated this debate on the horrors inflicted on children in war. The Security Council was determined to do more to stop the barbaric practice of involving children in civil conflict. The matter had already come up in the two most recent General Assemblies. Mrs. Graca Machel, former Minister of Education and First Lady of Mozambique, appointed as the U.N. expert on the subject had already given her horrifying report to previous sessions of the Assembly. Since then Olara Otunnu, former Ambassador of Uganda to the U.N., had been appointed as the Special Representative of the Secretary-General on

Children in Armed Conflict, and now he was invited to speak first at this unusual meeting of the Council.

Olara Otonnu, who had already personally visited three countries worst hit by civil wars—Sierra Leone, Sri Lanka, and the Sudan—gave an update on the fate of the children, "the most innocent and the most vulnerable" in recent civil conflicts. He said that two million children had been killed in the past decade; one million had been orphaned; twelve million had been made homeless. Half the total of the world's refugees were children.

The Special Representative said that the Security Council can lead the way in trying to ensure that the Convention on the Rights of the Child and the Geneva Convention on rules of war be implemented. But also at the local level anything should be done to prevent the collapse of the local value system. He instanced the concept of "lapi" in his own local Acholi value system in which, for example, there was a taboo against destroying crops. If this local culture failed then "everything was fair game in the struggle for power."

Olara Otonnu urged the Security Council to see that battle free zones were organized to protect children and schools and hospitals be kept out of the fighting.

Lastly he stated that after the end of fighting, peacebuilding arrangements put forward by the Council required special attention to the needs of children. Otherwise the cycle of conflict would never be broken. The Security Council should pay attention to this special need when creating a mandate for a new Peacekeeping Operation.

The fifteen members of the Security Council then affirmed the commitment of their countries to support the Special Representative in every way possible. Ambassador Weston of the United Kingdom, speaking on behalf of the European Union, said that negotiators for an International Criminal Court should be able to prosecute those who recruit children under age for war. Ambassador Dahlgren of Sweden and Ambassador Owada of Japan stressed the need to have a protocol to the Convention on the Rights of the Child to make the minimum age for the recruitment to the armed forces to be eighteen.[1]

If and when the Council applied sanctions, Ambassador Zmeevski of the Russian Federation stressed the importance of ensuring that children were spared their effects. Ambassador Amorim of Brazil spoke of the importance of this continuing disaster being given more attention by the General Assembly and the Economic and Social Council. Ambassador Andjaba of Namibia said a key role was being being played by the Committee on the Elimination of Discrimination against Women in bringing the sufferings of women and young girls in armed conflict to the attention of the world.

So what are the priorities in dealing with what Graca Machel has called "this desolate moral vacuum?" First the countries where civil wars have been raging have to re-establish national and local good governance. No amount of

U.N. intervention and supervision can ensure that this happens: nations must do it themselves. But the Security Council can and must exercise real authority when it creates a new Peacebuilding Mission. It will influence global public opinion when it debates the subject and exposes the latest atrocities against children by holding regular meetings with Olara Otonnu.

The Security Council, by itself, cannot destroy the dungeons of this world, but it can and must ensure that the ropes for climbing out of them are made stronger and more numerous than ever before.

Note

1. Security Council. News Coverage and Accreditation Service. SC/6536, June 29, 1998.

Part Seven

Economy

1. The Plans and Actions of the Economic and Social Council

What is more central to the U.N. than its work for a better standard of living for all? The Charter has affirmed the centrality of the U.N.'s development agenda by creating the Social and Economic Council. The General Assembly has confirmed this priority by passing a Resolution on the Right to Development and creating a whole series of development decades.

Now in the nineties, the Secretary General has stressed again and again that there can be no peace without development. He is, therefore, creating a whole new agenda for development to remind the world that poverty still dominates and diminishes the lives of millions. Something has to be done and done quickly to overcome its stranglehold on millions, and the U.N. is above all the institution which people trust to set the right policies in place to get it done.

The U.N. engine for this enormous task is the Economic and Social Council. In addition to its major task of setting the direction of economic and social policies, itself a huge task, the Council has a clutch of subsidiary bodies under its wing. It has commissions which report on population, social development, and narcotic drugs. It has regional commissions which initiate and coordinate U.N. work in Asia, Africa, and Latin America. It has standing committees which deal with Human Settlements and NGOs.

Yet in spite of this volume of useful work, almost everyone has something to say against this unloved engine of economic and social development. They say the council has no heart and no head. They say that with its fifty-four members it is not truly representative of the whole U.N. and that its work would be better handled by the U.N.'s one universal body, the General Assembly. They say the council tries to do too much and that it duplicates work already being done better by other U.N. agencies.

The Director of Policy Coordination for Economic and Social Affairs has been Miles Stoby, from Guyana. He was only too ready to agree that the Council is not perfect, and needs reforms, but he was also ready to defend what it does against unfair and ill-informed criticism. He stressed that development cannot be simplified. It is a complex business, and the priorities for making it happen are changing all the time. He believes that ECOSOC is the right body to get the job done.

Miles Stoby summed up the current situation in ECOSOC like this:

"Our key priorities used to be finance, the transfer of technology, debt. Now they are no less broad-ranging, but different. They are sustainable development, social development, the human rights agenda, crime and narcotics. And there is a new enthusiasm for the role of free enterprise and free trade enterprise in making development happen with efficiency.[1]

"The strength of trans-national corporations is that they can be a key engine for transfering technology. Their danger is that they can get too powerful and, from bases in just one or two wealthy regions, begin to control the whole world. The U.N. has the job of encouraging these businesses to be socially responsible in their investment policies. The U.N. also has to monitor trends in their actions so that governments can, when necessary, take action on the strength of trends—either encouraging or worrying—which U.N. monitoring reveals to them."

Stoby has a high regard for the work that Non-Governmental Organizations (NGOs) are doing in cooperation with ECOSOC. He asserted:

"In the old days the NGOs were patronized. Nowadays the U.N. needs NGOs as much as NGOs need the U.N. At Rio, NGOs made a tremendous intellectual and policy impact. They can offer position papers; they can caucus; they can lobby at ECOSOC and in all committees of the General Assembly, though the final decisions, of course, must still be made by Member States."

He feels there should be an increase in the staff that work with NGOs in the Secretariat, but he regrets that as long as the present financial crisis continues, it is unlikely to happen.

In order to perform its work properly ECOSOC has to be reformed, or as Stoby prefers, "modernized." Stoby outlined the modernizing process.

"ECOSOC needs to cut down on the number of its subsidiary bodies. The Security Council does not have subsidiary bodies: Why should ECOSOC? The Council needs to be more selective in subjects it takes up and meetings should continue throughout the year. The Secretariat is willing to adapt, to change, to experiment. But it is governments which have to give the lead in sharpening their own arrangements for inter-government relations."

No discussion of the international engine for economic development can be complete without consideration of the role of the World Bank and the International Monetary Fund and their relationship to the U.N. Here Stoby is optimistic. He believes that nowadays there is much more contact between the two organizations and, as a result, the bank is paying much more attention to human rights issues and to the need to tailor its economic policies so that they do not to come down too hard on the poorest members of society, especially in developing countries.

Miles Stoby concluded with a plea not to expect the Secretary-General to push through a great new program of integration of councils and agencies at the U.N.

"The specialized Agencies, like FAO and UNESCO, have been set up as independent bodies with their own boards. At best the Secretary-General is primus inter pares with the other heads of Agencies. Right from the start that is the way the governments wanted the system to function. This way each of the major governments gets an autonomous U.N. Agency in their own capital. It is useless to blame the Secretary-General for deficiencies in parts of the system over which he has no control.

"Meanwhile ECOSOC remains the spearhead of economic policies and economic action in the U.N. The United Nations Development Programme (UNDP) is ECOSOC's key action arm at work in more than 130 countries. ECOSOC was given its powers by the charter of the U.N. and, until something difficult is decreed by the General Assembly, ECOSOC is the best engine we have to make progress with multilateral aid for the poor."

Note

1. From an interview with Miles Stoby, Director, Division of Policy Coordination and Economic and Social Council Affairs. March 6, 1996.

2. Development—an Overview of the U.N. Perspective

Leaders from developing countries always insist that the battle for peace will never be won unless and until the battle against poverty is won first. That is why the United Nations for nearly fifty years has put such a great effort into creative thinking, staff, technical support, and financial resources for its development programs. The 1996 Agenda for Development, approved by the General Assembly, is the latest evidence of the U.N.'s tenacity on this matter. The spearhead of all this has been and still is the United Nations Development Programme (UNDP).

Richard Jolly, who was a Professor and Director of the Institute for Development Studies at Sussex University in England, is now the Advisor to the Administrator of UNDP. For thirteen years he was Deputy Director of UNICEF in charge of programs. He has already earned a high reputation as the mastermind of the now-famous Human Development Report.

Richard started his career doing community development work in Kenya. He was a pacifist and that added to his commitment towards building global peace and human security. During this time at UNICEF he continued to work relentlessly to ensure that aspirations and hopes for children and the world's poor were carried through into practical action.

189

Richard Jolly reacts vigorously to those who argue that all aid, especially multilateral aid, is largely a waste of money.

"Multilateral aid from the U.N. has played a crucial role from the earliest days—and has often been more successful than many realize. Look at the successful elimination of smallpox by the World Health Organization. Child mortality has declined dramatically. Access to education, especially primary education, has increased enormously. In the 1980s 1.3 billion people gained access to fresh water. Loans to the poorest countries at low rates of interest are helping them to build the essential infrastructure for development."[1]

Richard went on to explain how the U.N. has built up the means for States to monitor national housekeeping:

"From its earliest days the U.N. has played a key role in creating the statistical base for checking on the progress of nations. Of course these statistics monitor the growth of the national income and production (GNP). But they also provide details about life expectancy, and child mortality, and other indicators of social progress—or lack of it."

In answer to the question whether private enterprise could take the place of aid, Richard was just as forthright.

"Of course I am pleased to see the growing importance of private investment in developing countries—more than $250 billion at the latest count—but the trouble is that 80 percent of it goes to only 12 countries. There is no substitute for overseas aid from the richer countries to the poorest ones, especially the nearly 50 least developed countries. So it is unfortunate that in the nineties official development contributions, with the notable exception of the Nordic countries, have been declining.

"UNDP has played a crucial role in helping people to clarify development priorities. Even the World Bank has been influenced to adjust its own priorities and to give more attention to human development and the problems of poverty.

"In UNDP's human development reports we focus on what matters most, development as it affects people—the priorities for enabling people to live long, healthy, and creative lives. This leads us into many specifics—for instance the urgency of education and training for women and girls and a wide range and support for training and support for people in governance, especially in Africa. Our overall aim can be summed up in the expression, often used by our present Administrator Gus Speth 'Sustainable Human Development.' "

Richard pointed out that multilateral aid from the U.N.—as opposed to bilateral aid, from a developed country to a developing one—is appreciated because it has less of the national flag about it. Multilateral aid from the U.N. usually comes in the form of grants, not loans. Those administering U.N. aid are from many different nationalities and can often better appreciate what it means to be on the receiving end of assistance. Overall, multilateral aid, unlike loans with their inevitable conditionalities, makes it possible to build up real partnerships between the giver and the receiver.

Richard explained how UNDP provides support and exercises leadership in the field.

"UNDP has always been known for giving technical assistance. Nowadays assistance is mediated through UNDP's residential representatives in more than 100 countries. Africa is a region of special attention. UNDP has helped many countries to put together their own National Human Development Plans. More than 85 countries, including for example, Namibia, Egypt and Malawi, now have these plans which include UNDP insights in how to improve health and education, and mitigate the worst effects of inequality and poverty. National perspectives on development are being decisively changed and improved. These new ideas also influence other major U.N. agencies like the U.N. Population Fund (UNFPA) and the Food and Agricultural Organization (FAO), the International Labor Organization (ILO) and the United Nations Education, Scientific, and Cultural Organization (UNESCO)."

Richard Jolly concluded his comments on an optimistic note:

"I forecast a bit swing-back towards recognizing the pivotal importance of the U.N. The recent criticisms have been largely because the U.N. has been treated as a football by American politics. But the last two Secretary-Generals have steered the U.N. increasingly towards real-life issues. Reform is under way. The U.N. is not on the sidelines, and the current extensive coverage in the media world wide is a good sign that it is coming back into favor."

Update

In September 1998 James Gustave Speth, the Administrator of UNDP, underlined this bedrock role of UNDP at the heart of the U.N. system when he said, "If the U.N. allows its development presence to weaken, then the U.N. will be much weaker. The development presence of the U.N. around the world is the platform that builds the credibility of the U.N., the access of the U.N., the presence of the U.N., the respect for the U.N. And I would add the U.N.'s humanitarian work in those places where it occurs."[2]

And in October 1998, James Speth again stress that pulling people out of poverty cannot simply be left to the marketplace. Commenting on the 1998 global financial crisis, he said: "Gone are the notions that progress can be left to the market, that government is hardly necessary. If the state is needed to save the market from itself, how much more is it needed to save people?"[3]

1. Interview with Dr. Richard Jolly, Special Advisor to the Administrator of UNDP. September 23, 1997.
2. Interview of James Gustave Speth by Pranay Gupte, Editor of the *Earth Times*. P. 21 Vol. xi, No. 17. September 16–30, 1998.
3. James Gustave Speth. Address to the National Press Club. Washington, D.C. October 14, 1998.

3.   The Poorest of the Poor

Rarely do those who work at U.N. Headquarters get a chance to hear firsthand stories of how economic help can actually reach the grass-roots in Africa. Recently, however, there was a workshop at the U.N. on Informal Sector Development in Africa. This subject of Microcredit is fashionable nowadays when, as someone put it, "the whole world is being privatized." At this workshop the accent was on helping African women to create business.

Imagine a system of help which is so basic that the total amount of help it offers is precisely $100 and that's all! This grant is called a "Challenge Grant." It only comes to those who ask for it in installments—two of $50 each. These grants are only made available when the recipient has proved, after some training, that she has a business plan and can show she has a grasp of what making a business grow is all about. No regular bank would dream of dealing in such small amounts to such apparently unproven business people.

This very basic mix of money and training is the heart of the imaginative "Trickle Up Program" founded in 1976 by Mildred Leet, an American from New York. Every year she helps between seven thousand and eight thousand people in Asia, Africa, and the Americas. She claims by now to have helped 14,000 businesses in Africa and that 66 percent of them have been run by women.

There are so many tales about individuals who borrowed wisely from her Trickle Up Program. For example, this is a story of wealth beginning to grow from the humblest beginnings in Cameroon:

Helen, age 20, and her partner Martin decided to start a business in Dschang raising rabbits. But their first grant produced nothing. The mother rabbit killed all her offspring!

Not discouraged, they switched to chickens, produced eggs, and used the chicken droppings to grow tomatoes and other vegetables. Then they bought materials to make and sell crocheted antimacassars.

The business prospered and now they are selling cosmetics and provisions and have a stall in the market.[1]

Or consider the Sistrum Project in Nigeria. Ms. Seyi Olude first attended a Solar Box Cookers Workshop in Nairobi in 1992 and then went back to Nigeria to teach solar cooking technology. More than 20 groups now utilize Trickle Up grants to make and sell solar-heated box cookers.[2]

It is always difficult for small businesspeople to take those first hard steps. Especially for women who may be illiterate, who may not have their husband's approval, and who have, at all times, to keep a growing family and a household together.

Governments are often doubtful about these new grass-roots businesses. There is a suspicion that very small entrepreneurs evade the law and do not pay taxes. They are also often involved in smuggling. But these businesses continue to grow and a number are already on the brink of joining the formal sector.

The U.N. does more than take an interest in and encourage those who try to help the poorest. It has taken up the task of exposing the worst examples of poverty itself. Appropriately in 1996, in the Third Committee, a resolution was prepared for the Plenary of the General Assembly on Human Rights and Extreme Poverty. There is now a special rapporteur on human rights and income distribution who is encouraged to keep bringing the intolerable situation of the poorest before the Human Rights Commission for forwarding on to the General Assembly.[3] The U.N. is firm that it sees extreme poverty not as an appeal for charity but as a cry against a basic human right—the right to development for all.

And it is the women all over the world who most need to be able to claim this right to development. Khadija Haq from Pakistan has summed up the enormous scale of deprivation which women experience:

"Women, though one-half of the world's population, still do two-thirds of its work, earn one-tenth of its income, and own one-hundredth of its property. Worldwide, one out of every three women work for pay, earning 73 cents to a man's dollar and often in insecure, futureless, health-eroding jobs that no man would take on."[4]

Not long ago, Manfred Max-Neef remarked, "Economists speak of wealth trickling down from rich to poor. But the trickle down I know is garbage." There is now a new hope that trickle-up—of all kinds—can and will produce a real and valued end-product—wealth.

Update

Attention to the importance of micro-credit for the poor is growing all the time. In 1997 a Microcredit Summit was held in Washington. The United

Nations Development Programme (UNDP) has made available three times as much funding for micro-credit grants as ever before, and a website has been made available on the subject of poverty and sustainable livelihoods.[5]

In 1998, President Fujimori of Peru and Ms. Albertine Hepie, the Minister for the Promotion of Women in Ivory Coast, came to the U.N. to tell the story of how thousands of women in their countries can now get small loans without the usual security which commercial banks demand.[6]

The U.N., through the United Nations Development Programme (UNDP) highlights success stories in the fight against poverty in both developed and developing countries. One of their 1988 "Race Against Poverty Awards" went to a Frenchwoman and former metal-worker, Nicole Rouvet.

In 1990 Nicole created a program to help the very poor. Participants—typically women who were either homeless, alcoholics, drug addicts, or ex-convicts—received on-the-job training in ironing and alterations and worked in small shops run by her organization. In 1998 there were seven such shops—employing about 150 people—operating in her program, including a print shop and a handyman's service.[7]

Notes

1. Leet, Mildred Robbins, President, Trickle Up Program. "Types of Support Measures for Women's Participation in Informal Sector Development." June 1995, P. 3.
2. Ibid. P. 5.
3. A/C. 3/51/L.54 November 22, 1996.
4. Kadija Haq. Gender Priorities for the Twenty-first Century. The U.N. and the Bretton Woods Institutions. St. Martin's Press. 1995 P. 157.
5. UNDP 1996/1997 Annual Report. P. 7.
6. A Dialogue on Microcredit. The Friends of Microcredit. At the United Nations. June 26, 1998.
7. UNDP Press Release October 15, 1998.

4. The Regional United Nations

The U.N. has never been exclusively a New York organization. From the earliest days, vital activities, for instance human rights, have been centered on the offices in Geneva. A considerable amount of work in the area of economic and social affairs has been for a long time now concentrated in Vienna.

Nowadays with economic development and the battle against poverty in high gear, there are regional economic commissions in Addis Ababa, Bangkok, Beirut, Geneva, and Santiago. The U.N. Charter, in fact, has a whole chapter

(Chapter 8) on U.N. regional organizations, but it is only now, after the end of the Cold War, that it is being vigorously implemented.

Sulafa al-Bassam, an experienced U.N. Civil Servant from Saudi Arabia, is Chief of the office that services these regional expressions of the U.N. from her base at Headquarters in New York. She explained their importance as key building blocks in the U.N. system.

"There cannot be global development without the input of regional development. For instance at all the recent world conferences, such as the Social Summit and the Conferences on Population and Women, these commissions held regional preparatory meetings to set up regional priorities ahead of the global gatherings. And now the commissions are assisting in the implementation of the recommendations of those conferences at the regional level."[1]

Ms. Al-Bassam brought in a colleague, Kazi A. Rahman from Bangladesh, with extensive experience working with the Economic and Social Commission for Asia and the Pacific (ESCAP) in Bangkok, to give an Asian viewpoint. He explained how ESCAP, the Asian Commission, had been serving as the conduit for strengthening regional cooperation in a number of fields of common interest.

Mr. Rahman spoke about cooperation in the helping the disabled.

"The Commission has been energetically building on the U.N. Decade for the Disabled. Its work in this field is especially relevant for the victims of civil wars in Afganistan and Cambodia, who are in desperate need of artificial limbs, which they can afford.

"In cooperation with the commission, Non-Governmental Organizations are playing a leading part in a network of cooperative endeavors in getting this work done throughout Asia; the ones in China and Japan being especially dynamic. They have found that protheses equipments could be made much less expensively from indigenous materials. In traditional society with deep religious values, it is very important to be able to kneel for prayers and to attend to other customs, so they have modified the traditional western designs."[2]

Charles Kassangana, Ms. Al-Bassam's colleague from the Democratic Republic of Congo who had previously worked in the African Economic Commission (ECA), said the commission was concentrating on meeting the continent's basic economic needs:

"We urgently need to build up a network of roads across Africa. Without a proper transportation network in place we cannot hope to build up regional trade or even trade with Europe and other regions."[3]

Ms. Al-Bassam stressed the importance of the work of the economic commissions as essential to strengthen the foundations of peace, especially in regions that have to cope with major civil strife.

Regionalism is also growing to embrace other vital matters of concern to the U.N. For instance, in November 1996 Belgium co-sponsored a Resolution in the Third Committee of the General Assembly which calls for a regional approach to the protection of human rights.[4]

There was no complacency in Ms. Al-Bassam's summing-up:

"We are now seeing progress in many regions, but we have not yet solved the problem of how to deal with the sufferings of the absolute poor."

Her conclusion brings to mind the insight of the distinguished U.N. thinker and reformer Erskine Childers of Ireland who died recently, and who said, "Development is about people: all else is technique."

Notes

1. Interview with Sulafa al-Bassam.
2. Interview with Kazi A. Rahman.
3. Interview with Charles Kassangara.
4. A/C.3/51/L.62, November 22, 1966.

5. The Human Development Index

To introduce a note of drama even once into the subject of "Development" requires the skill of a conjurer. To introduce it over and over again throughout the nineties demands nothing less than wizardry. Yet that is exactly what two U.N. international civil servants, Mahbub ul Haq from Pakistan and Ingrid Kaul from Germany have been doing by producing the now-famous Human Development Report.

Every year their report has attempted to show that the wealth of a country can be and ought to be judged by measuring the development of human capital as well material capital. When this is done the apparently "richest" countries like the United States, Germany, and Japan do not come out on top in the league of "the wealthiest." Even President Bush of the United States called to find out how the U.S. had failed to come out top!

The Human Development Report has invented a new way of looking at the wealth of nations. To the usual measurement of goods and services (GNP) the report adds in an index of life expectancy and adult literacy, making it a threefold measurement of national prosperity which takes into account human as well as physical capital. In the words of the report the index is a measure of "productivity, equity, sustainability, and empowerment."[1]

What a furor was produced when the report first appeared! Every country sooner or later had to look and see how they made out. In 1990 the United

States only came in seventh. Japan came in first with Canada second. Now five years later, and with a more refined statistical system in place, Canada came out on top with the U.S. having risen to third place. Meanwhile the Netherlands, which was eighth in 1990, climbed to fourth in 1995.

Results for developing countries have been especially important. Some have done surprisingly well because they have a reasonable life expectancy and high rates of literacy. Near the top of the league throughout the nineties have been Barbados, Uruguay, and Singapore.[2] The idea that national wealth has to be measured in an altogether more inclusive way has caught on with governments. As the report is produced under the auspices of the United Nations Development Programme (UNDP) that is exactly what was supposed to happen. Guinea found itself at the bottom of the second successive year and a public debate began on how to get the national budget geared up to improve standards of health. The Philippines have set up a Human Development Network, and Bangladesh and Ghana, for example, have completed national human development reports.

The 1995 Report broke new ground and set about raising consciousness by making the main feature of its report the situation of women. Again nations rushed in to see how they were rated. Top on this rating come the Nordic countries—Sweden, Finland, Norway, and Denmark. When gender is the priority, countries like Argentina, Chile, and some Arab states come well below their overall rating because they do not give women equal job opportunities and equal pay for equal work. In 1995 Poland's Gender Development Index (GDI) was fifty places above Syria though both countries had about the same income. On the other hand, the fastest improvement in literacy rates has been in the United Arab Emirates.[3]

This report appeared just in time to provide well-deserved ammunition for the women gathering for the Beijing Conference to be armored with the facts, so that they could press for a fairer deal for women and for the girl child. Women still have a long way to go to come even close to men. In politics women fill only 6 percent of cabinet positions. In the agricultural sector women receive only three-quarters of the wages of men. It is still an unequal world.[4]

This is an age of mapping the human condition with unprecedented range and accuracy. One kind of map is the human genome, which should lead to the control of previously incurable hereditary diseases. Another kind of map is the statistical summary being made by the U.N. of the economic and social condition of humanity of every nation on the planet. Every nation will now be on stage, and a new global consciousness about levels of equality of opportunity is beginning to dramatize the political agenda everywhere.

Update

The 1997 Human Development Report makes a searching examination of all aspects of poverty and what to do to overcome it. The report is not all gloomy. It charts the great advances that have been made by 3–4 billion people since the 1950s. But it notes that still as many as 1.4 billion people have to exist on less than $1 per day.

In the 1997 Human Development Index the top seven countries were Canada, France, Norway, United States, Iceland, Netherlands, and Japan.[5]

Stop Press

Sadly, Mahboub ul Haq died in July 1998. He will always be remembered as a development economist who insisted that the priority for his discipline was not statistical results, but improving the lives of individuals. He wrote what is surely a definitive summary of the heart of Human Development: "The purpose of development is to enlarge people's choices and these choices extend to a decent education, good health, political freedom, cultural identity, personal security, community participation, environmental security, and many other areas of human well-being."[6]

Notes

1. Human Development Report 1995, P. 12.
2. Ibid, P. 1353.
3. Ibid, P. 81.
4. Ibid, P. 4.
5. *Human Development Report,* 1997, p. 152.
6. New York *Times,* July 17, 1998.

6. UNCTAD—A U.N. Engine for Developing Countries

What has the U.N. got to say as the tide of privatization and globalization sweeps around the world? Some would reply "not much." They would be wrong! The U.N. is at the center of these massive movements through its key multilateral organization, The United Nations Conference on Trade and Development, better known as UNCTAD.

UNCTAD, with a staff of 300 in Geneva, is financed from the main U.N. budget and is a core member of the U.N. family, controlled by the General Assembly. UNCTAD has its finger on the pulse of no less than $250 billion of direct foreign investment pouring into developing countries. But can UNCTAD do anything to stop this investment going to a tiny handful of already growingly rich countries, while the majority are left behind in poverty?

"It certainly can," says Georg Kell, an economist who joined the U.N. civil service from Germany and is head of the UNCTAD liaison office at U.N. Headquarters. Georg is passionately concerned that the poorer countries get a share of this huge and growing investment pie. He explained how UNCTAD tries to even things up:

"We see ourselves working in partnership with the developing countries. Globalization is, for us, a reality and we want to do all we can to integrate the less well off countries in the new economy. We want to get people to see why it can pay to invest in, say, Mali and Gabon, as well as the countries of the Pacific Rim. We produce country reports which give all the facts and possibilities about investing in the countries which for the moment are unfashionable.

"And more than that. We can steer the developing countries themselves in the directions that look most helpful for their exports, and we can also inform interested investors about special tax advantages offered them and also about insurance they can take out against political upheavals."

Many missions at the General Assembly—especially among the Group of 77 who now number more than 130 developing states—cannot afford to employ staff who know about trade and investment. So they arrange to meet Georg Kell. For instance, the Ambassador from Mexico asked him for a list of the 20 largest importers and exporters of textiles. China wanted the latest facts on the transfer of science and technology. Other delegates want to know how the new World Trade Center will arbitrate disputes and how it can be of help to them.

UNCTAD takes action, too. Small businesses are helped with know-how—in customs procedures, in finding new markets for exports, in listing the names of importers. When UNCTAD has an idea it cannot itself implement, it passes it on, as when it gives an impetus to the International Monetary Fund (IMF) to offer special financing to the developing countries. Oiling the wheels of trade with new kinds of funding is essential.[1]

UNCTAD also has a role in advocacy. Persuading developed countries to open up markets for goods, like textiles, where the poorer countries have a comparative advantage. Suggesting that the developed countries concentrate on developing and marketing the latest technology in telecommunications and software. In Eastern Europe especially advice and know-how is needed about how to turn businesses from being state enterprises into private enterprises.

And Africa, even South Africa, needs constantly to be brought to the attention of the investors.[2]

But not everything goes smoothly. UNCTAD can decide that the time is ripe for action on some fronts and find that the nations do not consider it is in their self-interest to agree. The idea of a Code of Conduct for multinationals is getting nowhere at present. The challenge of achieving international governance of large companies remains unmet. Commodity agreements for primary products—like coffee and copper—are not working well. Without controls for price fluctuations, the rich countries believe they can buy at lower prices and protect their idea of the free market.

These days UNCTAD, which has appointed a new Secretary-General, Mr. Rubens Ricupero from Brazil, is probably getting more, not less influential. And recently UNCTAD has led the way for other U.N. bodies by undertaking drastic reform in its organization.

The root cause of poverty, social tension, and mass migration is economic underdevelopment and as long as the gap between rich and poor trading nations remains so large, UNCTAD will be at the center of things.

In the latest U.N. budget, over 100 pages are devoted to UNCTAD. This is proof, if proof is needed, of how seriously the U.N. regards the arming of governments and businesses in the South with the basic research and the facts to enable them to strengthen their trading ability. If UNCTAD does not do it for them, then who will?

Notes

1. From two interview with Georg Kell. September 12, 1995 and 1997.
2. Ibid.

7. Economic Rehabilitation of Women under Exploitation

Asia had a strong presence at the Preparatory Commission (Prepcom) for the Women's Summit in Beijing. The Asian women seemed so well-prepared when they came to New York for this meeting. How do they do it?

Sister Soledad Perpinan of the Order of Sisters of the Good Shepherd from the Philippines is a typical example of an NGO leader from Asia. And a courageous one, too. She is in a wheelchair most of the time and can only walk with great difficulty because of arthritis, yet she goes up and down to her convent in New York on the bus without any escort.

Her work is to fight against sexual exploitation of women. Sexual tourism is a developed industry which feeds on unemployment and the poorest and the most vulnerable in the Philippines. It is fueled by nationals of Germany, Australia, Japan, and the United States. No one nation is more implicated more than others. New business companies offer sex holidays to their employees. The military, too, with their overseas bases, have been involved. So the personhood of women gets destroyed.

Sister Sole, as she is known, has two weapons. One is unfavorable publicity. Another is the jobs she creates for girls who turn away from prostitution often forced on them against their will. She has created a highly successful operation manufacturing colored candles.

She and her fellow NGOs have been working with the Economic and Social Commission for Asia and the Pacific (ESCAP), which is the largest of the U.N.'s regional offices, based in Bangkok with a budget of ninety million dollars. But very little of that money so far has been allocated for women's work. In fact there are only three women in the ESCAP office, which deals with women's affairs, and the way the work is accomplished does not yet match up with the affirmative action policies of the U.N. worldwide.

Nevertheless, the regional meeting in Bangkok made up of women from both governments and NGOs put together a document for the commission on the Status of Women which was every bit as strong and articulate as the paper put together in New York.

All around the world and especially in Asia where their numbers are so great, women have still to do so much to achieve equality and justice. In economic terms alone, it has been estimated that women do 60 percent of the world's work and receive one-tenth of its income. The UNDP 1995 Human Development Report estimated that the value of women's invisible contribution to the global economic output at $11 trillion out of the world $23 trillion total. Yet women, it has been estimated, own just 1 percent of the world's land that is in the commercial realm.[1]

Only the extraordinary persistence of people like Sister Sole, and the new strength and hope they give to vulnerable women by working regionally and internationally, can hope to overcome this great weight of injustice and discrimination against them.

Update

In October 1998, the International Labor Organization (ILO) produced a report on the theme of "More and Better Jobs for Women." One of their staff, Ms. Lin Lim came to U.N. Headquarters to discuss this report, which has had a controversial reception in those countries on which it has been concentrating its research—Thailand, Malaysia, the Philippines, and Indonesia. Many had complained that the report put too much emphasis on economic rather than moral factors in describing the plight of poor women. Ms. Lin explained that so much prostitution is in fact the result of desperate poverty and is brought on because there are so few jobs for women in Southeast Asia. She added:

"Countries are not gender sensitive or employment sensitive."[2]

She stressed that child prostitutes were victims, not practitioners and that all legislation to protect children must take boys into account as well as girls. She believed that gathering them together in groups was the way to help former prostitutes to get back some self-esteem. She said:

"Over and over again girls had told the makers of the report, 'We all do it with a heavy heart.'"

Ms. Lin concluded by warning that the 1988 financial crisis was causing a large drop in family incomes due to layoffs and the decline in value of local currencies. She felt this situation would make it harder than ever to create more jobs and training for women so that they would not need to turn to prostitution as a last resort.

Notes

1. UNDP Annual Report 1996-1997, Octdober 1997, P. 10.
2. Ms. Lin Lim at an ILO Seminar held at the U.N., October 16, 1998.

8.   Pledging Day for Aid for Development

A young girl with hands high above her head, launching a squawking bird of freedom into the air, dominates the Trusteeship Council Chamber. It is entitled *Mankind and Hope*, and the sculptor was Hendrik Starke. Encouraged by this symbol made by an artist from Denmark, one of the most generous of donors of overseas aid, hopes are high each year that a spirit of generosity will prevail in this room when the nations gather for their annual Pledging Day. Pledges are required every year for voluntary funds to support the regular budgets of three of the main U.N. agencies, the United Nations Development Fund (UNDP), the United Nations Population Fund (UNFPA), and the

United Nations Environment Programme (UNEP), as well as a number of smaller funds.

The Secretary-General sets the tone. "These are difficult times," he begins. "Yet," he adds, "1.2 billion people are living on $1 per day." He goes on to explain that, even though it is fashionable to expect business to take over the work which governments no longer feel is their responsibility, business cannot do it all.[1]

And there is so much to be done on issues which cannot, with the best will in the world, be turned over to private enterprise. How can business make a profit from funding for the Trust Fund for Aging or for Victims of Torture? Or for the Fund for Drug Control? So all this work, and there are more than 20 special funds outside the core U.N. budget, has to be funded voluntarily. The regular U.N. budget has never included these essential needs.

The proceedings in 1995 were typical. Ambassador Eitel from Germany said, "Development is the essential foundation for peace; it should get the highest priority from the United Nations." The Germans announced they were offering substantial rent-free accommodation in Bonn to the U.N. Volunteers Program.[2]

Ambassador Salander of Sweden said that the present system was simply not reliable. What was required was to put all these activities on "a more predictable, continuous, and assured basis." He noted, ominously, that negotiations about more reliable financing had so far, made very little progress.[3]

Fortunately no government wishes to be only on the receiving end of aid, so even the smallest and poorest countries, Bhutan, Antigua and Barbuda, and Lesotho—gave at least something to these voluntary funds. Many give funds in kind to provide accommodation for a U.N. Specialized Agency so it can operate economically inside their country. As with individuals, so it is with nations; giving and receiving need to be in balance.

What would happen if all the aid programs were closed down and it was left to governments to give in their own time and in their own way? Then all aid would become "bilateral" or would be given by a bloc like the nations of Latin America or Western Europe acting together, and of course a great deal of aid is given in that way already.

But developing countries would far prefer to receive "multilateral" aid for the U.N. Bilateral aid, or "bloc" aid inevitably has colonial overtones about it, and also special strings attached to it about buying equipment and hiring experts from the donor country. So Pledging Day at the U.N. is always very important to the countries of the South.

Update

In November 1998, the Member States gathered again to make their pledges which remain a vital reinforcement to the regular U.N. budget. Member States continue to dislike the system because the time for pledging does not fit in with the budgeting dates for many governments. Both the governments and the U.N. Secretariat would like to do away with the present system altogether. UNDP and UNFPA have already decided on a multi-year funding strategy which would make annual pledging irrelevant in the future.

As the regular U.N. budget gets slimmer, extra aid has to come from other voluntary sources. Meanwhile the level of Official Development Assistance (ODA) continues to decline—from $59 billion in 1995 to $48 billion in 1997.[4]

Notes

1. Speech by Secretary-General Boutros-Boutros Ghali. November 2, 1995.
2. Speech by Ambassador Professor Tono Eitel of Germany November 2, 1995.
3. Speech by Ambassador Henrick Salander of Sweden November 2, 1995.
4. Thalif Deen. Western Donors seek to end U.N. Pledging Conference. *Terraviva*. Vol. 8 No. 214. November 9, 1998.

9.   Reflections on Japanese Overseas Aid

During the Fiftieth Anniversary year Mr. Hiroshi Hirabayashi came to the U.N. to talk about the thinking behind Japan's overseas aid policy. This was a special occasion because Japan gives more overseas aid than any other country, including the U.S., and Mr. Hirabayashi is the Director General of the Economic Cooperation Bureau of the Ministry of Foreign Affairs. It is important that he thought it worthwhile to come personally to the U.N. to explain the latest trends in Japanese aid policies.

The Japanese program focuses on needs mainly in Asia and focuses on economic infrastructure (transportation, irrigation), education, and training, and meeting basic human needs (sewerage, public health). By the end of 1993, Japan had already sent 23,045 Japanese experts overseas and hosted 69,959 trainees in Japan![1]

Mr. Hirabayashi spoke about some of his special concerns.

"There is a major problem in getting the donors, the citizens of Japan, to realize that their sense of humanitarianism and global interdependence is recognized and appreciated. Thanks that are given in the U.N. hardly ever reach their ears. And when tourists travel hardly any of them realize, for example, that when they use the airport in Bali or the trams in Jakarta that these are products of Japanese aid, and nor do those who go to Thailand realize the same is true about Bangkok's airport and highways."[2]

204

Sometimes, however, recognition is achieved. For instance, President Ramos of the Philippines has visited projects completed with Japanese Aid fourteen times. Sometimes, too, there is international appreciation, as, for example, American public recognition of the "Parks in Peril" environmental program, targeting Latin America."[3]

But Mr. Hirabayashi stressed that more has to be done by the developing countries themselves if "aid fatigue" is not to influence the Japanese taxpayer. Corruption is still too prevalent. There has to be more land reform, better tax systems, and less military expenditure. If the latter is out of control then aid flows will be cut and the situation will be politely described as one of "negative linkage."[4]

Mr. Hirabayashi is optimistic that a target of reducing world poverty by half by the year 2020 is possible. He has hopes that aid fatigue can be more than offset by finding new donors—Korea, for instance. Private enterprise can still do much more and, with the increasing help of NGOs' aid, can be more efficiently used.

Japanese aid policies continue to be generous. But there is nothing complacent about Japanese interest in the battle against poverty. Indeed Mr. Hirabayashi says, "Japan is still a step away from being a truly leading donor." He also added frankly, "It is difficult to find people willing to work overseas in the new areas of Overseas Development such as population control, and the fight against HIV/AIDS and issues surrounding women in development."[5]

Aid for Development is and will remain too big a subject for any one nation to work out how to do it best. It remains to be seen if the U.N. can be the leading catalyst to make it all happen in unison.

Notes

1. Hiroshi Hirabayashi. Japan's ODA. Assuming Leadership in a New Era. Gaiko Forum. 1995. P. 72.
2. Ibid, P. 163.
3. Ibid, P. 164.
4. Ibid, P. 45.
5. Ibid, P. 17.

10.   The Special Initiative on Africa

It is unusual to see the President of the World Bank, Mr. James Wolfensohn, at the U.N. Headquarters in New York. But here he was in 1996 alongside a galaxy of top U.N. executives launching a new U.N. Initiative to help the people of Africa. As part of his orientation to his job he had recently been in Africa and he spoke glowingly how he can seen how the poorest people somehow found a way to survive.[1]

Commenting on this new collective initiative to help Africa, the President of the Bank added modestly, "We don't mind being coordinated and occasionally giving a lead." That was modest considering the World Bank is taking the responsibility to put together eighty-five percent of the funds for this new effort—twenty-five billion dollars over the next ten years.[2]

This occasion was also special in a number of other ways. Modern technology turned this event held in New York into a truly global occasion. The Secretary-General presided, but he spoke by satellite from the U.N. office in Geneva. The Prime Minister of Ethiopia, Mr. Zenawi, joined in and he was speaking from Ethiopia. So did Mr. Amaoko, Chief Executive of the Economic Commission for Africa, also speaking by satellite from Addis Ababa. All the dignitaries seemed united in their commitment to do something about the pressing and still unmet needs, in health and education, of the peoples of Sub-Sahara, Africa.

Another way that this was a special event was that all the different U.N. Specialized Agencies were at this event to give a public witness to their willingness to take this initiative together. The Secretary-General through the United Nations Administrative Committee on Coordination, better known as the ACC, had invited them to take part and they agreed. Therefore this new effort had even been given a new name, "A System-Wide Initiative" on Africa. The U.N. has always been a system, but it has not always behaved like one.

Everyone had sensed that nothing less than a System-Wide Initiative could possibly be big enough or comprehensive enough to do the job in Africa which lies ahead. A similar "Africa Recovery" plan had been launched in 1986 and achieved very little. Thirty-three out of fifty of the world's Least Developed Countries (LDCs) are in Africa. Mrs. Nafiz Sadik, Executive Head of the United Nations Population Fund (UNFPA) reminded the audience that the average life expectancy in Africa is still only fifty-four years. The average family is six, and half the labor force remains unemployed.

No amount of private enterprise investment can take care of the basic infrastructure needs of Africa. This new program of aid has named some twenty-two priorities and carefully listed which particular Agencies will pool resources for which particular project. For Household Water Security, for example, there will be a joint effort by UNICEF, WHO, UNDP, World Bank, and UNESCO. Top people do not much like being coordinated but rationally they can usually be persuaded that it is necessary. If coordination cannot be made to work better, then there is the alternative of a merger, which is even less to the liking of senior managers!

"The children of Africa will be a top priority," said Carol Bellamy, Executive Head of UNICEF. She said the funds would be used to improve health systems, give basic education, especially to girls, to provide a supply of safe water, and to protect children caught up in conflict situations. She added—and her words were a fitting summary the urgency of this new initiative—"Africa's children will hold us responsible for the outcome."

Update

The President of the World Bank continues to earn a reputation of not only caring about poverty, but making extensive visits to see for himself places where there is extreme poverty and where the World Bank is doing something about it. In September 1997, he said in his address entitled "The Challenge of Inclusion" to the Annual Meeting of the World Bank in Hong Kong:

"As I walked around a large water and sanitation project in Brazil, more and more women came up to me displaying pieces of paper showing charges and receipts for five or seven cruzeiros a month. I watched and listened to this until the Vice Governor said, 'What they are showing you, Jim, is that this is the first time in their lives that their name and address have appeared on an official notice. This is the first time their existence has been officially recognized. This is the first time they have been included in society. With that receipt they can get credit to purchase goods, with that receipt they have recognition and hope.' As I walked back down the hill from that favela, I realized that this is what the challenge of development is all about—inclusion."[3]

Notes

1. The World Bank comprises five organizations: the International Bank for Reconstruction and Development (IRBD), the International Development Association (IDA), the International Finance Corporation (IFC), the Multilateral Investment Guarantee Agency (MIGA), and the International Center for the Settlement of Investment Disputes (ICSID). World Bank Press Backrounder, 1998.
2. Enhancing Support for a Continent's Development. Publication of the Department of Public Information. March 15, 1996, P. 6.
3. James D. Wolfensohn, President of the World Bank, Annual Meetings Address, "The Challenge of Inclusion." September 23, 1997, P. 2.

11. The International Monetary Fund Comes to U.N. Headquarters

"It only lasts a certain while, like cherry tree time and the start of love." That is not exactly the kind of language that you expect to hear from one of the world's top bankers! But it happened when Mr. Camdessus, President of the International Monetary Fund (the IMF) came to New York for the first time in 1995 to address one of the U.N.'s most important bodies, The Economic and Social Council (ECOSOC). But what is it that only lasts "a certain while?"[1]

Mr. Camdessus was no doubt deploying his French sense of playful irony, as his subject was in fact—the global economic cycle! This cycle, he was saying, was now at its zenith.

One can usefully think of the two men who run the two main parts of the international monetary system established at the Bretton Woods Conference in 1944 and located in Washington, as the stern doctor and the kind doctor. The two separate parts of the system are the World Bank which was originally created to assist nations devastated by the ravages of the Second World War and which now lends to less developed countries to promote their economic growth and prosperity. The other part is the International Monetary Fund (IMF) which exists to promote international monetary cooperation and the balanced growth of international trade.

Mr. Camdessus runs the IMF and it is this body that prescribes, when its necessary, the nasty medicine "for the good of the patient." His medicine for nations in economic trouble is slimming budgets, cutting subsidies, not overspending on imports, and sometimes even encouraging devaluation of currency for the sake of exports. There are times, rather frequent times, when only this kind of medicine will restore a nation to economic health and strength.

Mr. Wolfensohn, who runs the World Bank, formally known as the International Bank of Reconstruction and Development is more like the kind doctor. His medicine tastes delicious, though like all medicine it does not come free. His bank gives loans for projects in every field—from agriculture to health and nutrition, from transportation to water supply and sanitation. Nations, of course, have to pay interest on their loans, but loans to the poorest countries can be offered by the bank under a special scheme which makes them virtually interest-free.

Mr. Camdessus was confident about the overall state of the world economy. Though he, in fact, began his remarks by saying how serious the recent financial crisis in Mexico had been. It showed everyone just how much the financial system is now irrevocably a global financial system. But the IMF had rapidly come up with an $18 billion credit to Mexico and the crisis which could have forced nations in Latin America to introduce exchange controls and so stave off hopes of new foreign investment, was nipped in the bud just in time.

Mr. Camdessus called the relationship of the IMF with U.N. Headquarters "lively." That was cheering, as there had been a feeling at U.N. Headquarters that it was little more than a formality. But Mr. Camdessus seemed to be taking the U.N.'s Economic and Social Council seriously.

He gave his views on making progress in the poorest countries. He emphasized that unproductive expenditure had to be cut out from their budgets, and he specifically targeted military expenditure. He also said he had met a minister in Mali who had told him that the most important person in the struggle to achieve development was not the Minister for Development, but the Minister for Justice. Without a proper legal framework to fight corruption, there could be no future for the poor nations.

So when the dialogue between the Bretton Woods Organizations, the World Bank, and the International Monetary Fund, the U.N. is gathering momentum. Dialogue and coordination of policies in the economic field is more than just a matter of courtesy and common sense. It is mandated in the U.N. Charter. In Article 63 of the Charter it is mandated that the Economic and Social Council *shall* do this work of coordination. Belatedly, it is now really beginning to happen.

Addressing the Economic and Social Council again in 1997, Mr. Camdessus stressed that, while emphasis on privatization should continue, the role of the state in good governance remains crucial.

"Many countries have reduced the negative aspects of state intervention in their economies, but they have yet to develop their public institutions into a positive force for growth and development. That process begins by increasing the transparency of government operations in order to limit opportunities for corruption and enhance public accountability.

"At the same time, countries must rededicate the state to fulfilling the tasks that are so essential to the confidence of private savers and investors and the smooth functioning of their economies—such as providing reliable public services; establishing a simple and transparent regulatory framework that is enforced fairly; guaranteeing the professionalism and independence of the judicial system; and enforcing property rights."[2]

Nations as well as individuals can never stop practicing the art of good housekeeping. But nations like individuals can and do let borrowing get out of control. It is the IMF's job to take the patient's hand and firmly to arrange matters in order to prevent a catastrophic economic collapse. The rest of the world relies on the IMF to use its long experience to judge when the time has come to prevent a nasty cold from turning into pneumonia.

Stop Press

In 1998, Mr. Camdessus's remarks about the good times not lasting forever are seen to have been prophetic! The sudden Asian crisis is now stretching the IMF's lending resources to the limit. But Mr. Camdessus is still insisting that the same medicine has to be taken by nations that have overstretched themselves, especially by unwise borrowing and overspending, if they want to find their way back again to economic health.

Notes

1. Mr. Camdessus. Managing Director of the International Monetary Fund. Address to the Economic and Social Council. November 6, 1995.
2. Mr. Camdessus. Address to the Economic and Social Council. July 2, 1997.

12. Helping the Palestinians

The United Nations Development Programme (UNDP), with a network of over 130 country offices and a budget of nearly one billion dollars made up from voluntary contributions by member countries, is the main engine of economic development for the United Nations. But this funding is no charitable handout, as the receiving countries often pay more than half of a project's costs in kind and in services rendered to donors.

UNDP, because it makes a special point of helping the most disadvantaged, has always given a high priority to its work for the Palestinians. This work has become even more urgent as the Peace Accord between Arabs and Israelis takes root. UNDP through its program of assistance to the Palestinian People (PAPP) currently is involved in some 80 projects in the West Bank and Gaza.

The man in charge in the New York office is Francis Dubois. He is French, from Alsace, and he has firsthand experience of working in Africa in the Ivory Coast Training Program for the Public Service. He has also lived in East Jerusalem for three years, where he was the Deputy Residential Representative for UNDP.

Francis Dubois stressed that the program had several unique features. First, and most important, all the UNDP programs are being led by the Palestinian people themselves and all new ventures are only put into action after full consultation and involvement of the local people at the planning stage.

This comprehensive ongoing program of assistance has four main features. With the help of aid from Japan, assistance is given to the Palestinian Authority to run a training program at the Palestinian Training Institute. The Authority has had to start absolutely from scratch. These new civil servants had no transport of any kind and UNDP had to provide 120 vehicles to the 17 Palestinian Ministries.[1]

Help for the economy was already underway. With Italian funding, a $9 million citrus processing plant has been established in Gaza. Now more than 600 requests to UNDP have been received for small business loans. Small factories to make curtains, foam mattresses, and potato chips are already opening up in the villages.

Sustainable Human Development is another priority and this is why the integration of Rural Development is crucial. The PAPP staff, for example, spent 10 days in the village of Kufr-Rai discussing what was to be done to revitalize the village. Eventually it was agreed that the priorities for this community were bringing water to the houses, a school, especially for girls, and road-making.

None of these developments can succeed without a proper infrastructure. That means, in effect, an efficient water supply and proper modern sewage systems to be put in place throughout the territory. These are not spectacular improvements, but they are absolutely essential and unfortunately very expensive. They are all the more necessary because more than half a million Palestinians are still crowded into refugee camps in Gaza and the West Bank.

But this is not the full story of the work of UNDP in these territories. The work that is being done with women in the community is also crucial. Not that the woman need motivating. They do not. Way back in the 1930s Palestinian women were already uniting in a Women's Federation to help themselves.

Mrs. Lina Hamadeh Bannerjee, also a member of the Staff of UNDP, has written a report on the special needs of Palestinian Women entitled "At the Crossroads." Their greatest problem, she concluded, has been isolation from the Women's Movement worldwide. But she was pleased that the position was improving under the transitional government. She also explained that they have been receiving valuable help from the Norwegian Government. She concluded:

"When I was in India I heard a proverb from Bhutan: 'Power without wisdom is dangerous. Wisdom without power is useless.' The Palestinian women, I believe, bring wisdom to the present situation and in their new networking they feel empowered by a new sense of unity."[2]

All these improvements add up to a multifaceted development program spearheaded by UNDP which benefits both men and women in the exceptionally trying circumstances of Palestine today.

Update

Highlighting the continuing stress facing the Palestinians, the Secretary-General in his 1998 Report to the 53rd General Assembly noted that relief and social services still had to be provided to 3.5 million Palestinian refugees in

Jordan, Lebanon, the Syrian Arab Republic, and the West Bank and Gaza Strip. Further, every year since 1993 the funds for this work had been steadily declining.[3]

The oldest and largest U.N. Agency in Palestine, the United Nations Relief and Works Agency for Palestinian Refugees (UNRWA), was founded in 1950 and has its Headquarters in Vienna. In its work for health, education, and social services, UNWRA employs some 22,000 persons and operates or supports 900 facilities.[4]

Notes

1. From an interview with Francis Dubois. UNDP. March 14, 1996.
2. From an interview with Lina Hamedeh Bannerjee. UNDP. March 25, 1996.
3. Secretary General's Report to the Fifty-Third Session of the General Assembly Supplement No. 1.(A/53/1)
4. Report of the Commissioner General of the United Nations Relief and Works Agency for Palestinian Refugees in the Near East. July 1, 1997 - June 30, 1998. To the Fifty-Third General Assembly. Supplement No. 13 (A/53/13).

13.   Sub-Saharan Africa in Crisis

The U.N. regards the situation in Sub-Saharan Africa as critical. There are three reasons why the world does not realize how bad the situation is. Peace has at last come to some of the major countries—Namibia, South Africa, and Mozambique. Democracy and free enterprise seem to be enjoying a new wave of popularity. Zambia managed a free election and a peaceful transfer of power to a new leader. South Africa has thrown off the shackles of apartheid in a spectacular manner. So it is concluded that things can't be all that bad. But they are!

For the last fifteen years the total wealth of the countries in Sub-Saharan Africa, and that includes Angola and Mozambique as well as South Africa, has been in decline. At present rates of very modest recovery it will take forty years to climb back to the level of 1975! Real wages have fallen 50 percent, virtually wiping out the middle class. Compare these figures with what has been happening in Singapore, in Korea, in Taiwan!

This situation, as Africans themselves will be the first to admit, is the result of the greed and bad management of those who seized power, such as President Mobutu who held on to it for so long. But factors outside the African's control have also been the cause of this decline. The value of agricultural produce, for example, went down in this period, not up. The economist Frances Stewart put it like this.

"A major problem for many low-income countries was the almost unprecedented fall in commodity prices which occurred over this period. Between 1980 and 1991, a weighted index of 33 commodities (excluding energy) fell by 45 percent. The deterioration in terms of trade for some countries was such that countries whose export volumes expanded at a respectable pace actually suffered a loss of export earnings. This was the case for cocoa production in Ghana, for example."[1]

Southern Africa is in a deep hole from which it cannot possibly extricate itself without help. Sub-Saharan Africa owes the world's banks $210 billion.[2]

There have been, in recent years, new terms offered to reduce and even cancel some of this debt. But the effect, so far, is marginal. It is estimated that only $7 billion of that debt has been canceled. Meanwhile Africa continues to pay $30 billion per year on its debt to the rest of the world which is estimated at $313 billion, excluding Libya and South Africa. Much more debt will have to be forgiven.

So what can be done? Africa fortunately has tremendous untapped natural resources. As the last century has been geology- and petroleum-based, the 21st century will be biodiversity based — and Africa has unmatched biological, animal, and genetic diversity. Adequate scientific training will be essential to take advantage of this potential natural wealth hidden in the forests of this vast continent.

The United States and Norway have committed new funds to do something about this enormous deficiency. The Report of the recent North–South Round Table summed up how this crisis affects women:

"The reality of the women's situation is feudal systems of landholding in which men are supreme; education systems based on a pyramid in which only a tiny fraction of girls can go forward to secondary schooling; rural credit going to men even though women are the main food producers; and inheritance rights on other legal arrangements slanted against women."[3]

Another key factor will be the formulation of National Plans of Action. African governments must choose their own priorities and restructure their civil services, and pay them properly, so that far less is spent in hiring in short-term consultants from outside.

The U.N. is passionate about the fight against poverty. James Gustave Speth, the able and thoughtful Administrator of UNDP, comprehensively summed up how he and his team feel about their struggle to abolish it.

"Human poverty is a condition as abhorrent as slavery and as repugnant as violence. Poverty is an evil in itself, as well as a source of conflict and political and social instability."[4]

This is a time to recall again the words of President Kennedy: "For the few to survive, it will be necessary for the many to prosper."

Notes

1. Revitalizing Africa for the 21st Century: an Agenda for Renewal. North–South Roundtable. Society for International Development. October, 1995. P. 8.
2. Ibid, P. 13.
2. Stewart, Frances. *Biases in Global Markets: Can the Forces of Inequity and Marginalization be Modified?* The U.N. and the Bretton Woods Institutions. St. Martin's Press. P. 168.
4. Speth, James Gustave. Administrator. UNDP. Message for the International Day for the Eradication of Poverty. October, 1997.

14.   A New Life for Refugees

There are at present more than 21 million refugees of special concern to the United Nations High Commissioner for Refugess (UNHCR). UNHCR is under the vigorous and tireless leadership of Mrs. Ogata, who joined the United Nations from Japan. In her latest annual statement to her Executive Committee, Mrs. Ogata said:

"I am becoming more than ever aware that repatriation is the main solution, but it is indeed a complex and difficult undertaking."[1]

In 1995 UNHCR released stories of resettlement from Central America, underlining the crucial role of local initiative. Stories from Africa could equally well make the same point.

Consider the story of Viviano Gonzalez who, along with with nearly 2,000 families, came home from exile in Mexico to rebuild a cooperative farm in the northern Ixcan region of Guatemala.

His return to a country torn by civil war but now at peace could not have happened but for the International Conference on Central American Refugees (CIREFCA) — essentially a regional initiative.[2]

Or, consider the case of Epifanio Lezcano and 14 members of his immediate family, who obtained permanent residency and a four-acre pineapple farm in the rolling hills of northern Costa Rica. CIREFCA made it all possible, too.[3]

Both these families found a new life due to an essentially regional initiative. Resettling refugees requires much more than just finding land for a family and leaving them alone to get on with it. The land has to be developed in the right way and that is why these new settlements have usually been a cooperative effort by UNHCR and the United Nations Development Programme (UNDP).

These new settlements have needed help with much more than just efficient farming practices. The new farmers were able, for the first time, to discuss the human rights issue between the government and NGOs without the fear of military intervention hanging over everything. Their wives felt more secure when left alone in the house. Their children could get safely to and from school. Doctors become available again. And the local police found it necessary to behave with more restraint now that they might suddenly come across U.N. personnel at work round the next bend of the road.

Does this mean that the U.N. can develop regional operations everywhere in the world? Certainly it is an encouraging sign that regional initiatives are beginning to take root. The Organization for Security and Cooperation in Europe (OSCE) has led this new development, and both the Organization of African Unity (OAU) and the Association of South East Asian Nations (ASEAN) are accepting that a whole range of issues, not least peacekeeping, have to be dealt with regionally.

Still, the regions will always need the guidance and support from U.N. Headquarters if they are to succeed. Crises, especially refugee crises, will often be too big for any region to cope with by itself. The U.N. is always going to need to operate both at a regional and a global level at one and the same time.

Update

Mrs. Ogata again spoke to the Economic and Social Council in 1988 and spoke of a world in which there are still more than 20 million refugees. She spoke of the great insecurity of so many in civil conflicts who return home to "insecure situations." She spoke about the difficulty of bridging the gap between relief assistance and development and cited Mali and Niger as two countries where reintegration is a crucial issue. She again stressed the importance of regions tackling their own refugee problems and she had been glad to co-chair a meeting with the Secretary General of the Organization of African Unity (OAU) and ministerial colleagues in Kampala on the refugee crisis in the Great Lakes area in May.[4]

Notes

1. Addendum to the Report of the United Nations High Commissioner for Refugees. (A/52/12/Add) 1997. P. 21.
2. Ibid. P. 12.
3. Refugees. Regional Solutions. United Nations High Commission for Refugees (UNHCR). 1-1995. P. 15.
4. Statement by Mrs. Sadako Ogata, Secretary-General of UNHCR at the 1988 Substantive Section of ECOSOC. July 28, 1988.

15. The Plight of the Least Developed Countries

The Preamble to the U.N. Charter has a striking phrase in its list of aims, "to promote better standards of life in larger freedom." "Larger freedom" stands for so much more than mere alleviation of acute poverty. It is not just giving people the ability to purchase more goods. It means giving people a sufficient standard of living so that they can begin to make choices, and not just live merely to survive. Making choices is what being "human" is all about.

Overcoming poverty then has always been a basic aim of the U.N. Sometimes the emphasis is on the social justice of relieving poverty. So in 1978 the General Assembly passed a Resolution on the Right to Development for all. Sometimes the emphasis is on self-interest, as illustrated by President Kennedy's remark to those who live in rich countries: "In order for the few to survive, it will be necessary for the many to prosper." And sometimes the emphasis, and this is especially the case in the '90s, is on our global interdependence. But always it's about every person having enough so as to be able to choose a future for themselves and their family.

Gradually, over the decades since World War II, the U.N. has been discovering, selecting, and improving both the tools for the fight against poverty and the places where they can most effectively be employed. At the Paris Conference of 1990, it was recognized that there are forty-two Least Developed Countries (LDCs). All have rapid population growth, and low levels of health, nutrition, and education. Thirty-three of the LDC's are in Africa. Their total population is estimated at 495 million.

The poorest countries suffer in so many ways. But, as the Foreign Minister of Uganda, Dr. Rugunda frankly explained, their plight is so much more than the fate of individuals who are compelled to endure grinding poverty:

"The deterioration of the socioeconomic situation of the LDC's is characterized by poor and weak physical institutional infrastructures, underdeveloped resources, widespread epidemics and disease, lack of food security and hunger, unemployment and under-employment, and widespread poverty and deprivation."[1]

Unfortunately in spite of "a solemn commitment" to the Program of Action at Paris in 1990, there have been few victories over poverty since then. Indeed the number of countries on the LDC list has grown to 48 even though Botswana has recently been taken off the list. Granted the '90s has not so far been a decade of prosperity for the developed countries, but that is more of an excuse than a reason for not doing more.

On behalf of the Group of 77—the Developing Countries—and China, Dr. Macaranas of the Philippines said:

"In the '90s in real terms the Gross National Product (GDP) of the Developing Countries actually fell by 1 percent.[2] And even worse the total debt stock of LDC's is estimated at $127 billion at the end of 1993, equivalent to about 76 percent of their combined GDP."[3]

So what is the response of the rich countries? At this stage aid is crucial to build up the countries' infrastructure. Private enterprise will not move into countries where roads, railways, storage facilities, and trained personnel barely exist and private enterprise will not pay for these basics to be put in place. At Paris in 1990, countries committed themselves to try to give 0.15 percent of their aid budget to LDC's. France and Portugal have reached that target and Denmark, the Netherlands, Norway, and Sweden have reached 0.20 percent, but the great majority have not made the target yet.[4]

The U.N. will keep on reminding the rich countries that there needs to be more debt relief and freer trade. There is still too much protection for textiles, vegetable oils, tobacco, and sugar. More bilateral arrangements could give help where help is most needed, to women, to street children, and for agricultural training and research.

As long as there is pervasive poverty, there cannot be fulfillment for individuals or stability and democracy for nations. Poverty and peace can find no harmony together.

Update

Access to the huge markets in developing countries is crucial in the fight against poverty. But we do not yet live in a world of completely free trade. Perhaps we never will. Nations, not least rich nations, jealously protect jobs on their home turf. Nevertheless, the new World Trade Organization is negotiating endlessly to get the barriers of protection lowered, and the trend is mostly in the right direction. But for the poorest countries there are still some dismaying barriers in place. Thus tariff barriers on footwear, leather, and leather goods are never less than 10 percent and can go to more than 50 percent. Sugar, tobacco, and fruit continue to face difficult hurdles to surmount. And these barriers are erected not just by the rich countries, but by the middle-range ones as well.[5]

Notes

1. Dr. Ruhakana Rugunda. Address at Mid-Term Review of Program of Action for Least Developed Countries. October 3, 1995.
2. Dr. Federico Macaranas. Statement on behalf of G-77 and China. September 26, 1995.
3. Paris Declaration. UNCTAD 1992. P. 26.
4. Ibid.

5. Secretary General's report to the Economic and Social Council on Market Assess prepared by the U.N. Conference on Trade and Development and by the World Trade Organization. E/1998/55

16. Developing Countries Can Trade with Each Other

"Poor nations should pull themselves up by their own bootstraps" used to be the slogan, to which the tart response was, "What happens if they don't have any boots?" In other words, without help from outside, no really poor nation can on its own win the battle against poverty. But nowadays, with the vast expansion of market economies and of opportunities for free enterprise, the emphasis is again on self-help. The answer to the question has become, "If they have no boots, let them find a neighbors who has, and sell them something which they themselves don't have."

The truth is, of course, that aid and self-help have to go hand in hand. Low-interest loans from the World Bank need to be in place alongside the efforts of poor nations to generate growth and savings themselves. But nowadays it is self-help which is getting all the attention.

Developing countries under the Chairmanship of Mr. Ali Katranji of Algeria have been holding a one-week discussion at the U.N. about how they can relate more closely to each other. These new links will be good for business and, if they do things regionally, their weak hand in bargaining with the rich countries will be strengthened. They will discover all sorts of opportunities close at hand they simply did not know about. And above all they will be creating their own trading networks and priorities and not simply reacting to the vast purchasing power of the North.

Take the example of Kenya in East Africa. Suddenly the people discover that they don't need to import nails and wire: it can be bought on the African continent. They find out that there are neighboring countries who are ready to buy their locally-produced detergents. And when a European market suddenly fails—for instance, the Europeans are now buying their beef from Eastern Europe—there are nations in Southern Africa who can and want to provide them with a market.

All over the world a network to encourage and develop this South–South trade and investment is emerging. Some parts of it are well-known like the South Asian Preferential Trading Arrangement (SAPTA) or the Latin American Southern Cone Common Market (MERCOSUR). Some arrangements are less well-known, like the preferential plans of the Arab Maghreb Union or the Melanesian Spearhead Group.

U.N. agencies are helping too. The United Nations Trade and Developmental Organization (UNCTAD) has its own database, which can be particularly useful on the subject of transferring technology to tropical countries. The United Nations Development Programme (UNDP) also has its own machinery for technology transfer. Developing countries, too, are also setting up their own data banks—in Zimbabwe and Malaysia, for example.

Progress will not be quick, but gradually an information framework for South–South cooperation is being put in place, which will be a crucial step towards regional economic freedom and viability, and furthermore decisive proof that the domination of colonial patterns of trade has ended at last.

Update

As globalization gathers pace, so do efforts increase by developing countries to trade and invest with each other. For example the largest investors in China in the nineties have been, not Europe and America, but Hong Kong and Taiwan. While Africa is still lagging, in this period mutual trade among all developing countries rose from $800 billion to $1400 billion or by 15.4 percent annually. Throughout the developing countries, trade in manufacturers has now taken the leading role over oil exports.[1]

Developing countries are also helping each with new technology and ideas for better agricultural productivity. In October 1998 the U.N. arrangement for Technical Cooperation among Developing Countries (TCDC) told how improved rice strains from Indonesia and the Philippines had been passed over to Africa; how Indian tea-bushes were being tried out in Iran; and how Chinese technology for small hydropower plants was being shared with other developing countries.[2]

In 1998 Ambassador Wibisono of Indonesia, Chairman of the Group of 77, announced he was placing high priority on arranging a South–South Summit as soon as possible. The Group of 77, which leads the effort by developing countries at the U.N. to overcome poverty, is actually 132 member nations at the U.N. who are determined to do more and more to help one another with trading and investing on a regional basis.[3]

Notes

1. State of South–South Cooperation. General Assembly A/52/402. September 29, 1997.
2. Technical Cooperation among Developing Countries. Exhibition at United Nations Headquarters, October 1998.
3. Journal of the Group of 77. Volume 11/2. Published at U.N. Headquarters, 1998.

17. Ten Commandments for Development

The corps of journalists at the U.N. are always throwing light into hidden places. Sometimes they come up with insights that illuminate a debate at the U.N. in a way the diplomats never could. "Papa" Menon, editor of the International Documents Review, does it as often as anyone. Earlier in the '90s he gave us a piece from Singapore, which was prophetic in 1992, and is still right up to date in 1997.

The piece was "Ten Commandments for Development" by Kishore Mahbubani, who is now Singapore's Ambassador to the United Nations. Here is a selection of these modern commandments for all who live in developing nations and who are dedicated to rapid social change, but who may not yet have realized that there is a price to pay, if the goal is to be attained.

Here are the first five of them:

1. Thou shalt blame only thyself for thy failures in development. Blaming imperialism, colonialism, and neo-imperialism is a convenient excuse to avoid self-examination.
2. Thou shalt acknowledge that corruption is the single most important cause for failures in development. Developed countries are not free from corruption. With their affluence, they can afford to indulge in savings and loans scandals. Developing countries cannot.
3. Thou shalt not subsudize any products. Nor punish the farmer to favor the city dweller. High prices are the only effective signal to increase production. If there are food riots, resign from office. Thou hast lost the mandate to rule because the population does not believe that only it should make sacrifices when leaders make none.
4. Thou shalt abandon state control of free markets. Have faith in thy own population. When its fetters are removed, it shall go forth and produce. An active and productive population naturally causes development.
5. Thou shalt borrow no more. Get foreign investment that pays for itself. Build only the infrastructure that is needed. Create no white elephants nor monuments nor railways that end in deserts. Accept the results of independent or World Bank feasibility studies. Accept no aid intended only to subsidize ailing industries in developed countries.

The next five commandments are equally, brutally realistic. But the author of this bracing message ends on an optimistic note:

10. Thou shalt not abandon hope. People are the same the world over. What Europe achieved yesterday, the developing world will achieve tomorrow. It can be done.

If, as some say, the present decade is turning out to be in the developed countries "the lean and mean nineties," then this advice is not merely useful, it is indispensable.

Walkabout:

Three

A tapestry of Picasso's famous painting *Guernica* commemorating the massacre of the people of Guernica in the Spanish Civil War. This tapestry depicting the disasters of war hangs in the UN on the way to the room where the members of the Security Council deliberate almost daily. (UN photo.)

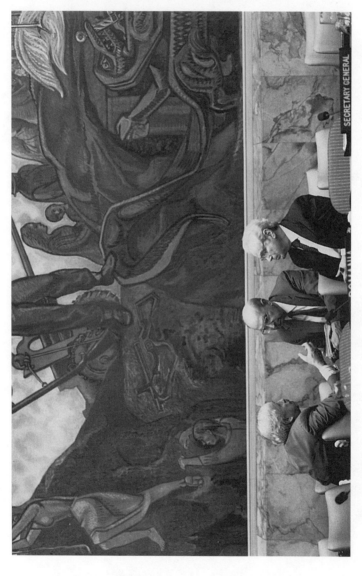

Left to right: Ambassador Penalosa (Colombia), Ambassador Pickering (United States), and former Secretary-General Perez de Cuellar, a former ambassador for Peru, confer at the security council in 1990 beneath the painting by Per Krogh of Norway which symbolizes man's struggle to climb out of barbarism into civilization. (UN photo: John Isaac.)

Mrs. Mary Robinson, High Commissioner for Human Rights and former President of Ireland, meets with Secretary-General Kofi Annan to celebrate the Fiftieth Anniversary of the Declaration of Human Rights, 1998. (Photo: UN.)

The handing over to Secretary-General Kofi Annan of the final document of the Oslo Conference, which negotiated in 1998 a total ban on anti-personnel landmines. Mr. Lloyd Axworthy, Minister for Foreign Affairs from Canada (second left), and Mr. Bjorn Tore Godel, Minister of Foreign Affairs from Norway (second right). At right is Mr. Stephen Goose, Program Director, for the International Campaign to Ban Land Mines. (UN photo: Milton Grant.)

Secretary-General Dag Hammarskjöld and Under-Secretary-General Ralph Bunche, both Nobel Peace Prize winners, 1955. (UN photo.)

Ivory carving of the Chengtu-Kumming Railway, which covers 1,085 kilometers. This carving was made from eight ivory tusks, and was presented to the UN by the People's Republic of China, 1974. (UN photo: T. Chen.)

Ambassador Fulci of Italy, President of the Security Council, confers with his colleagues on the mandate to extend the UN Observer Mission to Liberia, 1995. (UN photo: J. Bu.)

Delegates confer outside the General Assembly Hall. Above them is a kiswa, a black silk curtain embroidered in silver and gold, a gift to the UN from Saudi Arabia. (UN photo: A. Brizzi.)

1.   The International Art Collection at the U.N.

The buildings of the U.N. were always designed to be much more than a collection of office blocks. The aspirations of the Charter needed to be matched by the art with which the buildings were to be embellished. And for over fifty years now a unique collection of the art of all nations has been donated to the U.N. by a majority of the member states.

Assistant Secretary-General Alvaro de Soto from Peru has the unusual job of chairing the committee, which decides where to place the steady flow of artwork arriving at the U.N. from the member states. Each piece has its own special history.

Some pieces have the specific theme of peace, but many represent a nation's artistic achievement in a more general way. From Peru, for example, there is a marvelous royal burial mantle—a strictly geometric pattern in somber reds and blacks—from the Paracas culture of 1000 B.C. When the Peruvian Prime Minister gave it to the U.N., there was an explosion of indignation in Peru because he had given away a piece of national cultural patrimony, and his government actually fell soon afterwards!

In the same room there is an elaborately decorated and inscribed Kiswa, a black silk curtain embroidered in silver and gold from the Holy Kabaa, a gift from Saudi Arabia. This lounge, close to the General Assembly, is curtained off, as drinking is not permitted alongside such an important symbol of Islam.

Mr. de Soto remarked, "This is a delicate job, because we cannot select or reject a national gift. But we do give advice, and sometimes we are asked what would be most appropriate. We never accept offers from individuals or from the many artists who would like to give free gifts of their art. Probably under one hundred nations have donated up till now, so many more gifts may still be expected. Sometimes nations do not realize that the spaces they think most desirable—mostly on the second floor—are the ones where their art will be seen only by other diplomats, and not by the far larger general public who have their own route for touring the U.N."

"Because the U.N. is such a beautiful building, I believe we should take a minimalist approach to our collection. We owe it to our architects—Le Corbusier, Niemeyer, Harrison—to let the building speak for itself. Small pieces often fit perfectly. For instance the beautiful statue of Osiris given by Egypt looks exactly right on the second floor just where diplomats can enjoy it as they pass by on their way to the delegates' lounge. There is also a gold palm tree given by Bahrain that fits perfectly at the entrance to one of our conference rooms. But not everything fits. For instance, the abstract piece by the British sculptress Barbara Hepworth in the forecourt had to be increased three times in size to be in scale with the Secretariat!"

Tapestries look fine in the long passages and rooms with high ceilings. The Belgians have given, and recently had specially cleaned, the largest tapestry in the world. The designer Peter Colfs used 94,000 miles of yarn and 14 assistants to create a classical landscape entitled *The Triumph of Peace*. The Chinese government presented a gigantic tapestry which depicts the Great Wall of China and which dominates the Delegates' Lounge. On another wall of the prestigious second floor there is a superb Second Century A.D. mosaic of a Goddess, the presiding Genius of the four seasons, given by President Bourgiba of Tunisia, who was a great friend and admirer of Dag Hammarskjöld.

Of those works of art that celebrate peace, perhaps the most striking is the sculpture by Evgeny Vuchetich of a giant figure beating a sword into a ploughshare—a gift from the Soviet Union. There is also a remarkable modern piece in our gardens unveiled jointly by American Secretary of State Baker and Russian Foreign Minister Shevardnadze in 1988, depicting St. George sticking his long destructive lance into the shards of two actual missiles, a Soviet SS-20 and an American Perching 2, lying on their sides.

Then in the passage leading directly to the room where the Security Council meets, there is a tapestry copied from Picasso's famous painting of the massacre at Guernica during the Spanish Civil War. Picasso personally supervised its creation. It is on an extended loan to the U.N. from Mr. Nelson Rockefeller. Mr. de Soto proposed that it be placed exactly at this spot to focus the hearts and minds of members of the Security Council, who wrestle day by day with grave decisions about war and peace.

Mr. de Soto concluded, "My hope is that the art at the U.N. will always be a celebration of cultural diversity and a symbol of the universality of man and his creativity." Then he added in a lighter vein, "We have just received a new work of recent art from Estonia. The composition depicts a tower of skirts with a pair of beseeching hands wearing white gloves on top of the column. Its meaning is not clear to me, but it is a piece of folk art, and adds to our House a note of color and levity."[1]

Note

1. From an interview with Assistant Secretary-General Alvaro de Soto. December 14, 1995.

2. The Dag Hammarskjöld Memorial Library

The Dag Hammarskjöld Library was not dedicated until 1961, but it is a focal point at U.N. Headquarters. The Director of the library is Angela Kane, a member of the Secretariat from Hamlin, Germany. She studied at the Universities of Munich, Bryn Mawr, and Johns Hopkins and has served the U.N. in Indonesia, in the Department of Disarmament, in the peace negotiations for El Salvador and most recently in the Secretary-General's Cabinet. She spoke about the inspiration she draws from Dag Hammarskjöld, the Secretary-General after whom the library is named:

"I see him both as a philosopher and a revolutionary. Or should I say 'visionary.' He pushed out the perimeter of the U.N.'s concerns and work. He orchestrated the U.N. operation to preserve the unity of the Congo. And he did that at the height of the Cold War. After his death there was a long period of stagnation."[1]

Angela Kane presides over a staff of 120 whose primary task is to enable the missions—all 188 of them—to obtain U.N. documents "with the greatest possible speed, convenience, and economy." Increasingly that means servicing diplomats and the wider world by means of the electronic highway. More and more documents are also being made available on CD-ROM.

Apart from the main documents concerned with U.N. business in the General Assembly and the Security Council, the Library is responsible for substantial Legal, Statistical, and Map Collections. There are more than 80,000 maps in the collection.

There is also a Woodrow Wilson collection, a unique repository of documents relating to the League of Nations. It is good to be reminded of the name of the famous U.S. President Woodrow Wilson, whose vision played a crucial role in the creation of that organization. Addressing the people of Omaha, Nebraska, in 1919, President Wilson, whose portrait hangs in the library, spoke about the Covenant of the League in words that could equally well be applied to the inspiration that should be generated by the U.N. Charter.

"My fellow citizens, this is one of the charters of human liberty, and the person who picks out the flaws in it, for there are flaws in it, forgets the magnitude of the thing, forgets the majesty of the thing. . . ."[2]

The Maps and Cartography Collection is much in demand to cope with present-day territorial disputes. It has a strong archival section going back to the 1940s, and this can be very important with regard to border disputes in an area like the Middle East. Recently, as a political storm began to brew, two small and obscure islands had to be urgently located by the staff on the best map available. One was called Imia in Greek and Kardak in Turkish, and another one in the Red Sea called Harish was the focus of a dispute between Eritrea and Yemen.

The maps are also especially in demand by the Department of Peacekeeping Operations (DPKO). Up-to-date maps of Bosnia and Liberia have been urgently needed. "One of our staff," said Angela, "recently prepared a map, which showed the roads in the interior of Sierra Leone. This was apparently available nowhere else."

Like all other parts of the U.N., the Library is feeling the financial pinch. Budgetary constraints affect repairs to the building, number and quality of the staff, and the ability to initiate staff training of many different kinds. The Library deposits its materials in more than 300 libraries worldwide.

Due to the staff shortage, one Indian staff member was asked, while on leave, to visit all the Indian depository libraries and see if they needed help and advice. As it turned out, they were well on top of the job. Other countries with shorter library traditions may not manage so well, and they need staff to visit and advise them on how to cope with the unceasing flood of U.N. material arriving for them from Headquarters.

Until all countries pay their arrears, the Library, like all other parts of the U.N., will continue to struggle to deliver the all-round service that 188 nations expect of it.

Notes

1. From an interview with Angela Kane. April 15, 1995.
2. *The Messages and Papers of Woodrow Wilson.* Review of Reviews Corporation. 1924. P. 804.

Part Eight

Environment

1. Rio + Five—An Evaluation

"Hot Air" was the dismissive way the *Wall Street Journal*, a U.S. newspaper, dealt with the major U.N. event of 1997—the Special Session of the General Assembly to evaluate progress since the great Environment and Development Conference of 1992. Jonathan Porritt, a British environmental expert, had a sharp response for this kind of airy dismissal of the movement to create sensible planetary housekeeping:

"Just how idiotic this throwaway contempt sounds when set against the principal outcomes of those two frenetic weeks in Rio five years ago."[1]

The *Wall Street Journal* is just plain wrong. Since the Rio Conference in 1992 produced its marching orders—better known as Agenda 21—there have been all sorts of practical outcomes to safeguard the planet and to hand it on to the next generation in viable good order. Working out the practical implications of the conventions signed at Rio to deal with the dangers of global warming and with the threat of extinguishing species on a terrifying scale are perhaps the most important. But the preservation of other resources—for example fish, forests, and water—has been receiving lots of attention, too.

Those who say dangers to the environment are exaggerated and that the scientists are still not unanimous, should have heard the Minister of Foreign Affairs of the Solomon Islands, David Sitai, speak at this Special Session. In an upcompromising manner he proclaimed the urgency of the U.N.'s evaluation of global threats to the environment.

"The economy of the Solomon Islands rests largely on agriculture, fishing, and tropical forest products, so climate change, ocean pollution, and the loss of biodiversity are serious threats. For us, Agenda 21 is a life and death matter."[2]

And further, to prove that an ounce of practice is worth a ton of rhetoric, the cover of the minister's speech showed a solar panel at work in the village of Sukiki on Guadalcanal which, courtesy of the U.N. Fund of renewable energy and the Italian Government, is now being lit and heated by solar energy. Many more villages will follow this example and the solar energy movement will gather strength wherever the sun can fuel it.

Worldwide, however, there is still so much to do. Fish are being harvested from the sea quicker than they can breed and trees are being cut down far quicker than they can replace themselves. And a particularly shocking statistic is the estimation that 50,000 animal and plant species are likely to become extinct over the next decade.[3]

Who will pay for all this, and will the rich be helping the poor to pay for the technology to cut down on harmful emissions into the atmosphere? Unfortunately at this conference, there was little fresh evidence that all the debate at the Special Session had turned on a new financial tap.

239

The U.N. estimated at Rio that the developing countries would need $600 million per annum until the end of the century to do all that is necessary. It was suggested that the developed countries could reasonably provide $125 billion of it. In fact, since Rio the developed nations have averaged only $60 billion in overseas aid. It has been argued that as the amount of private investment since 1987 has gone up from $25 billion to $200 billion, this sum more than offsets the shortfall of government aid promised at Rio. Of course investment from private and commercial sources helps, but private investment tends to go to the richer rather than poorer countries and it can increase or decrease at short notice, depending on market forces.[4]

That is the bad news. The good news is—and the varied attendance at the Special Session reinforced this—that the safeguarding of the planet is now in the hands of not just governments, but a whole range of pressure groups who are now known as "stakeholders." These citizens, as the result of the U.N. Conference, are taking things forward in their own ways. In nations, in cities, in villages, and in homes all over the globe, these stakeholders have been "thinking globally and acting locally."

These stakeholders, women, children, indigenous people, municipalities, and of course the business sector, usually belong to some group or other. These groups are all specifically named in Agenda 21 so they are aware of what they have to do to save the planet. With the help of electronic communication, they can bring continuous international pressure on national governments as they have never been able to do before.

Business has a special role to play in all this. But Rio + Five revealed how far the partnership between the U.N., governments, and the business sector has still to develop in order to fulfill the demands of Agenda 21. But it is encouraging that voluntary codes of conduct for business are now coming into existence which will help to set common environmental standards, and that codes of conduct are already emerging from numerous trades and professions.

At this Special Session, it proved impossible to put together terms for a possible Forest Convention. It was still not possible to make much progress in establishing some sort of Environmental Security Council. Meanwhile the Commission on Sustainable Development, working within the Economic and Social Council, will have to do the best it can.

In this special week at the U.N. the *New York Times*, explicitly contradicting the tone of the *Wall Street Journal*, headed a leader "No Hot Air on Global Warming." So there is hope that some Americans do indeed realize the dangers ahead. As they are the largest polluters of the atmosphere, they have the most to do to decide what targets to set to control atmospheric pollution for their own sake and for the world.

The Special Sessions concluded that while in a few areas progress has been acceptable, in many others it has not. Meanwhile, the U.N. goes on giving the movement to protect the environment a steadily global focus and ultimately a universal moral legitimacy.[5]

Stop Press

Slowly and painfully in 1998 the nations and not least the United States are coming to terms with a common policy to prevent global warming. It is generally agreed that emissions have to be cut around 8 percent below 1990 levels. A sticking point has been that the developing countries have been refusing to make any commitments of their own until their industrialization has caught up with the developed countries. However Argentina has agreed to a target for lower emissions and others may now follow.

Notes

1. Agenda 21. Chapter 33. "Financial Resources and Mechanisms," p. 251. U.N. Department of Public Information, 1993.
2. Edited by Felix Dodds. *The Way Forward. Beyond Agenda 21*. Earthscan, 1997. Introduction Jonathan Porritt, p. xvi.
3. Ibid. Barbara Bramble. Financial Resources for the Transition to Sustainable Development. P. 191.
4. The Honorable David Sitai, MP. Address to the Special Session of the General Assembly to Review and Appraise the Implementation of Agenda 21. June 1997.
5. Earth Summit + 5. Department of Public Information Fact Sheet, June 1997.

2. The NGO Perspective on Rio

"In many respects, the U.N. is only six years old, rather than fifty, due to the gridlock imposed upon it during the long Cold War," says Bill Pace, the Director of the International Office of the World Federalist Movement. What Bill means is that, during the Cold War, Non-Governmental Organizations (NGOs) could not really be independent minded, because of the enormous pressure on them to line up with one side or the other in the struggle.

Bill outlined the very different post-Cold War situation now developing:

"Most successful NGOs now operate through multi-regional and cross-sectional alliances, networks, and caucuses. The most powerful new agents for global change are the partnerships forged when progressive NGOs of the North and South combine their efforts with progressive governments in the North and South."

Bill Pace first became involved in international politics during the Vietnam War. Some years later he was working for Amnesty International as a Director of the "Human Rights Now!" campaign, promoting awareness of the Universal Declaration of Human Rights. This campaign and concert tour took Bill around the world four times in two years. While in Amsterdam he met up with the World Federalists and subsequently he became their executive director.

"We are at a rare historic crossroads," said Bill, "when the world's governments are deciding whether the U.N. will finally be allowed to become the institution envisioned in the charter, or one which will fail and go the way of the League of Nations. Will we create the kind of emergency and crisis mechanisms at the U.N. that humanity needs for basic survival and protection? Or will governments continue to heap more and more demands on the U.N. while denying it the barest of financial resources and political authority and capacity?"[1]

The defining landmark, Bill believed, in this new post-Cold War era was the 1992 Rio Conference on Environment and Development.

Bill summed up its unique importance.

"It was the largest summit in history, dealing with the largest number of issues ever addressed in a summit, and involving the greatest number of representatives of civil society, even including previous international inter-governmental negotiation.

" 'Agenda 21'—the program of action of the summit—represents a triumph of North–South diplomacy. To get it established, though, the Southern NGOs and governments had to confront the hypocrisy of the Northern NGOs, governments, trans-national businesses, and financial institutions, who sought to impose growth and development restrictions on the South—in the name of saving the global environment—restrictions which they were unwilling to apply to themselves.

"This crisis is misunderstanding had, in fact, already emerged long before at no less than four preparatory conferences for Rio. In the end, coalitions of progressive Northern and Southern NGOs turned out to be the key factor in bridge building to overcome these two irreconcilable positions. Governments, while they certainly found the NGOs 'awkward,' had to recognize the strength of their expertise, and their growing interest. NGO numbers were up from just 14 at the First Prepcom to 5,000 at the fourth and last one!

"When the time came to go to Rio, no less than 35,000 attended the parallel NGO Conference and more than 2,000 were present at the official Conference!"

242

Bill recalled how the diplomats at Rio were willing to work so much more closely with the NGOs.

"Due to the good offices of the Conference's Secretary General Maurice Strong, and with the support of key Ambassadors, especially Tommy Koh of Singapore and Ambassador Razali Ismail from Malaysia, NGO participation in the negotiations was unparalleled. For example, during the last Prepcom and in Rio, the legal and institutional issues caucus organized NGO plenaries and NGO-government dialogues, often with U.N. interpretation. For the first time NGOs could debate common positions among themselves in the NGO plenaries. Working group chairs, heads of government delegations, and other leaders participated in these extraordinary NGO-led dialogue sessions."

During the Prepcoms, Bill and others began to see that only if the right legal, financial, and institutional arrangements were in place would there be any hope of fulfilling the goals of Agenda 21, and in protecting the legitimate interests of the developing nations. Only if new funds were made available by the North for sustaining the environment, could the South be expected to resist the kind of wholesale short-term exploitation of their natural resources, which represented their only gateway to prosperity.

Then, as the conference neared its end, there came a crucial moment. The NGOs pressed for a commission to follow up the conference's huge program of action to ensure that both Environment *and* Development got an equal share of attention. Many powerful nations did not want this commission — including some from developing countries. It sounded too much like "interference" in domestic affairs. But a formidable coalition of governments led by Malaysia, France, Canada, the Netherlands, and others, stood firm and the doubters were convinced. And so the Commission on Sustainable Development was born and it was given its marching orders in the unique follow-up document called Agenda 21.

Agenda 21, the action program for the Commission on Sustainable Development (CSD) is a massive, intimidating document, but it is nothing less than a pioneering blueprint for environmental survival. It has a whole chapter on the role of women in promoting sustainable development. Local authorities and trade unions are mobilized, too.

It will take a decade or more to work through everything that is in Agenda 21 in the General Assembly in all of its main committees, in the Bretton Woods' financial bodies, and in disarmament work. This formidable assignment must not just be left to the commission to undertake by itself.

Since Rio, NGOs have had a much greater share of the action at subsequent summit conferences. At the Women's Conference in 1996 in Beijing, the women's caucus became even stronger and better organized with a global reach. NGOs are now actively campaigning to take part in the General Assembly and all the main U.N. Committees, and not just in the work of the Economic and Social Council (ECOSOC). Every step of the way will be a struggle.

But governments are getting used to the idea that there is a conference of NGOs (CONGO) based in Geneva and when it speaks, it represents literally millions of members of the widest coalition of NGOs. It is the voice of "We the People" and it represents a weighty range of worldwide opinion.

"The age of global governance is upon us," concludes Bill Pace, "NGOs are now poised to participate in U.N. debates in a multi-dimensional way—operating at a local, national, and international level—and to bring to birth a truly international democracy."[1]

Note

1. From an interview with Bill Pace. November 5, 1995 and November 20, 1997.

3. Financing Global Environmentalism

There are two world crises that are too big for any one nation to solve by itself. One is the protection of the dwindling numbers and variety of animals, birds, insects, and plants on the planet. The other is the danger of global warming. Therefore at the Rio Conference in 1992, the U.N. community signed Conventions on Biodiversity and on Climate Change. Now, five years later, most nations have signed these Conventions and a major fund has been set up and begun to give some teeth to the good intentions of governments to help each other to overcome these great environmental problems.

The fund to prevent these potential disasters is called the Global Environmental Facility (GEF). Nations have put more than two billion dollars into it, which, in fact when shared between five continents is not a large sum. But it is a solid financial result of the Rio deliberations and it is of utmost importance that it work successfully.

The GEF has already done some interesting things, such as supporting large projects and small ones. A typical large project has been to assist in stopping pollution of the ozone layer by old-style industries located in Belarus, Bulgaria, Hungary, and in a wide swathe of Eastern Europe. A small project has been helping to establish solar power in rural areas of Zimbabwe and Indonesia which are outside the range of standard electrification.

Its projects are usually incremental. That means helping nations to do things they would do anyway, but enabling them, when they do it, to use the most up-to-date technology. Projects have to have a regional or a global dimension. Thus harmful weed control on Lake Victoria benefits, not just Kenya, Tanzania, and Uganda, but all the countries who use the waters of the Nile basin.

The Fund is pioneering all sorts of new ways of doing U.N. business. First its implementation is the work of a new kind of three day partnership—between UNDP, UNEP and, surprisingly, the World Bank. In the council they have set up a new voting system in which membership from the developing countries outnumbers membership from the donor countries. Both sides have come up with majorities for a project to be able to go ahead. This is a shift from the World Bank's weighted voting arrangement which is sometimes described as "One dollar, one vote." So far, due not least to good staff work, all decisions have been reached by consensus.

Another innovation in the way the GEF does its work is to involve NGOs. They are invited to come up with ideas for projects, take part in the council's deliberations, and do everything except actually vote. But first they have to get the host country or countries involved in a possible project to give their agreement to go ahead.

Dr. Mahammed El-Ashry, Chief Executive of the Fund, summed up progress so far. He said he was proud that this was the first "strategic alliance" between the U.N. and the World Bank. He was pleased that already more than 15 percent of the projects were being run by NGOs. He noted that not all the first tranche of money in the Fund had been spent, not because of bureaucratic delays, but because there had not yet been enough viable projects put forward. Lastly he regretted that not much progress had been made with plans relating to desertification and deforrestation.[1]

Predictably the largest donors to the GEF so far have been Japan, easily the biggest donor, the larger countries of Western Europe, Canada, and the United States. These countries realize that if they let some of the environmental sores around the world left to fester, it will not be long before the ill effects spill over to effect them, too.

A new attitude to nature is permeating governments and business. Human beings are ultimately not in charge, but we are, nevertheless, very much responsible. As the then-American Under Secretary of State Tim Worth put it, "The economy is a wholly-owned subsidary of the environment."

Note

1. From a speech by Dr. Mahammed El-Ashry, Chief Executive Officer of the Global Environment Facility at the United Nations. March 4, 1997.

4. Managing Population Growth

In the modern world, successful populations are smaller populations. Latest figures on growth rates reveal the encouraging fact that the number of children per family is getting smaller in practically every country in the world. This is an essential trend in a world where the population is growing at the rate of ninety million each year. But how can the world's population stay a reasonable size?

The U.N. through its United Nations Populations Fund (UNFPA) gives a high priority to this vital work. The Population Division in the Secretariat meets regularly to discuss progress and make future plans for action.

One of the delegates to their meetings is Cecille Joaquin-Yasay who heads the Commission on Population in the Philippines. Her views are especially valuable because she began her career working in the United Nations Children's Fund (UNICEF) and in the United Nations Population Fund (UNFPA) in New York, and now has moved to live permanently in the Philippines. She now sees the practical effects of the work done by UNDP, UNICEF, and UNFPA in her home country and her enthusiasm about its value is even greater than it was when she worked at the Headquarters of these big organizations in New York.[1]

For Cecille the Summit Conference on Population in Cairo in 1993—known for short as the ICPD—was a landmark event in the creation of right thinking about managing population growth in all nations. It was clearly seen for the first time that population policy had to come from the bottom up, and not the top down. Problems caused by population growth was not a matter to be dumped on governments and U.N. agencies. Certainly governments had a part to play, but fundamentally the policies had to be a people-centred community concern. This especially applied to the crucial issue of the size of families. No amount of sanctions or punishment could influence a couple's decision about this matter.

And Cairo stressed that creation of a healthy family was equally a matter for the men as well as the women. Now that women were increasingly employed, men had to become aware that they also would have responsibilities in household management and childcare, something they never had before.

In the Philippines there is a problem about the Roman Catholic Church's view on methods of controlling the size of families. Cecille commented on this important issue.

"We agree with the Church with their stress on the importance of the family in society and with their views on the status and health of women. They are right, too, that matters of population have to be dealt with in the context of sustainable development as a whole."

The Population Commission reviews all the policies on population in the Philippines. It has found that the first priority for successful advocacy of the policy since Cairo is essentially work done on a person-to-person basis. Cecille agreed with Dr. Nafis Sadik, Director-General of the UNFPA that the subject may be "sensitive and difficult."[2] No less than 50 percent of the population in the Philippines is under 18, so programs are needed to reach young people both in and out of school.

Major funding for the Philippines Population work comes from UNFPA. Cecille commented regarding more funding for development programs.

"The main problem, as I see it, is planning, allocation, and elimination of waste, not more money. This applies to the U.N. itself as well. We need to make it a leaner operation and get more of its work done at the regional level. In the Philippines we are now making increasingly good use of our U.N. regional Economic Commission (ESCAP) in Bangkok."

Cecille Yasay believes population policies in the Philippines are more effective than they have ever been, but she cautions, "Anyone who has lived in the West for some time should never forget the huge difference in attitude in developing countries like mine. There is a wholly different attitude to money, to poverty. The emphasis is on survival, not accumulation. If we do have something extra, we will share it, while we can. In my language the very word job means 'Looking for life.' We do not emphasize efficiency and punctuality. In pushing for changes in attitudes—and sometimes expecting too much—we must constantly remind ourselves how deep-rooted these cultural differences really are."

Update

In November 1998, UNFPA announced its latest plans for helping the management of population growth in Madagascar. The facts of the current situation there are worrying. The annual population growth at 2.9 percent means the population of 12 million will double every 25 years. The infant mortality rate at 96 per thousand live births is high. The use of modern contraceptive methods is low (14 percent in urban and 7 percent in rural areas). The literacy rate for both men and women is barely over 50 percent.

With the support of the Ministries of Finance and Economic Affairs and the Ministry of Foreign Affairs in Madagascar the UNDP proposes to reinforce its previous three programs of work in Madagascar with a $14.4 million program putting a special emphasis on reproductive health and population and development strategies.[3]

Notes

1. From an interview with Cecille Joaquin-Yasay, Executive Director, Commission on Population, National Economic and Development Authority. March 1, 1996.
2. Dr. Nafis Sadik, Executive Director, United Nations Population Fund (UNFPA). Dispatches, February, 1966, P. 2.
3. Executive Board of UNDP and of UNFPA. DP/FPA/MDG/4. November 20, 1998.

5. Demography—a Key to the Future

Jofret Grinblat is a French demographer who serves in the Population Division of the Secretariat. He can eloquently demonstrate that the study of population statistics is far more than simply a scientific summary and analysis of the results of population censuses. The progress of nations and even the fate of the planet itself depends on the rate of population growth. Jofret explained that if the world population kept growing at the present pace, in a few centuries the volume of the weight of the world's population will be greater then the volume of the earth itself!

This is, of course, impossible and shows just how abnormal is the current population growth in the larger perspective of human history. "Either fertility goes down or mortality goes up," concluded Jofret bluntly. He should know as he is Chief of the Estimates and Projections Section of the Population Division. He went on to explain just how extraordinarily rapid the growth of the world's population has been in the past hundred years compared with all previous centuries. And this state of affairs cannot continue. If it did, civil disturbances would cause the disintegration of nations.[1]

Jofret Grinblat is cautiously optimistic. He believes that if people can see a better life is possible with smaller families they will opt for fewer children. A decline in the birthrate has already happened in Thailand and Korea, where artificial means of controlling the birth rate are now popular.

In Pakistan and in Sub-Sahara Africa, however, the growth rate continues. A part of Jofret's work for the U.N. is to try to see what factors might be producing these very different scenarios. And in developing countries the problem is made even more difficult because of the unreliability of the statistics. But the U.N. is working hard to achieve a common standard in the way censuses are conducted and in the methods used to compile the statistics.

Population statistics often have a sharp political edge. For instance in Nigeria there has not been a reliable census that has been accepted by the world scientific community since 1962, and even that one has not been officially published. The results of any new census could have an explosive effect on the way the wealth controlled by the federal budget is distributed to the states, and so the figure are either distorted or they do not get released.

Another territory where the work of the demographer has a political dimension is Western Sahara, a former Spanish colony in which the U.N. is trying to keep the peace between the Polisario freedom-fighters and Morocco. A census was taken by the Spanish in 1974 and there is no reason to doubt it was done in good faith. The problem is the interpretation of the details.

Jofret Grinblat went there personally in 1991 and 1993 and found that in Arabic the spelling of a name can be done in different ways depending on where the name is being used. If there were to be a referendum in Western Sahara, it would be difficult to identify individuals from their name on the census. He explained to the officials that the technicalities of arranging a fair and true referendum on the future of the country were going to be greater than even they had imagined.

As a schoolboy in France, Jofret won an essay prize which brought him together on an exchange encounter with fellow African competitors. He became fascinated with Africa and worked for a while in Niger. He is typical of many U.N. civil servants who have the highest qualifications in their chosen field of expertise, and who combine their intellectual and technical skills with practical experience and concern for people struggling against poverty.

The U.N. standardized system of national accounting is the foundation of the assessment and evaluation of the economic progress of nations, and the demographic division is an essential part of this process.

Demographers are seldom seen, but without their steady analysis, development work, and planning, the U.N. would quickly degenerate into speculative ventures and misjudged expenditure.

Note

1. From an interview with Dr. Joseph Alfred Grinblat, Population Division, U.N. Secretariat. April 23, 1996.

6. Saving Forests for the Next Generation

How can the great majority of people on this earth become much wealthier without at the same time reducing the planet to a treeless, plantless desert? It was to answer this pressing question that the nations and peoples gathered at Rio in 1992 to hold a great summit on Environment and Development.

Forests, not surprisingly, were one of the key issues at this meeting. But agreement on how to treat forests was hard to reach. The developed nations put the emphasis on saving the forests for future generations. The developing nations put the priority on exploiting them now in order to achieve a decent standard of living for millions still living in poverty. It seemed an unbridgeable gap.

The conference eventually agreed that the only way they could find some common ground was to agree on just a Declaration of Forest Principles and even that was to be a non-binding agreement. But a Declaration of Principles is, of course, much too vague and completely unenforceable.

So in 1997 the U.N. played host to a new intergovernmental Panel on Forests in an ongoing attempt to get more common understanding on rules for forests. There is a hope that in a few years' time there could actually be a global law, a Convention about forest conservation agreed and signed by all. Only a convention, the Canadians argued, would ensure that member states are implementing a mutually agreed-on set of rules of the road for forests.

In spite of the difficulties, there is still a determination to reconcile the points of view of developed and developing nations. So the Panel on Forests appointed two co-chairmen, Sir Martin Holdgate from the United Kingdom and Mr. Kristin from India, one from the developed and one from the developing world. The members of the Panel were determined to find more common ground than seemed possible at Rio.

But even if these co-chairs could ensure a harmonious meeting, the whole subject, like all matters before the U.N., is far too complex to resolve in four days. It will only be much further down the road that the two Chairmen who will have to work with the different national groups, like the Latin American bloc and the European Union, and can hope to bring about a new consensus. For now they have to get all the latest facts about the exploitation of forests into the discussion—and a great deal has been happening since Rio to take into account.

The U.N. Secretariat gave the following intimidating list of all the relevant U.N. conventions that have to be looked at in order to get an overall view of the crisis situation with regard to forests:

The Convention on Biological Diversity
Convention to Combat Desertification
Convention on Climate Change
Convention on International Trade in Endangered Species of Wild Flora and Fauna
International Tropical Timber Agreement. . . .[1]

Nitin Desai, the Under-Secretary General in charge of Sustainable Development, added a personal touch to the debate when in 1995 he said to the Commission on Sustainable Development:

"Forest management has to be inter-generational. My grandfather and his brothers planted one mango orchard whose benefits accrued largely to my father and his brothers. They planted a second mango orchard whose benefits have accrued to me and my brothers. And right now my brothers and I are planting a third mango orchard whose benefits are not going to accrue to us, but to our children."[2]

Nor is that all. Nowadays the views of indigenous people who have made forests their home for generations have to be taken into account, too. As the World Conservation Union points out, these forest dwellers are the ones who know how falling timber can influence fish-spawning sites in remote tropical river basins.[3]

Once there is an agreement to protect timber, there has to be a system to mark whether a log has been taken from a sustainable forest site or not. Logs can be stamped that they originate from a properly managed forest. They call this "eco-labeling" and it is already being worked out by the Forestry Stewardship Council and the International Organization for Standardization.

Forests, like every other major natural resource nowadays, have to be nurtured and exploited by reference to a whole range of new environmental laws and principles.[4] Slowly, diplomats are making that happen.

Notes

1. Commission on Sustainable Development. Panel on Forests. Program of Work. August 16, p. 16.
2. Statement by Mr. Nitin Desai, Under-Secretary General for Policy Coordination and Sustainable Development at the opening session of the CSD Intergovernmental Panel on Forests. September 11, 1995, p. 3.
3. IUCN World Conservation Union Forum Summary Paper. September 13, 1995, p. 4.
4. Commission on Sustainable Development.

7.   Lobbying by a Group of Dutch NGOs

The international community of Non-Governmental Organizations (NGOs) determined that it would take advantage of the unprecedented way it had been encouraged by governments to be in the forefront of the work of the U.N. at the Rio Conference on Environment and Development in 1992. The NGOs aimed to make as strong a showing, or an even stronger one, at the follow-up to Rio which was now grounded in the Commission on Sustainable Development (CSD). In 1995, Simone Lovera from the Netherlands came to the meeting of the commission in New York on behalf of 17 NGOs from her country.

Her particular concern was the lifestyle of rich countries, particularly "Patterns of production and consumption"—that meant the wasteful way food is often produced in the West and the way oil is being used up by gas-guzzling cars.

To make an impact on the commission, Simone had to use a whole range of negotiating skills. It is not just diplomats who need diplomatic skills. NGOs need them, too, and they usually have far less back-up staff to help them. Simone worked to get the hang of the "process" of a U.N. commission. She discovered how the meeting moved on relentlessly from general statements of intent to hard negotiations on a final text. Time, she realized, was of the essence. She had to have a perpetual sense of urgency and to be ready at the very last moment to rush across to a diplomat and tactfully persuade him to put forward her proposals. And she found out that, like members of all NGOs, she had no voice in the content of the final text. That still remained the prerogative of the professional diplomats from the different nation states.

Simone had also to be a very good listener. At times it might be possible for her to put two different proposals for a text from different governments into fresh words and carry them across to a delegation for their consideration. Suddenly, as the final text for the Conference Report took shape, her compromise wording might find favor with the officials—if she could come up with new language knitted together in just the right way.[1]

Personal contacts have to be gradually built up over time with a huge cast of diplomats. This is not easy as the staffing of missions keeps changing all the time. Further, NGOs are often felt by governments to have two faces. Sometimes their fresh ideas are welcome. At others, they will seem to government officials to be hopelessly idealistic and out of tune with the negotiations in progress.

Simone's special interest was in the relationship of biodiversity to patterns of consumption and production in the rich countries.

The whole subject is much more complicated and international than might be expected. Simone explained that a recent report had explained how important part of Dutch cattle feed is soy beans which are grown in Brazil. Twenty years of increase in production in this crop in Brazil have caused a wave of unemployment in some rural areas, because soy bean production requires seven to eight times less labor than other forms of agriculture. Some migrate to the favellas of Brazilian big cities. Others take up shifting cultivation and so the Brazilian forests get cut down at record speeds. Now if the Dutch were to decide to eat less meat, that would help Brazilian peasants to keep their livelihoods in the rural areas.[2]

The intensive Netherlands agricultural policy produces greenhouse gas emissions and it has been estimated that these must be reduced by 60 percent if serious harm is to be avoided to the biodiversity of other nations. Furthermore, the country's huge surplus of manure causes acid rain, which destroys European forests and damages their biodiversity.

So production for the modern industrial lifestyle is harmful both to humans and the environment, and it affects not only for the Netherlands, but also for the rest of Europe, and worldwide.

Simone remarks that while in the Netherlands there is considerable awareness of the social cost, of being a meat eater, there is much less willingness for governments to do anything about it. The same goes for the government's attitude to carbon emissions from motor vehicles.

Simone notes that in America, the position is reversed. Americans are far less socially aware of pollution, yet government is doing more to legislate in favor of unleaded gas and to fine people heavily for dumping waste on the street.

The heart of these recommendations put forward by the NGO caucus is to get the Commission on Social Development to produce a report which will focus on this central issue of production and consumption. Simone and her colleagues in the NGO's caucus eventually put forward their own wording on this subject for governments to consider:

"The Commission recommends that, beyond the preparatory work of improving understanding and analysis, each country must commit itself to identify priorities and set specific, measurable, and time-bound targets for achieving sustainable production and consumption patterns in all pertinent sectors (for example including agriculture, chemicals, energy packaging)."[3]

It is one thing to produce a well-worded recommendation, which would, if accepted by governments, raise the consciousness raised by Rio a small step further. It is quite another to get it accepted by the European Union drafting committee.

Simone tried her text on the Dutch Delegation who might take it to the European Union. But in the European Working Group, where the Dutch were members, they had other equally important topics to think about—demography, poverty, trade. But she believed that about half of what she and her group proposed might get accepted by the European Union.

If only this clause on patterns of production and consumption is successfully promoted by the European Union, then NGOs would have an effective new tool by which they could legitimately find out what exactly their governments were doing about changing ways of production and habits of consumption in Western Europe.

If her text failed then Simone, as a last resort, might approach an independent country like Norway and see if they would carry her words forward to the final Plenary. Whatever the outcome she felt, and still feels strongly, that the U.N. in the future has to begin to pay much more attention to economic and social affairs and to make the whole world aware of what it is doing. NGOs must keep on lobbying to make this happen.

In any case Simone would be returning again to the next Sustainable Development Commission Meeting and would no doubt be urging her government and others from developed countries to remember the saying, "The rich must live more simply that others may simply live."

Notes

1. Lovera-Bilderbeek, Simone. *The Challenge of Integration: Biodiversity and Consumption and Production Patterns.* Netherlands Committee for IUCN. 1995.
2. Major Groups Caucus on Sustainable Consumption and Production. Recommendations. Third Session of Commission on Sustainable Development. April, 1995.
3. Interview with Simone Lovera, April 10, 1995.

8.   Straddling Fish Stocks

One Monday morning in 1995 saw one of the great conference halls at the U.N. almost transformed into a courtroom. The occasion was the start of the United Nations Conference on Straddling Fish Stocks and Highly Migratory Fish Stocks, and this seemed like a good time to get on with refining rules for fishing on the high seas, which had already been laborously written into the 1982 Convention on the Law of the Sea.

Instead, Mr. Brian Tobin, Minister of Fisheries and Oceans for Canada, chose to use this occasion to put the case against Spanish fisherman, who in the past year had been grossly overfishing for cod on the Grand Banks just outside the 200-mile Canadian territorial limits.

He spoke with some feeling as 40,000 Canadian cod and flounder fishermen had already been put out of work and were sacrificing their livelihoods in order to give the fish stocks time to regenerate. Canadian patience with distant water fishing fleets had run out, and so the Canadian government had decided that year to arrest a Spanish vessel, the *Estai*. What they found on board confirmed their worst suspicions. The catch was almost entirely juvenile fish, who had had no time to spawn. When it was arrested, the *Estai* cut its net and sent it to the bottom of the sea. But the Canadians recovered it and found it was made up of an illegally small mesh exactly right for catching juvenile fish.[1]

Commissioner Emma Bonino, on behalf of the European Union, speaking for the Spanish, objected strongly to this case for the "prosecution" and put the case for the "defense." This unilateral seizure of a ship on the high seas was, she declared, simply illegal. Further, the Law of the Sea, which had recently come into force, laid down rules to be followed in a dispute. She claimed the story about the net was a fabrication and no one except the Canadian authorities had actually seen it after it was recovered.

The real culprit, she argued, was the Canadians themselves who had been grossly overfishing the cod in their own waters and now the world had to suffer because of their failure to preserve these fish stocks, which she said were the heritage of mankind, a part indeed of the Global Commons like clean air and unpolluted oceans.[2]

This argument between two countries who are usually allies was surprising and disturbing, but no doubt would be resolved before there was further violence.

Meanwhile this latest dispute highlights the urgent need of this conference to draft an agreement which can follow through on the Law of the Sea where it comprehensively says (Article 25), "States have the obligation to settle their disputes by negotiation, enquiry, mediation, conciliation, arbitration, judicial settlement, resort to regional agencies or arrangements, or other peaceful means of their own choice." This gave the conference plenty of detailed work to do and the arrangements they would make for the policing and settlement of disputes for overfishing on the high seas would be crucial.

But what of the larger picture? This incident highlighted the simple fact that worldwide in 1995, too many ships were chasing too few fish. And more than that. The overall supply of fish from the oceans was in serious decline. The Food and Agriculture Organization of the United Nations had reported that, "At the beginning of the nineties about 70 percent of the world's conventional fish species were fully exploited, over-exploited, depleted, or in the process of rebuilding as a result of depletion."[3]

Fishermen themselves confirmed that since 1989, catches on the high seas had fallen from 9.1 million tons to 4.7 million tons. The Minister said that some countries, like Japan, had made the necessary transition and now operated responsible distant water fleets. Others had yet to learn what the concept of sustainable development really means when applied to global fish stocks.[4]

The Law of the Sea finally came into force in November 1995, and that convention, which took twelve years to negotiate, will begin to influence the fish diet of everyone, especially city dwellers, now living on this planet. But who knew if tempers would cool, and the current negotiations would succeed?

Notes

1. Address by the Honorable Brian Tobin, Minister of Fisheries and Oceans for Canada. March 27, 1995. P. 1 and P. 3.
2. Statement by Commissioner Emma Bonino for the European Community. March 27, 1995. P. 6.
3. Statement of Ambassador Satya Nandan, Chairman of the Conference. March 27, 1995. P. 2.
4. Address by Tobin.

9.   An Indian Perspective on the Fisheries Dispute

There is a crisis over the world's fish supplies. Greenpeace says it is caused by "massive overfishing, declining and collapsing fish populations, enormously wasteful levels of discarded bycatch, and tens of billions of dollars lost annually because too many factory boats are competing for too few fish."[1]

So the nations came back to the U.N. in 1995 trying to produce a treaty which will guarantee a livelihood for all, not least, of course, for the fish. At a meeting of such importance NGOs concerned about the future of fishing gather around. One key figure is Sebastian Mathew from India, who works for the International Collective in Support of Fishworkers. His organization, based in the south India Port of Madras, but also with a regional office in Brussels, exists to protect the livelihood of fishermen who catch fish inshore, and who run small family businesses. Such people fear the greed of big foreign factory ships and their style of catch-all fishing.

Sebastion is an economics graduate who became involved in the battle against pollution in the '70s. He fought the battle against big dams in India and then, one day, saw the pollution created in coastal waters of the Indian Ocean by a local factory which was making titanium. He realized that the livelihood of the local fishermen was at stake. He soon found that there were other fishing communities in the Philippines, in Malaysia, in Madagascar, who were also under a similar threat. He began to realize the plight of small fishermen was a world problem, and that big and small fishermen might soon be coming to blows.

Sebastian wants to see the factory fishermen compelled to use selective fishing gear. He wants to see the long-term sustainability of the global fishing industry maintained. And he wants to see fishing fleets monitored, and those who break the rules by over-fishing brought to court. But he also knows that the big owners will fight hard to tone down the regulations, which are being negotiated.

256

But his special interest is in the working conditions of the migrant workers who man the big fishing fleets. They are often cheated out of the pay and expected to work outrageously long hours. He feels nothing less than a special U.N. Conference should be called to take up their cause. The International Labor Office (ILO) in Geneva cannot do it, because the owners of the fleets refuse to join in the ILO system. This current U.N. Fisheries Conference is already arguing that the exploitation of migrant workers falls outside their terms of reference.

Sebastian remarked that but for the great U.N. Rio Conference on Environment and Development in 1992, he probably would not be present at U.N. Headquarters. Rio set the tone, created the precedents, and made the involvement of NGOs alongside governments possible. As result, Sebastian noted that the bureaucrats, whether in Brussels, Manila, or Dakar are learning to listen to the fishermen. As he put it, "Nowadays from a fisherman's viewpoint, the oceans of the world are one big lake."[2]

Notes

1. Greenpiece Press Release. July 26, 1995.
2. From an interview with Sebastian Mathew. August 2, 1995.

10. Day for a Fisheries Treaty

The atmosphere in the Trusteeship Council Chamber was almost festive one morning at the end of 1996. In a message, the Secretary-General said everyone should have "quite a feeling of elation." And the reason? This was the day to sign the Final Act of a treaty, just negotiated, on the Conservation and Management of Straddling and Highly Migratory Fish Stocks. Of course the treaty will not come into force immediately. Parliaments have to ratify treaties, and that might take a year or more. In this case, thirty states have to ratify before the treaty becomes law.

But the signing would get the treaty well and truly launched. And it is a treaty which is needed for very important reasons.

First, the Food and Agricultural Organization (FAO) has warned that fish stocks worldwide are in serious trouble. More than 70 percent are over-fished, depleted, or slowly recovering. Admittedly highly migratory fish are only 20 percent of the total, but new rules for how to treat them will set a standard for all kinds of fishing, and will stop the abuse of uncontrolled fishing in all the world's oceans.

Second, this Treaty is a part of a detailed implementation of the much larger Law of the Sea Treaty, which was finally passed in 1982. This monumental treaty was first proposed by Malta, one of the U.N.'s smallest member states, in 1967. Negotiations under the able and indefatigable Chairmanship of Ambassador Tommy Koh of Singapore were finally brought to a close sixteen years later in 1982. Even then difficulties over sea-bed mining rights took another ten years to be resolved satisfactorily.

This Treaty on Fish is part of a huge map—the new Law of the Sea—out about how best to look after that vast area of the oceans which fall outside the jurisdiction—normally a 200-mile-limit—of any nation. This is what is called protecting the Global Commons—plants, fish, mammals, minerals, which exist in the oceans outside the jurisdiction of nations.

The Treaty on Fishing and Fish Stocks is coming at the end of a year in which there was a serious confrontation between Canada and the European Union about cod fishing rights in the North Atlantic. Both sides needed a law to restrain them, and both needed an arbitration process to settle disputes. Now they have both.

This Treaty comes at the end of three years of intense negotiations. And no wonder, because the Treaty adopts a *precautionary* approach to over-fishing. It will work out fishing limits and fishing protection *before* fish stocks have been reduced to practically zero. So it will be a treaty which has, at its heart, the aim of making all fishing in the oceans indefinitely sustainable.

So the simple ceremony began. The chairman, Ambassador Satya Nandan of Fiji, who had steered these difficult negotiations, begun in 1993, to a hopeful conclusion, said a few words of welcome. He expressed his pleasure that the agreement had finally been reached by consensus. A small table was set alongside the dais. States who were ready to sign, signed in alphabetical order. Among the first to sign were Antigua and Barbuda, Argentina and Australia, and that gave an immediate and encouraging global spread to this new commitment of nation states towards a common future under the rule of international law.

This Treaty sensibly curtails the absolute right of nations to fish where and when they like on the high seas. It also establishes the way for regional organizations to set up a workable procedure for settling fishing disputes. So far, so good.

But the Treaty does not solve all the difficulties of modern industrial fishing. There are still too many fishing boats, often receiving subsidies from their governments, chasing too few fish. Fishing near the shore, for shrimp for example, continues to damage the coastal environment. But this Treaty is a start—and it ought to lead on to still better arrangements for sustainable commercial fishing on the oceans worldwide.

Everything will now depend on the regional arrangements which will now be put in place by the Member States to monitor fishing in deep waters and to operate a dispute procedure as laid down in the Law of the Sea. According to the treaty, NGOs have an opportunity to take part in the future meetings as observers. It is certain that bodies like the World Wildlife Fund will be playing an important part in keeping governments committed to go ahead now and put the practical and legal arrangements in place. This will ensure the long-term protection of this vital oceanic source of food for millions.

11. Water Follow-up

The follow-up to Rio is a gigantic task. All the issues—saving forests, clean air, protecting mountains, fighting deserts, preserving clean oceans—require urgent and sustained work on them. But none deserves more urgent attention than getting fresh clean water to the millions who do not yet have it.

Water may often be free, but that does not prove it is unlimited. Far from it. Indeed 97 percent of the world's water is salty and undrinkable, and 2 percent is groundwater and not easily accessible. That leaves only 1 percent freshwater on the planet and most of that is tied up in glaciers or icebergs!

In following up all Rio issues, the partnership between governments and NGOs is proving essential. But it is not a smooth partnership and never will be. Governments tend to praise their own achievements and be vague about what they have not done. NGOs are likely to be negative and critical. NGOs concentrate on how much there is still to do. But so far both sides have been meeting fairly amicably at the Commission on Sustainable Development (CSD), which has been set up by the U.N. to turn the words and proposals from Rio into actions.

Meanwhile, the Stockholm Environment Institute has been asked to do a world survey of fresh water and report to the CSD in 1996. On the face of it all that is necessary is to determine what parts of the world have the water; who has too much; who has too little; and most difficult of all, how the supply can be fairly shared among the nations.

The Stockholm Institute will certainly do that. There will be some surprises. For instance, the South Pacific has been called the aquatic continent, but it hardly has any pure water! Antartica, which looks such a vast area of pristine snow, actually is a desert, receiving only two inches of snow a year.

The real difficulty comes when water *use* is evaluated. What people do with it—that's what counts. For instance, what about water harvesting in dry lands? At present both collection and distribution is woefully inefficient and wasteful in situations where every drop is vital, in Israel or Mali for example.

The quantity, or lack of quantity, of water and its use cannot be discussed apart from the price of *supplying* it. Too often those who can least afford it are paying the most for it. Distribution costs are essentially a political issue and a controversial one. Indeed Secretary-General Boutros-Ghali once said that if there is another world war it might well be over water.

Looming over the whole issue is the pressure from the growth of population. Even now the numbers of people in urban areas are causing prodigious pollution of water supplies in urban areas. For instance, 1.3 billion people lack access to safe water to drink, while 1.7 billion lack adequate sanitation services. The cost of boiling water averages 20 percent of family income in developing countries.[1]

The Earth Summit Watch Report sounds the alarm, as the world population increases 92 million each year.

"Worldwide, more than 250 million cases of water-related diseases such as diarrhea, malaria, cholera, and schistosomiasis, are reported annually—resulting in about 10 million deaths a year. These water-borne diseases, which have their roots in bacteria, viruses, or insects, can be controlled and in many cases eradicated by improving water quality and sanitation services."[2]

With all this information and with equally important data gathered on such subjects as lead pollution and hazardous wastes, the CSD should be able to draw up a list of priorities for expenditure so that spaceship Earth can sail on without fatal drainage of the most precious of all its life-giving commodities—water.

Notes

1. 1994 Earth Summit Water Report. Editor Jared Blumenfeld. A project of the Natural Resources Defense Council and Campaigns for Action to Protect the Earth-Cape 21. P. 10.
2. Ibid, p. 10.

12.   Advocating for the World Wildlife Fund

Who doesn't know that the World Wildlife Fund (WWF) wants to save the panda? But much more than that, the whole of nature is the province of this major NGO with fifty field offices around the world. WWF exists to warn the world about the scale of the environmental hazards which these days confront us at every turn.

But just to warn is not enough. WWF is also in the business of providing the world with expert knowledge on key environmental issues, making positive suggestions for the fight to preserve biological diversity, even negotiating compromises with governments to save the planet. And so, of course, the fund is constantly building up its special links with the whole United Nations system.

Working at the U.N. on behalf of the WWF is Joy Hyvarinen from Finland. Joy has two degrees in international law and is the WWF's International Treaties Coordinator.

One of Joy's major preoccupations is the Law of the Sea. This comprehensive treaty took ten years to negotiate and only in 1994 did it receive enough ratifications from member states to come into force. Its provisions now require protocols to put teeth into the treaty. For example, the Law states that fish stocks must be preserved, but the arrangements about how exactly the different regions of the world will do it have not yet been put in place. Yet the governments made a collective commitment in 1995 to make detailed arrangements to deal with countries which overfish stocks, and they have not acted yet.

Another area where WWF is intensely involved is the likely effect of pollution on climate change. Here again the problem is to give teeth to a recent general commitment, made at Berlin to stock to a planned reduction of gases from industry which will create global warming. WWF is trying to get the developed countries, especially the oil lobbies, to realize the dangers and to see that the developing countries are not going to consider slowing down their own industrial progress unless the rich countries are themselves prepared to make some sacrifices in their own levels of consumption.

Unfortunately it is the General Assembly which handles the debate about Law of the Sea and the General Assembly is still one of the areas where NGOs can neither speak nor circulate their proposals for making progress. Joy can and does speak with individual Ambassadors, but that is not enough. Now in 1996, as the General Assembly prepares to debate the subject and to end up with a harmless ineffectual resolution, she is highly critical of the lack of progress.

"This is one of the worst examples of decision-making by the lowest common denominator of agreement I have seen. We must see to it that next year the General Assembly really delivers a proper set of global priorities for the ocean."[1]

On behalf of WWF she spoke out equally strongly on the slow progress in negotiating the details of the fish agreements, recently worked out by the U.N.

"The world's fish stocks are in a catastrophic state. A key criterion for the success of the U.N. Fish Stocks Agreement is its implementation by regional fisheries bodies, most of which seem to be both unwilling and unable to undertake this. The Assembly should treat this as an emergency."[2]

But Joy has not lost faith in the U.N. She still feels that Headquarters in New York is where all the big decisions are made. She still sees the U.N. as not only the place to strive for global consensus, but also the center where forward thinking on the Global Agenda, often fed into the system by the NGOs, can take root. She regrets that the U.N. is still preoccupied with national security issues and has not yet discovered a way to give environmental issues the priority they require and deserve.

Update

In August 1998 the World Wildlife Fund issues a report, confirming its fears about worldwide overfishing. The report suggests that the fishing fleets are too large and that they are now capable of catching 155 percent more fish than can be replaced by normal reproduction.

A possible way to deal with the present potentially disastrous free-for-all would be to issue tradable rights to a percentage of the catch. This had worked well in New Zealand, Australia, and Iceland.[3]

Notes

1. Interview with Joy Hyvarinen, International Treaties Coordinator for the World Wildlife Fund. December 6, 1996.
2. "Should the U.N. General Assembly Debate on Oceans Be Abolished?" WWF November 29, 1966.
3. *New York Times*. August 23, 1998.

13.   A Citizen Activist from Sri Lanka

Mr. Uchita de Zoysa came to a spring meeting in 1995 of the Commission for Sustainable Development from Sri Lanka. In the past few years in his own country he and his colleagues have won a battle against the construction of a coal-fired power station, stopped thirteen containers of toxic waste being dumped and incinerated in his country, has used the arm of the law to halt fishing with illegal nets by rogue fishermen. He comes, then, to the U.N. with firsthand knowledge of a whole range of the key issues that came up at the Environment and Development Summit at Rio.

But does that make him feel good about the Rio process? Definitely not! He feels that at Rio in 1992, a great chance was missed to come up with something visionary "to save the world." He wanted to see a plan evolve which would safeguard the planet for the next four generations—perhaps for one hundred years.

But he feels there was no vision at Rio. Instead the official Program for Action—Agenda 21—does little more than plan ahead for not more than the next twenty years. He sees the plan as no more than an outline to follow, in order to monitor various parts of the earth's environment. And even then it is not a complete agenda. He sees it as a plan to compel the third world to adopt a market economy drawn up to benefit the rich countries.

But for him the priority remains in getting things right at home in Sri Lanka. He believes "the South" has to develop itself. He has a vision of his own society holding on to its rural roots and building up a network of villages made up of extended nuclear families. He believes that the rush to the cities is already slowing down. And in his communities there will be less travel and so less need to consume fuel for travel. He considers that in the alternative society he envisions, the nation state should dwindle both in power and influence. And groupings should emerge based more on social and regional differences.

His vision for the future is not the same as the currently fashionable "Civil Society." He believes the majority have an unreasonable faith in the market and in the business. He wants to develop an alternative economy in which Sri Lanka is no longer chained to the ups and downs, mostly downs, of a world market geared to cheap labor and low prices for primary commodities. He feels sure that the people—and the people are not the same thing as the NGOs, the Non-Governmental Organizations—will know how to get this new society in order. For him the very term NGO has a certain limiting tone about it. His vision will produce a self-sustaining society which will be right for Sri Lanka, but others may gain some insights from it.

He knows it will be hard to get people to follow the path he favors. Since the Gulf War, CNN, with its consumer emphasis, has made great inroads into the culture of Sri Lanka. And the present emphasis on the wonders of the free market will certainly not do much to divide wealth fairly between the rich and poor.

But coming to the U.N. is still useful for him. He meets people from all over the world, who have had different experiences. He is not enthusiastic about meetings in New York and prefers Geneva. The meetings in America, he says, get dominated by too many Americans, whom, he thinks, argue too much amongst themselves.

The Commission on Sustainable Development will meet for three weeks. Uchita de Zoysa will continue to feel an uneasy tension between his own vision for the future, and the plodding sectoral analysis about environmental issues—the follow-up of Rio—of the bureaucrats and diplomats.[1]

Note

1. Interview with Uchita de Zoysa. Commission on Sustainable Development. April 16, 1995.

14. Fighting Desertification

The United Nations Development Programme (UNDP) is in the business of fighting deserts. Most of the time people think of deserts in terms of Africa and the Sahara desert, a great empty space endlessly whipped by terrible sandstorms. They think of stopping the relentless southward march of sand dunes by building miles of fencing, by planting shrubs and grasses. But this is less than half the desert story.

Deserts and arid lands are on all continents. Some even call Antarctica a desert. But the biggest problem is not the deserts but the huge dryland areas along their borders. People live in them. These lands, always short of water and often afflicted by droughts, are the borderlands where the people live and struggle to make a living. These borderlands are in nearly 100 countries all across the globe and these harsh conditions affect the lives of nearly 900 million people. Seventy percent of these lands are over-exploited by the inhabitants and their livestock and so the U.N. always talks more accurately of fighting, not deserts, but "desertification."

So how does UNDP and its special desertification arm, the Office of Combat Desertification and Drought (UNSO) tackle this vast problem? Experience has taught that the experts from Head Office are very often not the experts! The real experts are the local inhabitants. Not only do they know their animals and their crops, but they also know where the grazing rights are and who owns the cultivable land. Behind them stand the regional government and even, at a distance, the central government itself.

Mr. Firuz Sobhani is Chief of the Technical Unit of UNSO. Born in Iran, he spent 17 years in Burkina Faso on the edge of the Sahara. He felt so much at home in that young country that he eventually became a citizen of this

264

French-speaking West African State. He told a story which illustrates the kind of mistakes made by "the experts" in the old days.

"In one country I know well they put in a large plantation. There had been a great shortage of firewood. Things went well for a while. Then suddenly the young trees started to die. Experts were called in, but they could find nothing wrong. Only that the roots of all the trees that failed did seem unaccountably disturbed. Eventually, the explanation emerged that the local inhabitants were creeping out at night and shaking the roots. They wanted to kill the trees, because they believed they would all now belong to the government, and not to the original owners of the land on which they were planted!"[1]

Firuz Sobhani stressed that everything done by his unit was done in close consultation with the local people. He gave the example of how areas undergoing severe degradation in Mali had been rescued by replanting a local aquatic grass called bourgou. It thrived on the flood plain and provided fodder when all else had dried up. With the help of funds from Australia and Norway, plant nurseries were established. Rootlings were carefully grown and transplanted. Areas that had been denuded of grass came back to life. And most important, those people who had the right to graze the land and to harvest the crop before it became degraded, took back their traditional rights.

Mr. Sobhani explained that lessons about how to achieve involvement and consensus with the local inhabitants in new projects could be translated to other parts of the world. Lessons learned in Africa were now beginning to benefit people in the semi-desert regions of Bolivia, Mongolia, and Uzbekistan. In order to succeed, projects now involved several different U.N. Agencies—FAO, UNICEF, UNEP—for example, and the United Nations Development Programme (UNDP) had the job of coordinating and integrating these different specialist inputs.

The greatest step forward in getting on with the fight against desertification in the nineties has been the Convention on Desertification which came about as a result of the Rio Conference on Environment and Development. This convention now has more than 40 participants. They include countries which have deserts and dry lands, and those that do not, but who feel a responsibility to help. A global consciousness about deserts and desertification now exists and a global mechanism to do far more about this constant threat is emerging. If the U.N. has anything to do with it, deserts can and will halt and turn back.

Postscript

With 50 signatures, this desertification Convention came into force in October 1996. All those nations who have signed it have to take concrete steps to fight desertification and to report periodically to the U.N. about the progress they are making.

Note

1. From an interview with Firuz Sobhani. March 15, 1996.

15. Domination by Drugs

The drug problem with its inevitable links to international crime and terrorism, will not go away. Mr. Giorgio Giacomelli, Director of the U.N. International Drug Program (UNDCP) based in Vienna, spoke out about this essentially international crisis at the Third Committee of the General Assembly in 1996 where he said:

"Today drug abuse and illicit traffic have emerged as one of the major threats to public safety and national security. The danger is not only to the individual but to the very fabric of society."[1]

Since the start of the twentieth-century, international cooperation in the field of drug control has been increasing all the time. In 1909 the first attempt to limit the shipping of narcotic drugs was in force. Since that time a whole range of Treaties have been put in place. The 1998 U.N. Convention marked a climax to this work. This Treaty bars all havens to drug traffickers by making provision to extradite drug traffickers, to confiscate drug assets, and to provide mutual assistance between states on drug-related issues.

In 1997 the Chief of the New York liaison office of the United Nations International Drug Control Program (UNDCP) was Ms. Sylvie Bryant, an American. She showed more than ordinary dedication to her job through her networking with other departments at U.N. Headquarters, with specialized Agencies such as the United Nations Children's Fund (UNICEF) and the World Health Organization (WHO), and with civil society. She recalled her first encounter with the world of drugs when she was growing up in New York.

"I saw young women addicts doing a heroin dance on the street. They nodded their heads as if they were about to fall over and collapse in the street. It was frightening. They were so vulnerable. I always have believed drug dealers are merchants of death."[2]

She went on to explain her view of the future shape of campaigning against drugs.

"You have to combine carrot and stick. Sometimes, I believe, we overstress the role of the police and the military angle. There has to be education for public health as well. And we must create new development plans which include incentives for growing alternative crops, together with the creation of a whole new range of social services for local communities. UNDCP in Lebanon and now in Myanmar is pioneering these kinds of alternative agricultural development programs."

The New York office of UNDCP is one of twenty offices around the world which are part of the global network centred on Vienna. More than 90 percent of the funding is coming, not from the U.N.'s regular budget, but from voluntary funding by concerned nation states.

The Austrian government financed a young Austrian, Sabine Bauer, as an associate expert to assist in the New York office. She is a graduate in law and keen to work in the international field. As a result of her experience, she concluded: "The drug problem is respecting no national boundaries. Therefore it cannot be solved by one nation alone, but they have to join their efforts. We are only the facilitator and advocate of their efforts. Without member states' political will to do something against all global threats—such as the drug problem in all its dimensions—nothing moves. To me the U.N. is most like an elephant which moves slowly forward, one foot at a time."[3]

Both worldwide and in the U.S. most people don't yet know about UNDCP, and what it seeks to do. They are simply not aware of the legal commitments, which the nations of the U.N. have already made to combat the menace of drugs. So in 1988 the General Assembly held a Special Session on the whole subject to heighten global awareness and renew the collective commitment of member states to combat this formidable and persistent menace.

Dr. Klaus Kinkel, Federal Minister for Foreign Affairs for Germany, summed up the scale of the problem when he noted that the annual turnover of the international drug cartels totals $400 billion—8 percent of world trade. And he added "Behind this figure is a tale of untold suffering."[4]

The Drug Summit of 1998 confirmed that the governments were solid in their view that no one nation acting alone could solve the drug problem. Indeed they made a special political declaration to that effect, affirming that they did indeed have the political will to overcome the scourge of drugs by international cooperation. But they went further and affirmed that states acting alone could never solve the problem. Regional attention to the issue would be crucial, as would public opinion and the work of concerned Non-Governmental Organizations. Governments are passionate that they will collectively achieve "real and measurable results" in this war which threatens both individuals and ultimately the stability of nations.[5]

Notes

1. Speech by Mr. G. Giacomelli, Executive Director, UNDCP. Information Letter. December 1996, p. 10.
2. From an interview with Ms. Sylvie Bryant.
3. Ms. Sabine Bauer. January 28, 1997.
4. Speech by Dr. Klaus Kinkel, Federal Minister for Foreign Affairs, Germany, on the occasion of the United Nations "Countering the World Drug Problem Together," p. 2.
5. Political Declaration. Resolution 1 A/S-20/4, June 1998.

16. Cities for the Twenty-first Century

The U.N.'s series of summit conferences in the nineties begun in Rio and ended in Istanbul turned out to be a sort of continuous planetary parliament. These gatherings of thousands caught people's imagination far more than the annual meetings of the U.N.'s General Assembly have ever done. The final conference in the series, The Cities Summit in Turkey, turned out to be a fitting climax which pulled together everything that had been learned over the last five years. It was held in 1996 and some called it "Doorstepping the Millennium."

Dr. Uner Kirdar, the Special Representative of the Secretary-General at the Summit, spoke about his reasons for being optimistic about the way ahead. Appropriately he is himself from Turkey, where his father was a famous Mayor of Istanbul.

"This conference was much more than simply a 'Cities Summit,' as the press sometimes called it. All the insights of the previous conferences could now be slotted together and assembled as the last building-blocks in a building designed to make Human Security possible for the very first time for the whole human race.[1]

"Let me tell you about these building blocks. First we recognized that economic and social development have to go forward side by side. At the Social Development Summit in Copenhagen we had seen the necessity for that parallel progress so clearly, and at Istanbul we were glad to see industrial companies, including Turkish companies, who were also realizing that *social* responsibility was in their own self interest.

"There is a new recognition, not least by government, that they cannot do it all by themselves. What is needed is more governance and less government. Iniatives must come at least as much from the bottom up as from the top down.

"But what is 'governance'? Governance is a partnership between all who have authority to get things done in the cities and in the nation at large. Governance is all the arms and legs of the civil society working together in a new kind of harmony. In particular, in cities especially, local authorities have to be the social innovators—in some cities they practically run things anyway.

"But there are other building blocks in creative governance. Business has to be involved. Furthermore, businessmen are now developing their social awareness through organizations like Rotary International. There are many other partners in emerging city and global governance—professional organizations, labor unions, media networks, civic bodies.

"And then there is also a whole range of Non-Governmental Organizations. Since I ran the first Habitat Conference in Vancouver in 1976 I have seen NGOs grow enormously in numbers and expertise."

Dr. Kirdar enthused about the way NGOs and the other parts of this new partnership with governments dialogued in special gatherings at the Istanbul Summit. He said that in the old days, NGOs took part in informal activities such as lobbying governments. Now they have moved from indirect participation to direct participation! At Istanbul as the Plan of Action emerged, NGOs were involved all along in working at it. The NGO text of suggested amendments to the official Conference Text was, for the first time ever, printed as an official document.[2]

Being a Turk himself, Dr. Kirder was particularly pleased that the arrangements in Istanbul worked splendidly. And even though Turkey is a Moslem society, he was pleased to note that no one seemed to object to the presence of groups made up of people of different faiths, like the Wisdom Keepers, speaking about their commitments.

Dr. Kirdar, who has himself been a pioneer for the U.N. in thinking creatively about development in recent decades concluded on a thoughtful note:

"We still have to find a way of carrying the poor along with us in all our new partnerships. In a generation we shall have twelve million people in Istanbul. Other world cities will be larger still. These people have their own dignity. And their own wisdom. If we do not lift them along with the rest, then the social fabric of our great cities will be too fragile to survive the frustrations of the masses."

Update

Mr. Klaus Toepfer is the new Executive Director of the United Nations Environment Program (UNEP) and was responsible for the Habitat Center at Nairobi. In October 1998, he came to the U.N. to emphasize the crucial importance of cities in the 21st century. Mr. Toepfler, a former Minister for the Environment in Germany, said: "Marshall McLuan introduced us to the concept that we all live together in a 'global village,' but now it is surely much more appropriate to talk of a 'global city.' By the time my daughter reaches fifty, 70 percent of the world's population will be living in cities. And much more than that, the peace of the whole planet depends on our creating cities for the public good, cities which are not segmented into different areas for the rich and poor. I am glad our center is located in Nairobi. We see poverty every day and we know without the involvement of the women in the urban community we cannot overcome it."[3]

Notes

1. From an interview with Dr. Uner Kirdar. October 9, 1996.
2. A/Conf. 165/INF/8.
3. Mr. Klaus Toepfer at a Second Committee Seminar on the implementation of the Istanbul Human Settlements Conference. October 29, 1998.

Walkabout

Four

Professor Tono Eitel, ambassador of Germany to the United Nations. (Photo: German Mission to the UN.)

Mr. Vadim Perfiliev, Director of the General Assembly and ECO-SOC Affairs Division in the Secretariat from Russia and his secretary Ms. Isabelle Martinez from France. In the background is a painting of the monastery of Zagorsk in Russia. (Photo: W. Grey.)

UN flag raising ceremony by steelworkers topping out the Secretariat Building, 5 October 1949. (UN photo.)

In September 1996 President Clinton signs the Comprehensive Nuclear Test Ban Treaty on behalf of the United States. The United States Congress has yet to ratify the treaty. (UN photo: Evan Schneider.)

The interior of the meditation room inside the United Nations. The design was inspired by Secretary-General Dag Hammarskjöld. (UN photo.)

Mr. Giandomenico Picco, former Under-Secretary-General and hostage negotiator from Italy, meets with Rosemarie Waters, President of the UN Staff Union to Commemorate the Day of Solidarity with Detained Staff Members, 1998. (UN/DPI Photo: Eskinder Debebe.)

Thirty-eight volunteers from Greenpeace, an organization which campaigns for greater protection of the environment, chain themselves to UN flagpoles in a protest against the United States for its reluctance to sign UN treaties pledging to reduce its emissions of greenhouse gases, 1992. (UN photo: M. Tzovaras.)

Non-Violence. This bronze sculpture by Karl Fredrik Reutersward was pre-sented to the UN by Luxembourg. (UN photo: M. Tzovaras.)

1.   At the U.N. Post Office

It is not possible to buy a United States stamp inside the U.N. This is as it should be, as of course the United Nations is international territory with the right to issue its own stamps. It does six times a year and visitors flock to the U.N. post offices to pounce on the latest offering and then to take it to be stamped as a First-Day Cover with either a New York, a Vienna, or a Geneva postmark.

And U.N. stamps have an important extra dimension. Since 1966, the World Federation of United Nations Associations (WFUNA) has produced a limited edition series of art prints by the world's best modern artists which appear alongside the stamps on the First Day Covers. The creator of this imaginative idea was Annabelle Wiener, the Deputy Secretary General of WFUNA. Since 1966 she has put her unique knowledge and enthusiasm for contemporary artists at the service of the U.N. Annabelle calls each stamp and cover design "a tiny message of peace." Each print which she commissions is tied in to an agency, accomplishment, program, or aspiration of the U.N.

The program originally began with a presentation of an original watercolor by Salvador Dali to mark WFUNA's twentieth anniversary. Since then there have been contributions from Alexander Calder, Victor Vasarely, Krisna Reddy, and Andy Warhol, and even Jacques Cousteau offered a drawing which he said had been inspired by the Irish Book of Kells.[1]

Marc Chagall, a Russian who lived in France, was one of the most famous artists invited by Annabelle to contribute. His drawing of angels are world famous and he did one especially for the U.N. in 1967. At that time the fashion for stamp-collecting was at its height, and the day of the issue there had to be extra security at the office of WFUNA.

Most recently Yuri Gorachev has made a drawing for the endangered species issue and Rudolf Mirer from Switzerland has produced a set of drawings to be used for the fiftieth anniversary of WFUNA in 1966.

Annabelle recalled that sometimes artists did not quite come up with what was required. She asked William Gropper to do a drawing on the theme of racial discrimination. Everything was fine, except the white man looked and dressed just like Uncle Sam. She tactfully told the artist that she wanted "a generic white man." He found the expression baffling, but he substituted a less American figure in the drawing instead.[2]

A recent highlight has been the work of the famous Chinese artist, Ting Shao Kuang, who did a special set of imaginative drawings for the Women's Conference in Beijing. Although he now lives in America, the Chinese had a reception for him in Beijing while the conference went on.

281

Each year WFUNA distributes nearly 100,000 press releases and information sheets which highlight some aspect or other of the work of the U.N. A
whole team of volunteers help to sell the stamps and so project the work of
the U.N. worldwide. For First Day Covers, great care has to be taken to tear
the sheets exactly in the middle of the perforations.

The Secretary-General celebrated the importance of the work of the World
Federation of United Nations Associations in his own words, "WFUNA has a
central role to play in democratizing the United Nations."[3]

Notes

1. From an interview with Annabelle Wiener. Deputy Secretary General of WFUNA. December
   17, 1995. 1. Ibid.
2. Ibid.
3. WFUNA Art and Philatelic Program. November 1995.

2.   A Visit to the Thirty-eighth Floor of the Secretariat

For most of the eight thousand people who work in the Secretariat, the 38th
floor is forbidden territory. This floor is entirely given over to the Secretary-
General. There are only two elevators that go up there and security is very
tight. This is the office of the man many would call a secular Pope.

When the elevator finally reaches there, the corridor is wide and the whole
floor is quiet. Through the windows, New York City and Long Island stretch
out to the horizon. The Atlantic Ocean is in sight. Immediately you sense that
the S-G, as he is usually known, has surrounded himself with a dedicated team
that is hard at work. It does not matter that he himself may be a continent away
on a diplomatic mission: he can be reached by telephone or fax almost instantly.

It *was* a surprise to discover that when Boutros Boutros-Ghali of Egypt
was the Secretary General that, though English is the predominant language
throughout the Secretariat, the working language of the S-G's personal staff
was French. Although he was fluent in both English and Arabic, he preferred
to speak and write French. He liked short sentences and simple language.
Besides a small group of senior staff in the Secretariat, he had with him two
long-standing friends and colleagues from his days in legal and government
circles in Egypt.

It was often simply not possible to make literal translation of his speeches from French into English and vice versa. The result would too often be unbearably awkward. David Stephen, who was his speech-writer in English, who was also completely at home in French, explained, "For his speech to the Social Summit in Copenhagen we had to render into English 'un neuveau projet de vie collective.' Literally that would translate into 'a new project of collective life.' That would be almost meaningless. So we really struggled to render it better, and finally came up with simply 'new ways of relating to each other'."[1]

There was and is also a continuing problem with the difference between English suitable for Europe, and English suitable for America! Professor Herve Cassen covered French; David Stephen European English; and Professor Charles Hill American English.

And then again, the U.N. was and is awash with yet another kind of English—U.N. bureaucratic English. This often turgid style of reporting the progress of diplomacy pervades most U.N. official documents and did not mix at all with the way the S-G liked things to be expressed. Finally, U.N. texts of all kinds always have to be translated into the other official U.N. languages—Arabic, Russian, Spanish, and Chinese by the professional U.N. translators. This, too, is no work for computers: it requires the personal touch.

It is fitting that the corridors of these offices on the thirty-eight floor should be dominated by a fine series of etchings—presented by King Juan Carlos of Spain—celebrating the five hundredth anniversary of the birth of Father De Las Casas, who, in the name of what is now known as "universal human rights," so fearlessly condemned his own nation state, Spain, for its genocidal treatment of Indians in the New World.

Note

1. From an interview with David Stephen. November 9, 1995.

Part Nine

Media

1. Information at the U.N.

Seven million people every month visit the U.N. site on the World Wide Web! That is a measure of how much progress the U.N. has already made in making its work available on the Internet to the global constituency.

The General Assembly has chosen Ambassador Ahmad Kamal from Pakistan to head the working group to develop further the U.N.'s expertise in this age of Infomatics. Ambassador Kamal has spent most of his career in multilateral diplomacy and has been Pakistan's Ambassador in New York for the past three years. Before that he was the Ambassador to the U.N. Regional Office in Geneva where he was especially concerned with issues of Human Rights and with trade negotiations. He knows the U.N. inside out.

The Ambassador explained that the entirely new way of looking at things that the Internet is now making available to all has to be seen in the context of the first fifty years of U.N. history. The Ambassador gave a summary of the way the victorious powers expected the U.N. to work in 1945.

"The victors of 1945 made the assumption that they would be the victors forever. That's why they arranged permanent seats for themselves on the Security Council and claimed the perpetual right of veto. Permanence, I believe is an attribute of God, not of human beings! This was never a democratic arrangement. It has often been abused by nations seeking their own national interests. As time has passed the wars that have occurred have been within states rather than between them and that is a situation that the charter did not foresee. Indeed since 1945 more people have died in the two hundred local and regional wars than the total in the two World Wars together.

"I believe the U.N. cannot relate effectively to the future unless changes are put into motion which are generally recognized to be feasible, periodic, and genuine.

"The Charter's arrangements have failed to provide the means to overcome the world's poverty. Indeed the gap between rich and poor has been growing greater than ever.

"And now we are seeing the rise of civil society. Governments are no longer the only actors on the world stage. Non-Governmental Organizations—through academia, through think tanks—are raising fresh voices. Citizens now have instantaneous access to information on a global scale and it makes no difference whether they are sitting in Tierra Del Fuego or the Gobi Desert. They are a tectonic force and if governments try like King Canute to resist this force, they are bound to fail.

"And business, the private sector—again not well-recognized in the charter—is moving more than a trillion dollars a day around the globe without consulting governments at all. That is why the Secretary General recently called a meeting of thirty top business executives to meet with U.N. officials to see how the U.N. can relate more effectively to the vast power of the multinational business community."[1]

The Ambassador described how he had been conducting his own "jihad" to create an awareness that eighteenth-century ways of doing diplomacy were completely outdated. He noted that all the permanent missions to the U.N. were now hooked up to each other and linked to the Secretariat. The Africa group and the European Group could exchange information by computer in complete confidentiality. People had instant access to the texts of all General Assembly resolutions since 1974. Connectivity has increased exponentially. These developments would probably result in a savings of 25 percent of the amount of paper currently used in the conduct of U.N. business.

Ambassador Kamal has also been in the thick of negotiations to make it possible for Non-Governmental Organizations to take a greater part in U.N. deliberations. At present their right of access and the right to speak is formally limited to only one of the five main committees of the General Assembly—the Economic and Social Council. He has found these negotiations very difficult so far.

"Governments find the idea of power-sharing very difficult. Yet the people want to act and not necessarily relate all the time to their governments. So I believe there has to be a new partnership between governments and civil society at U.N. Headquarters.

"Of course there are problems to overcome. Non-Governmental Organizations at the U.N. are still too dominated by Western NGOs. We have to find a way to correct this global imbalance and make it possible for people from the developing countries, who outnumber those from the North by four to one, to attend.

"We have, too, to strike a right balance in the representation of NGOs. We can't let fringe organizations speak for more people than they actually represent. It is up to NGOs themselves to sort out their representation in a fair and responsible way.

"I support the idea of holding a People's Assembly. But it must not just be a one-shot affair. It must set in motion a process, leading to action. It can be an important way of alerting everyone in our civil society of what is at stake for the future of the U.N.

"The U.N. is the only universal multilateral organization we have. We have to reform it now. Reform includes doing away with waste and duplication. Also future recruiting must bring in younger technologically competent staff: the average age of the present professional staff is around fifty. Only if we carry out wide-ranging reforms will we create a U.N. that will be truly credible and useful for the next fifty years ahead."[2]

Ambassador Kamal has demonstrated that every month the U.N. is refining and improving its commitment to the information revolution. But no one can yet tell which part of the U.N. will benefit the most from this new technology. Governments and the Secretariat will undoubtedly be able to share information and points of view far quicker than in the past. But probably more significant in the longer term will be the way that everyone, and especially women, will be able to find out instantly how the U.N. is handling their interests. The peoples will be enabled to be vastly more in control of their future and their fate.

Note

1. Interview with Ambassador Ahmad Kamal. April 9, 1998.
2. Ibid.

2. Telling the U.N. Story by Radio

Communicating the U.N. message by radio has been going on for more than 50 years. In spite of all the emphasis on television, computers, and the Internet, radio is still the main way to reach people all over the world.

U.N. radio is now big business. Eighteen hundred stations worldwide receive U.N. broadcasts in 6 official languages and 11 other. Portuguese, for example, has recently been added to the list. U.N. Radio produces more than 1,000 features and documentaries every year, though nowadays the emphasis is rather more on news coverage and wider dissemination. More than 70 United Nations Information Centers around the world monitor the effect of these regular broadcasts on thousands of local communities.

But as the U.N. gets bigger and more complicated, how on earth do the broadcasters decide the content of the broadcasts? They are greatly helped about deciding priorities by the standing Committee on Information, made up from the member states, who decide the priorities. For instance in the nineties, the committee decided to put the stress on advancement of women, children, drugs, crime, and human rights. And now, reflecting hopeful changes, especially in Africa, Latin America, and Eastern Europe, the latest progress of the emergent and restored democracies has been chosen as a special high-profile subject.

Most recently the conference about commercial sexual exploitation of children in Asia held in Sweden has been given special attention. This conference was a three way cooperation between UNICEF, the government of Sweden, and the NGOs. At this time of acute shortage of funding the U.N. is finding new ways to carry out its programs by creating partnerships with others who care about the same crises as does the U.N. itself. Child prostitution was exactly this kind of subject.

Each broadcaster has latitude to concentrate on subjects judged to be of special interest to their own special audience. For example, Peter Mischenko, a citizen of Ukraine, broadcasts to a large Russian-speaking audience in Russia and Eastern Europe. He knows his particular audience wants to hear about progress in dealing with the Chernobyl tragedy and what UNDP, WHO, and UNICEF are doing to help the recovery from this disaster. His listeners are also especially interested in human rights, environment, and peacekeeping in Georgia and Tajikistan.

Interviews are an important component of U.N. radio programs. To mark International Women's Day, twenty-five women who have done remarkable things to protect the environment were honoured at the U.N. Maria Cherkasova came from Moscow to see her portrait on display and tell her story to Peter Mischaneck. Maria is an ecologist, famous for her part in leading a campaign to halt construction of a hydro-electric dam on the river Katun.

Peter Mischenko is in no doubt that U.N. broadcasting has its own special aims and its own flavor.

"I believe U.N. radio complements national broadcasting. We try to give a multi-dimensional picture. From the letters we receive people often expect the U.N. to do impossible things for them, like mending the roof of their house! Another person who had heard our program on micro-credit wrote to complain that something ought to be done about the stingy lending policies of banks in his region. These responses, even if sometimes misguided, at least show that ordinary people do have faith in the U.N. and believe it can help them to live better lives."[1]

Peter himself is proud to be a citizen of Ukraine.

"We are a country of fifty million people. We have always been a nation, but only now have we become a state. During the Cold War, Ukraine always had a separate seat at the U.N., as did Belarus. This meant we kept going some training of diplomats and we had a degree of international exposure and experience. Indeed I believe that without our special U.N. status since 1945, when the Soviet Union broke up, we probably could not have become a functioning independent state so quickly.

"I am glad to be working at the U.N. in this first century of its creation and growth. I feel I have been, and I still am 'in at the creation.' This is an inspiring feeling which never leaves me as I daily strive to communicate from our broadcasting studios what the U.N. is doing around the world."

Note

1. From an interview with Peter Mischenko. March 7, 1997.

3.   Making Development into News

David Lascelles from the *London Financial Times* came to a meeting at the Sustainable Development Commission together with other media experts, to discuss how the U.N.'s current agenda can reach the press. He quickly puts his finger on the problem: "Sustainable Development can never go in a headline." Quite!

Almost all economic and social development—the heart of more than half the work of the U.N.—is not news, because it is not 'immediate.' As Barbara Pyle of CNN put it, "News is what happens today; not what might happen tomorrow." The media wants to report crises. The fact that the planet, that the whole global environment may be one gigantic crisis is not news at all. Barbara Pile put it another way, "The present situation is like trying to warn a blind man about to walk off a bridge. But it is not news till he actually jumps."

Worse still, the actual slow forging of sustainable development policies in the U.N. chambers with endless chopping and changing of words and texts is even less newsworthy than stories from the field. Again Barbara Pyle put it exactly, "You'll never get the media to cover a room with men in dark suits talking about brackets around words." And yet it is in these chambers that the global community is revealing just how much or how little it is prepared to put financial muscle behind the fight against world poverty and in favor of conserving the global environment.

"Relate it all to people—that will link it to the political agenda, and that is the media agenda"—that was the message of Maurice Strong, the eminent Canadian, who was the architect of the Rio Summit in 1992.

Maurice is right. The abstract generalized language of U.N. documents turns people off. Concepts like 'system wide approaches,' 'linkages,' 'internal resource mobilization,' even 'empowerment' and 'gender equality' are all dead in the water when it comes to interesting journalists.

291

The Security Council, on the other hand, can make news because its business is so often to tread along the thin line dividing war from peace. But the continuing problem is how to make the battle against poverty newsworthy.

There are other difficulties too. Sometimes as Michael Keats of Interpress pointed out, the country which is absorbing a major developing project like a dam may prevent journalists getting close to it. They may fear that news of harm to indigenous people affected by the project will leak out. They may fear there will be a taint of corruption somewhere and someone will 'talk.'

The U.N. finds it almost impossible to report controversy. There is, as Ian Williams, the doyen of U.N correspondents, put it, "a blanding machine" at work in the U.N. Department of Public Information. So the tales of hard-wrought compromises worked out late at night at the last minute by skilled diplomacy never get told by the media. Civil servants cannot present "news" and journalists mostly not wish to read their handouts.

Development stories will only "fly" if the light in them is balanced by the shade. Human nature cannot bear to read about unadultered success. It is said that we all have enough strength to bear our friend's misfortunes. But it will be a brave civil servant or administrator who will risk offending his boss and dare to tell the tale of a project "warts and all." But at a stretch, development can be made readable and the U.N. has to keep trying to do it both in pictures and in words now through the electronic media.

4. Reflections of an African Broadcaster in French

"You see, when you first come to the U.N. you are full of ideals, energy, and goodwill."[1] Those are the words of Philippe Gouamba, who has just retired after twenty-three years as a U.N. civil servant. Philippe was the first person from his country, the Republic of the Congo, to serve in the U.N. Secretariat. But was he as full of enthusiasm about the U.N. system when he left as when he arrived? Unfortunately not!

His career, while it had its good moments, was tarnished by disappointment and frustration. In fact things started off well enough. He worked in the Office of Technical Cooperation and went abroad to see the fruits of development plans, hatched at Headquarters, in action. In Africa he saw and heard of all sorts of good things happening—more education of women, making essential bore-holes for water in Chad, taking the first census in Upper Volta. Even now he singles out for special praise the work of the World Health Organization

(WHO) and the work of the United Nations Educational, Scientific, and Cultural Organization (UNESCO) on illiteracy.

But when he moved over into the Department of Political Affairs, he began to experience the atmosphere of the Cold War. Things should have gone well, as he had already had experience of working in the Ministry of Foreign Affairs in Brazzaville. But they did not. He felt frustration in this new job because there was no visible result of his work for the Security Council. In a department with a Soviet Russian in charge, Philippe commented on those years.

"I worked with the Soviets, not for the Soviets. I always thought of myself as an international civil servant. I was proud to work with the Soviets—intelligent people."

These were the days when the veto was used frequently. Philippe saw the U.N. then as a double-edged institution in which there was intensive use and abuse of power by the five permanent members of the Security Council. Philippe recalls that when Rhodesia declared unilateral independence and Mozambique was attacked, the whole world was against this illegal act, but no less than three of the nuclear powers on the Security Council used a triple veto to prevent any effective action to protest the invasion of Mozambique. Further, from the personal perspective, Philippe Gouamba felt that in the daily course of office politics, his color was definitely a disadvantage.

But a welcome break came when Philippe was seconded for a year to be Head of the Namibia Commission's Office in Luanda, capital of Angola. As a civil war raged on, he saw the confrontation of the two superpowers from a different angle and realized that in that struggle there was only one victim—Angola. He worked hard to find ways to arrange training for Namibians in exile and when finally independence came to Namibia under U.N. auspices, he was proud to have worked with the government-in-exile.

When eventually the Cold War ended, there was an enormous reorganization in the U.N. Philippe felt like a victim of the collapse of the Soviet Union, and found himself moved sideways. He noted that countries that became free and independent like Poland, Hungary, and South Africa began to make their influence felt at the U.N., but the permanent members still continued, as before, with the use and abuse of power to protect their interests.

While he would much prefer to have remained in the political mainstream—he had an additional degree in political science from St. John's University, Long Island—he found himself in the French language section of U.N. Broadcasting to Africa.

To his surprise, this work turned out better than he had hoped. When travelling abroad he even found people recognized him on airplanes and commented favorably on his broadcasts. He remarked about this new experience late in his career, as a sink-or-swim journalist.

"Broadcasting was fun. But we had to stick strictly to the official press handouts put out by the Spokesman for the Secretary-General. These texts came to us in English. We had to wait 24 hours for the official French version and by then the subject was often not news anymore. I am bilingual, so I can understand the English version of things, but I still had to wait for the official translation. I am afraid the French language feels to me like the poor relation at the U.N. And the present financial crisis only makes it worse for French, because translation is always expensive."

Although his career in the U.N. did not live up to his original high expectations, Philippe declared he still has a positive view about its future and he feels glad to have dedicated those years of his life to the U.N.

"The U.N.—especially the Agencies—is doing a tremendous job. Going back to my own country, Congo, I can see how basic services are improving. As we say, 'No politics on an empty stomach.' Now we have to make people much more aware of the practical improvements that the U.N. is making all over the world. So many people still don't realize that it is so often the U.N. that is providing the things which they really need and want."[2]

Notes

1. Interview with Philippe Gouamba. October 9, 1996.
2. Interview with Philippe Gouamba. November 6, 1966.

5. Televising the Global Agenda

In recent times, the image of the U.N. on world television has not been a good one. Mostly the U.N. has been seen in the midst of muddles—in Somalia and in Bosnia-Herzegovina. Peacekeeping operations have got all the publicity. Somehow all the other work the U.N. has been doing—on development, on the environment, on issues of family life—has simply failed to make any impact on the public imagination. So what has gone wrong?

Has in fact anything gone wrong? Here are the views of Steve Whitehouse, a member of the Secretariat from New Zealand who is a television producer for the Department of Public Information. He makes a convincing defense that given the small scale of its resources, the U.N. has, all along, been doing quite a lot right in telling its stories to the world. Steve put it like this:

"In the early days, the U.N. had an easier run. Nowadays the climate has changed. There is more realism, even skepticism, about expenditure on international activities. But above all television networks today are much more selecting and ratings orientated. We in the U.N. have to be professional, too.

"We have to stop being too much like a fifties-style bureaucratic operation. If we give the networks stories that are timely, well-presented, and marketable, they will show them. There is, for example, an entirely new interest nowadays in the environment and in women's issues. Every year our unit produces some sixty three-minute 'shorts' on all sorts of U.N. issues and every one of them gets shown in one country or another.[1]

"We cover stories that show U.N. involvement which the other networks—Reuters, Worldwide Television Network—may be overlooking. For instance, recently we did a story on Burmese refugees in Bangladesh. We covered the plight of whales and penguins in Patagonia. We focused on the campaign for re-afforestation in Cape Verde. We keep a watch on U.N. peacekeeping operations that are not currently in the public eye, like in Angola or Western Sahara, and we are steadily building up an archive on peacekeeping activities worldwide. People want to see stories videoed in the field. Television is not a good medium for showing stories about diplomats and international bureaucrats in suits meeting in conference rooms."

Steve Whitehouse went on to point out other ways in which, contrary to the ill-informed critics, the U.N. is getting good coverage. The recent spate of U.N. summit conferences got surprisingly broad coverage by outside companies. People did want to hear about global population and housing issues. They did not want generalizations. They did not want hand-wringing. But they did want to hear about practical solutions to deal with the problems.

Steve explained that, perhaps because Ted Turner, CNN's founder and chief executive, is an idealist, CNN has always been pro–U.N. Over the past eight years, CNN World Report has shown some 500–600 items filmed by the U.N. and CNN will use U.N. material on its American news channel if it is noteworthy and well-produced. Ted Turner spoke passionately at the U.N. about his support for the U.N.'s priorities, saying, "I don't want a world in which Arnold Schwarzenegger mows down everyone in sight."[2]

There are problems, of course. One is that the budget for U.N. filming operations is so small. Steve put it this way.

"You wouldn't launch a toothpaste in Chicago with the kind of money the U.N. system budgets for video. Or," said Steve, "to put it another way, the U.N. craft is not like a giant battleship, more like a small boat, rowing frantically."

Another problem, as Steve explained, is that diplomats and civil servants are inclined to blame U.N. public relations when, in fact, it is often the lack of substantive progress that is the real weakness. Diplomats rather like secrecy, so it might help if the work of the Department of Public Information (DPI) could be set up to operate more independently under an intergovernmental board, rather like the way the BBC handles its publications arm.

In spite of the constraints, U.N. filmmaking keeps on going. Steve Whitehouse says of himself:

"New Zealand is a rich, developing country. I was brought up in an atmosphere where prosperity depended on the price fluctuations of primary products. So understanding the economic problems of the developing world did not require a great leap of my imagination. We have a lot more stories to tell of the U.N. in action around the world, and, within the constraints of our budget, we shall keep on doing it."

Notes

1. Interview with Steve Whitehouse, Television Executive of the Department of Information (DPI). November 4, 1996.
2. Ted Turner at the U.N. World Television Forum. November 22, 1996.

6. A South African's Odyssey

Climbing up into the ranks of professionals in the U.N. is never easy, and sometimes the obstacles seem almost insurmountable. But the story of Sindiwe Magona is proof that however formidable the difficulties, it can happen. Sindiwe was raised in the slums of Cape Town, South Africa, and was forced to leave high school early, because there was no money to pay her school fees. She had only the lowest qualifications to teach the youngest children. Then at twenty-three, when she was expecting her third child, she was deserted by her husband. Sindiwe described the agonizing situation in which she found herself:

"How on earth was I going to bring up three children? I was motivated by only one thing—pure, naked fear. I was reduced to getting hold of sheeps' heads from the local butcher on credit and scrubbing them clean to sell as meat."

For Sindiwe, these were the worst years of apartheid and she was not even a citizen in her own country, South Africa. Later, in order to survive, she struggled through four years of domestic service. Eventually she just managed to scrape together enough money to resume her education. She completed high school, took a degree by correspondence from the University of South Africa, and finally with the help of a scholarship, she earned a master's degree from Columbia University in New York.

She was asked to join the U.N. as a part-time translator of her South African language, Xhosa, and eventually she was made a permanent member of the Department of Public Information. Her job was to broadcast to South African exiles in North America, the Soviet Union, Zambia, and Zimbabwe, and to inform them about all the things the U.N. was doing. She broadcast about educational opportunities for exiles and told the story of how sanctions were building up against apartheid South Africa. Later, she wrote and broadcast her own scripts in English for a worldwide audience. She commented on those years:

"I knew the U.N. was dealing with all sorts of other useful things—human rights, the status of women, de-colonization, but I was happy to be locked into this anti-apartheid work. I found myself a member of a vibrant unit. We were keeping people's spirits up—even inside South Africa itself they would risk listening to us—and that helped their morale. Feedback from our listeners, and from people I met in South Africa, proved our usefulness."

Occasional visits to South Africa reminded her of how pervasive poverty still was for the vast majority in her country.

"I remember one visit in the Transkei where one woman begged me to see what I could do about getting a communal tap for her village. It simply did not occur to her to ask for an individual tap for her own house! Rural destitution is a terrifying and humbling thing."

Apartheid finally came to an end and Sindiwe was so happy that her people were free at last. She was then transferred to the work of librarian for the video section. There she has been in charge of a vast amount of footage of development initiatives, which record how the U.N. has intervened all over the world to improve people's lives.

Her particular passion now is to strengthen and expand all efforts being made to educate the girl-child. She welcomes projects, such as those UNICEF is undertaking for them, but she believes there is still so much more to do.

"We have got to expand the horizons of the disadvantaged child. We must bring children into the modern world. Girls must not be doomed to a lifetime of domestic work. There is work out there for them in the sea, in the air, in the wild. If a miracle could happen in my life, it can happen in theirs, too. Let them meet with professionals and see at first hand what they do. To them and to their teachers, organizations such as the U.N., the World Bank, and the World Health Organization (WHO) are mostly still a mystery. We can and we must open the world to them so they can fulfill themselves as has never been possible before."[1]

Note

1. Interview with Sindiwe Magona. Audio/Video Section. Materials Library Department of Public Information. July 17, 1997.

7. The *Earth Times* Alongside the U.N.

The U.N. has its own publishing house, the Department of Public Information (DPI). It is huge, and it reaches out to the whole world via its own information centers located on every continent. The DPI puts out "facts" not "comment." If it expressed opinions it would inevitably offend one or more of the 185 nations who pay for its existence. Therefore the U.N. also needs friendly, but essentially independent publications with offices located near U.N. Headquarters who can make independent evaluations of U.N. affairs. The *Earth Times* provides exactly what is required.

Founded five years ago by Maurice Strong, the Canadian leader who gave the lead address at the Earth Summit in Rio in 1992, the *Earth Times* is under the able editorship of Pranay Gupte of India. Pranay was trained by the *New York Times* and his paper now has a readership of 30,000 global syndication, and an electronic edition. The paper covers, in its own words, "the great issues in environment, development, and population." It covers them from a global perspective, and always finds space for the specifically U.N. perspective in all its reporting.

Pranay Gupte believes the series of U.N. Summit Conferences—on Environment and Development, on Human Rights, on Population, on Women—were something entirely new on the planet:

"I saw them as global town meetings. They focused attention on pressing issues, clarifying them, quantifying them where necessary, and creating machinery for everyone—government, business, and people to implement them. We publish every day while they are going on.

"Diplomats used only to do things behind closed doors. But these conferences were a sort of public global conversation. Things are now out in the open, and the presence of Non-Governmental Organizations at them all added to the public interest and awareness of the issues at stake. I believe more global summits—on Migration and Food Security, for instance, will soon follow before long."[1]

The *Earth Times* takes a positive view of the increased involvement of private enterprise in environment issues. The editor considers the good points of private enterprise are that it has to respond to its shareholders, please its customers, and usually it has to be, and usually is, more economical than governments. Nonetheless, Pranay Gupte stresses that individual countries, especially developing countries, have to increase their skills in monitoring multinational businesses so that the corporations do not by default "take over" the economies of developing countries. Pranay Gupte summed up his hopes for the U.N. in the nineties:

"During the Cold War, peacekeeping was center stage. Now what really matters is the elimination of poverty and environmental security for every citizen on this planet. The Nordic countries and the Netherlands are leading the way in holding up this new vision of things. From now on development simply cannot be divorced from peacekeeping."

Notes

1. Interview with Pranay Gupte. Editor, The *Earth Times*. December 12, 1995.

8.   U.N. Bashing—Nineties Style

U.N. bashing is primarily an American phenomenon. It is a serious disease, but, so far, it has not proved either contagious or fatal. But as the U.S. is the largest single contributor to the U.N. and as long as U.N. headquarters remains on U.S. soil, the disease deserves close and continuous examination. Senator Jesse Helms (R–N.C.), Chairman of the Foreign Relations Committee, summed up his negative view of the U.N. as follows.

"Its bureaucracy is proliferating, its costs are spiraling, and its mission is expanding beyond its mandate—and beyond its capabilities."[1]

Blunt words. But fortunately they are mostly simply untrue! The bureaucracy has in fact been reduced some 10 percent over the past two years. The budget for the next biennium shows a nil increase from the previous two years. Lastly, the mission of the U.N. cannot expand beyond its mandate on security and peacekeeping affairs—and that is surely the area Senator Helms is referring to—without American agreement. The U.S. with its permanent veto in the Security Council, can veto any plans for intervention which it considers not in the American interest.

If Senator Helms has got his facts wrong, why does his summary still strike a chord in the American psyche? The reasons are numerous and all influential in one way or another. Millions of Americans have ancestors who emigrated to America to get away from the troubles of other countries. Their descendants do not want to be drawn back into the problems of these countries. Only reluctantly was America drawn into the two World Wars, and then only when the wars had been raging for a number of years.

Also the memory of the conflict in Vietnam still lingers in the nation's consciousness. Vietnam seems proof that if America gets drawn in to international ventures, Americans will lose their lives in unacceptably large numbers and no lasting good will come of it. Another telling reason for skepticism about the U.N. is the feeling that it does not do a clean clear-cut job in sorting out problems for the international community. Recently it has seemed to fail in Somalia and in Bosnia, and once again there was a high cost in terms of lives lost and money spent. Peacekeepers, as in Kashmir and Cyprus, seem to have to be maintained for years on end without visible result and America has to keep on paying its substantial share of the bill.

Unfortunately the vision of the U.N. as the modern white knight in shining armor rapidly riding in to do what no nation can do by itself holds no water. U Thant, the former Secretary-General from Burma, expressed the real truth of the matter when he wrote the following.

"Great problems usually come to the United Nations because governments have been unable to think of anything else to do about them. The United Nations is a last ditch, last resort affair, and it is not surprising that the organizations should often be blamed for failing to solve problems that have already been found to be insoluble by governments."[2]

This is a much more realistic way of evaluating what the role of the U.N. really is. The U.N., in fact, requires sympathy rather than ill-judged criticism. A Canadian recently put it like this.

"The U.S. acts like an abusive husband toward his wife—using her when expedient (in Iraq, for example), ignoring or beating her when he disagrees with resolutions (in the examples of Israel and Lebanon, East Timor, and Indonesia)—and withholding support payments (or, in this case, dues) like a 'deadbeat dad.'[3]

Fortunately most members of the U.N.—all 185 members states—continue to give steady support, if sometimes qualified support, to the U.N. and its agencies. And all is not lost as regards the U.S. Recent surveys in the U.S. have demonstrated that well over 60 percent of the people support the U.N. and the back-payment of dues. President Clinton came to the U.N. in 1996 and gave the official support of his administration to the organization.

Fortunately there are Americans who take trouble to articulate the importance of the U.N. to the U.S. A recent report by the Council on Foreign Relations has this to say:

"The U.N. gives expression to world community; it helps establish international law; it enjoys attention and support, and appeals to idealism among Americans and people around the world, and it realizes, however imperfectly, its charter aspiration to represent 'We, the Peoples' by affording ever-increasing roles to non-state actors and citizen movements in its policy and programs."[4]

Increasingly global problems can only be solved with global solutions and whoever takes up the cause of U.N. bashing, there is no escaping, not even for Americans, the interdependent world in which we all have to co-exist cooperatively.

Notes

1. Jesse Helms. *Saving the U.N.* Foreign Affairs. Sept.-Oct. 1996. P. 2.
2. U. Thant. *View from the U.N.* Garden City, N.Y.: Doubleday and Co., 1978. P. 32.
3. *The U.S. and the U.N.: Can This Marriage Be Saved?* Boston Research Center for the 21st Century. Fall Newsletter. 1996, Number 6, P. 5.
4. American National Interest and the United Nations. Sponsored by the Council on Foreign Relations. 1996.

Part Ten

History

1. The Day of Celebration of the U.N.'s Fiftieth Anniversary

Twice in this century the city of San Francisco has had the privilege of hosting two great milestones in the history of the United Nations. And twice it has risen splendidly to the occasion. But this second time was more difficult than the first.

As the war in Europe came to an end, there was a worldwide wave of joy and relief. On June 26, 1945 half a million cheering citizens welcomed President Harry Truman at the Golden Gate. At the signing of the charter, their acclamation banished a nightmare, and welcomed a vision.

Now, fifty years later, a different kind of celebration was required—more thoughtful, more questioning, yet with an undergirding of thankful achievement running through it. The citizens of San Francisco, under the leadership of Mayor Frank Jordan, set out to create such a ceremony—once again using the Opera House as the stage for the finale. They did it by interweaving the main speeches into a tapestry of words, pictures, and music.

The celebration began with a procession by the ambassadors and a roll call on the screen of the 188 countries which now make the United Nations a truly universal organization. The climax of the event, as in 1945, was the concluding speech by the President of the United States.

There were sad moments of remembrance. Searing pictures of the devastation of the war were flashed on the screen. At the closing ceremony in 1945, Mr. T. V. Soong from China had eloquently summed up how the original parties gathered to sign the charter felt at that time:

"We, of the Chinese Delegation come from a part of the world with teeming populations whom the cataclysm of this war has stirred to the very depths of their souls. They have witnessed the rise and fall of mighty empires: they have gauged by the precepts of their own philosophies, the depths of villainies perpetrated by the exponents of brute force, and they have appreciated fully the majestic surge of the power of free men joined in comradeship."

To mark the unique importance of the signing of the charter in 1945, the Chinese insisted on bringing their own brushes and grinding their own ink before they signed the document.

There were pictures, too, of Franklin and Eleanor Roosevelt. Without the vision of President Roosevelt, there would have been no United Nations. Without the negotiating skills of his wife, there might well have been no Universal Declaration of Human Rights.

There was reflection. Secretary-General Boutros Boutros-Ghali from Egypt said that the United Nations had made it possible for millions of world citizens to win their right to shape their destiny as independent nations. He reflected that the Charter had been flexible enough to allow the creation of peacekeeping, which was a new manifestation of the idea of international solidarity. He considered that much more had still to be done to give women their rightful place on the U.N. Agenda.

President Clinton called on the U.N. to outlaw international terrorism and, addressing especially his American audience, he said that while reform of the U.N. was necessary, that did not mean "turning one's back on the system as a whole and going it alone." He made a commitment to see that the U.S. paid its dues and he proclaimed "on every continent the U.N. has played a role in making people more free and more secure."

There was resolution—in words and in music. David Brinkley, who chaired the ceremony, called for the banishment of "a kind of bloodless, genteel isolationism." American Ambassador Madeleine Albright said, "Let us vow to go forward from this ceremony so that the children in this beautiful city living on the highest hill and also those in the deepest valley in the remotest land will have something precious to share and to safeguard."

The American President concluded, "Let us say No to isolation, and Yes to a brave, ambitious new agenda and, most of all, Yes to the dream of the United Nations." Singers from the San Francisco Opera and the Scarborough Schools Choir accompanied by the Orchestre de L'Opera de Lyon sang Leonard Bernstein's *Make Our Garden Grow.*

There was rejoicing. A fanfare from the herald trumpets of the United States Army rang out. Time and again the audience of 3,700 people punctuated the optimistic speeches, with their sustained applause.

A prayer by Archbishop Desmond Tutu from South Africa and a moving poem by American poet Maya Angelou entitled *A Brave and Startling Truth* lifted the spirits of all who were fortunate enough to be at this finely-crafted ceremony. And when it all came to an end, everyone present was re-inspired to respond to the call of Ambassador Essy from Ivory Coast, President of the General Assembly, "Let us set out on the highway to tomorrow."

2. A Miracle from 1945

October, 1995—the month of the U.N.'s 50th birthday—was the perfect moment to look back to 1945 and recall the words of American Dorothy Robins about the birth of the U.N.:

"How the United States came to ratify the United Nations Charter in 1944–1945 is a story that seems to resemble historical fiction more than history. In some respects it has the elements of a fairy tale. The adherents of international organization conquered the dragons of public indifference and Senate resistance only after intensive labors, and secured the hand of the princess for which they had been fighting. In overcoming obstacles, the heroes gained in knowledge, in stature, and in strength. It is a romance of modern times."[1]

But just how was it achieved when just after the first World War the League of Nations was debated in the American Senate for nine months but then failed to win approval from an isolationist majority? And in both cases, the two Presidents involved—Wilson and Roosevelt, both supporters of new international institutions—were incapacitated at critical moments.

The second time, however, two things were different. First, President Roosevelt started to plan for a new world order back in 1941 before the U.S. had even entered the war. What came to be known as the Dumbarton Oaks educational campaign was the result of four years of imaginative postwar planning by the legendary Leo Pasvolsky and his team who planned the shape of the U.N. on behalf of the American President. The planners, unlike the situation at the end of the First World War, could count on the seeds of a global outlook that were planted as far back as 1935 through the work of the National Peace Conference, other agencies, and far-sighted individuals.

Second, the number and quality of citizen organizations ready and willing to mount a sustained campaign of public education in favor of a United Nations was extraordinary. Their campaign took off, culminating in the Dumbarton Oaks Week. The Union of Democratic Action, for example, released one million copies of a new cartoon-illustrated pamphlet with a catchy title: "From the Garden of Eden to Dumbarton Oaks."[2]

A select team of American women were active in this educational build-up—Vera Micheles Dean, Jane Evans, Rita Kleeman, Mrs. Harrison Thomas, and Dorothy Robins. Joined by the League of Women Voters, they trained 5000 discussion group leaders, who were all to the fore in the intense program of seminars, manifestos, exchanges, and pamphleteering which took place in the lead up to the San Francisco Conference in April 1945, which went ahead while the war was still going on.[3]

It was notable, especially at that time, the way that the American State Department set out to cooperate with the citizen groups and the Secretary of State Edward Stettinius became known as the 'darling' of the concerned citizens.[4]

The government officially appointed 42 consultants, and some 102 others were in San Francisco as observers. The government was taking a risk, as they knew that whoever they chose would inevitably mean that others, more or less suitable, would be excluded. And more than that, this was the first time that "the People" not merely had a ringside seat at a conference on foreign affairs; they were inside the ring itself. The "People" made the most of it!

When Stalin, Roosevelt, and Churchill met at Yalta they concentrated on how to develop and sustain, by military means—traditional "Collective Security." But the "People" at San Francisco wanted to deepen and extend the notion of security. So they insisted that Economic and Social Affairs become an integral part of the charter, and they were far-sighted enough to propose that the whole subject of human welfare and security be linked up with the creation of the World Bank and the U.N. Agencies. They also pressed for the preamble of the Charter to proclaim importance of human rights and fundamental freedoms. Finally they pressed for an article—Article 71—to be in the Charter, which established continuing dialogue between governments and citizen organizations as a matter of right. Never before had "the People" been formally involved like this in a great international Congress.[5]

When the Charter finally came to the United States Senate, it was ratified 89–2 in just five days of debate with the full support of both Democrats and Republicans. It did all turn out to be a political miracle of modern times.

Notes

1. Robins, Dorothy. *Experiment in Democracy*. The Parkside Press. 1970. P. 151.
2. Ibid. P. 93.
3. Ibid. P. 143
4. Ibid. P. 103
5. Ibid. P. 128

3.   Forgotten Founding Father of the U.N.

"Let us now praise famous men and our fathers that begat us." But who deserved that kind of special recognition at the U.N.'s 50th Anniversary? Obviously in their different ways, no reputations as Founding Parents stand higher than those of Franklin and Eleanor Roosevelt. But Roosevelt could not lay the foundations for the birth of the U.N. all by himself. As his health deteriorated, he depended more and more on his Secretary of State, Cordell Hull.

But Hull today is a forgotten man. No picture of him hung at the San Francisco Celebrations in 1955. No stamp was ever issued to commemorate his unflinching international vision for the post-war world. Yet in 1945 he was the sole winner of the Nobel Prize for being *the* Founder of the United Nations.

So who was he? He was an American, born poor and in a log cabin in Tennessee, and he was a lifelong Democrat. In Europe between the wars and even more in Latin America he worked to bring about peace through the avoidance of trade wars. He sat at the right hand of President Woodrow Wilson. As the Second World War raged on, he worked hard to develop an international framework that would be stronger and better than the defunct and discredited League of Nations.

Throughout his life Cordell Hull was a serious and often outraged student of history and biography. In a speech in 1933 he remarked: "It is an amazing commentary on the human race that international law was virtually unknown during the first three thousand years of history . . . the common lot of ninety percent of the human race within the last two hundred years was that of slavery, serfdom, and enforced war service, mainly to gratify the ambition of rulers."[1]

In 1944 Hull succeeded in promoting, at Dumbarton Oaks, the U.N. preparatory conference in Washington, a document which would lead to the establishment of the U.N. in 1945. By that time Hull's health had compelled him to retire as Secretary of State, but his inspired workmanship had made the birth of the U.N. possible.

Cordell Hull's father could not have known how prophetic he would be when he said of his son: "Cord wasn't set enough to be a school teacher; wasn't rough enough to be a lumber man; wasn't sociable enough to be a doctor, and couldn't holler loud enough to be a preacher. But Cord was a right thorough thinker."[1]

Cordell Hull's 'thoroughness' ensured that tricky crucial issues like use of the veto in the Security Council were successfully negotiated with the Russians and the Chinese. And more than that, due to his influence the U.N. was set up as, first and foremost, a global organization, and regional bodies, whose importance Churchill had promoted, were not given equal status in the Charter.

Cordell Hull also took great pains to see the American Congress, especially the Republican members, were kept fully informed about the shape of the new international organization that was to be promoted at Dumbarton Oaks. He always preferred the term "Nonpartisanship" rather than "Bipartisanship" and in that spirit he cultivated the support of leading Republicans like Senator Vandenburg, Governor Dewey, and John Foster Dulles. As a result, when it came to the vote, Congress, which had felt unable to support the constitution of the League of Nations after World War I, gave a ringing endorsement to the birth of the United Nations.

He positioned the U.N. in the framework of viable international politics exactly when he said: "The U.N. deserves and must have the unwavering support of the American people. . . . Let us not on the one hand insist that the U.N. cannot work and we must therefore return to nationalism and isolationism, nor

309

on the other hand urge that the U.N. is inadequate and we must therefore replace it with a world government."³

Cordell Hull was not well enough to attend the Peace Prize Ceremony and that may be one of the reasons why his name has sunk into obscurity. But he sent a message to be read out loud—a message which still resonates today in the midst of so much politics shot through with expediency and drift.

This was Cordell Hull's message to the world.

"The crucial test for men and for nations today is whether or not they have suffered enough, and have learned enough, to put aside suspicion, prejudice, and short-run and narrowly conceived interests in furtherance of their greatest common interest—peace."⁴

Notes

1. *Autobiography of Cordell Hull*, Vol. I. Macmillan. P. 176.
2. Gunnar, Jahn. Nobel Prize Presentation. December, 1945.
3. *Autobiography of Cordell Hull*, Vol. 2. Macmillan. P. 137.
4. Cordell Hull. Acceptance speech for the Nobel Prize. Read by Lithgow Osborne, American Ambassador.

4. A Fiftieth Anniversary Balance Sheet

In the life of an individual, middle age is not the ideal moment to draw up a balance sheet. Too much of a person's life and achievements hopefully still lie in the future. Winston Churchill did not become the British Prime Minster till he was sixty-four and Nelson Mandela did not become President of South Africa till he was in his seventies. But institutions are not individuals. Institutions deserve evaluation much more frequently, and when they are creative and pioneering like the United Nations they deserve a searching examination as they enter middle age.

In 1945, people felt very differently about the U.N. People felt a sense of euphoria about the U.N. Their critical faculties were suspended. But now in middle age, the U.N. has a track record. There are successes; there are failures. The U.N. is itself a mirror of the world and of the nation-states of which it is composed, and for that very reason it cannot but be found to be a flawed instrument for delivering peace and security to Planet Earth. So the question is—just how much is the U.N. flawed?

Its successes have been remarkable. To have carried us through the Cold War without a third world war was notable. But much more than that, the U.N. has now grown into a truly universal body. Millions through their Ambassadors for the first time have a voice in the counsels of nations. The peoples of former colonies can now help to shape international conscience and consciousness. In all of previous history the citizens of the new nations—numbered in millions—were absent in the counsels of diplomacy.

"We, the People," the citizens' organizations which so often transcend national boundaries and national loyalties, have yet to find their full and proper place in its counsels, but the new post-Cold War civil society is giving "the Peoples" opportunities in the processes of the U.N., which in earlier decades would have been unthinkable.

Human Rights Law is another great success. Taken as a whole, it elevates the status and importance of the individual to a completely new level in world politics. But full implementation of covenants and protocols to protect justice for individuals remains unfinished business.

The Universal Declaration of Human Rights launched in 1948 triggered an enormous corpus of declarations, covenants, and protocols which is affecting the laws of all nation-states. Crucially, protocols allow individuals to appeal over the heads of their own nation to a higher tribunal. This law, as Professor Schachter of Columbia University aptly put it at San Francisco, is "soft law." It is law not yet backed up by courts, but nations usually find it in their interest to take notice of the finding of the U.N.'s major bodies and the work of its legal experts.

Peacekeeping must also rank among the major successes of the U.N. Recent events in Somalia and Bosnia, however, have tarnished its image. But peacekeeping can save, and has saved, hundreds of lives. It can and does diminish conflict and the suffering of civilians caught up in civil disturbances. But U.N. peacekeeping does not always proceed smoothly. Inevitably, blood has been shed, and more than 1,000 U.N. peacekeepers have already died in peacekeeping operations.

Now for the flaws:

The first thing wrong with the U.N. is that too many nation states still do not pay their bills! At the latest count, the 185 nations owed their "offspring" $2.8 billion. The U.N. system is not a viable system as long as it teeters on the edge of bankruptcy. And in some areas, like human rights, which receives barely 2 percent of the U.N. regular budget, the U.N. is grossly underfunded.

Although Secretary-Generals love to point out that the U.N. spends 70 percent of its income on economic affairs, it cannot yet be claimed that the U.N. has won the battle for development. True, the United Nations Development Program (UNDP) runs many good projects in over 100 countries and U.N. agencies do a great deal of fine work worldwide. But there is a fight against world poverty still to be won, and it is not clear the U.N. has found the formula to make this happen.

Time and again all who have said what ought to be done to reform the U.N. have come back to the matter of democratizing it. The U.N. in its charter proclaims that "We the People" are the driving force of all its ideals, yet the rest of the charter speaks only about the responsibilities of nation states.

And there are plenty of areas in the machinery itself that are not democratic. Membership of the Security Council has to be increased, especially now that the U.N. has 185 members. The General Assembly neither in composition, debate, nor voting could be described as a democratic assembly. Too many meetings which are labelled "closed" could quite well be made "open" to the press and to civil society generally.

The health of the U.N. cannot be properly calculated without consideration of the current strength of American support for the organization. The American undergirding for the U.N. cannot be underestimated. Without the vision and work of President Roosevelt, there would not be a U.N. and, if there were, it might well not have its Headquarters in New York. The U.S. remains the largest single donor, and each American actually pays $7 per head per annum towards its costs.

Fortunately the latest poll shows that as high as 67 percent of the American public have a favorable view of the U.N.[1] But the fever of isolationism—some prefer to call it parochialism—is never completely quenched. Even President Roosevelt back in the 1940s recognized this. At this time of trying to balance the American budget, the U.N. seems, in the short term, an easy place to make cuts. Another disaster like the death of American peacekeepers in Somalia, could prejudice an uneasy public opinion against the whole U.N. system. But if American support were to falter seriously, the U.N. itself would fall victim to the old saying, "If America catches a cold, the rest of the world catches pneumonia."

This mirror of ourselves may be cracked, but we can still see through it and glimpse the rungs of a ladder up to a world in which justice and peace can prevail as they never have before. We have no choice but to keep climbing up the ladder towards this better world.

Update

The creation of tribunals to try cases of suspected genocide in former Yugoslavia and Rwanda and now the passing in Rome in 1998 of a treaty to create an International Criminal Court are encouraging signs that the U.N. legal system is at last acquiring some teeth.

Note

1. News Release. Times Mirror Center for the People and the Press. June 25, 1995.

5. Reflections of the First Secretary-General from Norway

Forty years ago, the first U.N. Secretary-General, Mr. Trygvie Lie, from Norway, published his memoirs. An exploration of what he said then reveals how little changes in the way politics are conducted at U.N. Headquarters in New York.

But of course one thing has changed—Communism has come to an end! How delighted and relieved Trygvie Lie would have been. The rivalry between the two superpowers during the Cold War overshadowed everything he was trying to do. Both sides, and especially the Russians, used the veto constantly. Lie found himself, as he put it, "attacked from left, right and center."[1] Americans accused him of harboring Communists in the Secretariat, and the Russians, during and after the Korean war, became more and more hostile to him personally, boycotting social events in which he was involved and accusing him of being a lackey of the Americans and of the Western powers. Indeed, after seven years in the job he had had enough, and he resigned.

But apart from the political behavior of Communists and some others, Lie's memoirs find him agonizing over just the same things that the Secretaries-General of the nineties complain about. He complains he has so little real power. He complains that he has difficulty in merely bringing matters to the attention of the Security Council. He writes how the nations are ambivalent about even the limited powers which the Charter gives to the Secretary-General:

"I know that there were—there still are—many traditionalists in the foreign chancelleries of the world who would like to see Article 99 of the Charter, and all the political power deriving from it, consigned to an unused constitutional corner to gather dust."[2]

He discovers that the Americans simply cannot understand, when he has a viewpoint which is different from theirs:

"Washington did not seem to recognize that the Secretary-General of the U.N. might, in all honor and intelligence, take a view of a problem legitimately at variance with that of the U.S."[3]

After his first visit to Latin America, he suddenly realized that the biggest battle yet to be fought and won in the post-war world was the battle against poverty:

"A message was handed to me in Latin America, not by statesmen, but by the thousands of dirty, ragged figures that never attended a reception or raised their voices in any fine declaration of faith."[4]

Unfortunately this battle is still far from won. Declarations, policies, options on how best to fight poverty still stream forth from the U.N. And never more intensely than at the 50th Anniversary Year when the latest Agenda for Development was being thrashed over at enormous length by a Group commissioned by the General Assembly.

Over and over again, Lie agonizes over exactly the same difficulties that confront the Secretary-General today. He also muses over the same things that even today are still considered desirable, but not yet possible. Thus on the creation of a U.N. standing force, he said way back in 1948:

"It is possible that a beginning could be made through the establishment of a comparatively small guard force, as distinct from a striking force."[5]

In 1997 that beginning is still only "a possibility," though, due to Danish and Canadian initiatives, standby forces are at an all time high state of readiness.

There has been little change in the powers of the Secretary-General over the past forty years, because that is the way the big powers want it. They want to keep the real power firmly in the hands of the Security Council. Indeed, that is how things are arranged in the charter itself. No one, including Secretaries-General, can get far who does not work with the U.N. system the way it is, and not the way they wish it would be. The system has its strong points; not least that it reflects the realities of politics, the power politics of nation states. Perhaps the last word to those who have disappointed expectations about the U.N. is the saying, "It's the best U.N. we have."

Notes

1. Lie, Trygvie. *In the Cause of Peace.* The Macmillan Company, 1954. P. 417.
2. Ibid, P. 42.
3. Ibid, P. 75.
4. Ibid, P. 325.
5. Ibid, P. 98.

6. Remembering Eleanor Roosevelt

In 1995, Hillary Rodham Clinton, wife of the President of the United States, visited the U.N. in honor of Eleanor Roosevelt, who was being remembered on International Women's Day. She was escorted to the podium by the U.N.'s first female protocol officer. In a clear and committed speech, Mrs. Clinton said her favorite quotation from Eleanor Roosevelt was "We must comfort the afflicted and afflict the comfortable!"

The object of this Women's Day was to link Eleanor's name to the campaign to end "discrimination and class distinctions within the U.N."[1] The words of Secretary-General Boutros-Ghali from last year's Women's Day were recalled, "In November 1992 in my address to the Fifth (Legal) Committee, I said the ideal would be parity for women in policy-level positions by the time of the 50th Anniversary. This target is ambitious."

Certainly it was. And it has *not* been reached; but, slowly, equal opportunity *is* entering the consciousness and the conscience of those who decide U.N. personnel policies. Meanwhile the Group on Equal Rights for Women inside the United Nations is getting stronger, and more impatient, every year.

Stories of how Eleanor Roosevelt made her way in a world dominated by men stirred this audience. Widowed at 61 when President Roosevelt died suddenly before the Second World War was over, she found herself nominated by President Truman to take part in the first U.N. General Assembly in London. The appointment shocked many and someone at that time described her as "an emotional rat-brained woman." Her fellow Americans "dumped" her in the Third Committee where they thought she could do no harm dealing with Social and Humanitarian affairs.

They got a surprise! The Committee hummed with urgent activity and had to try to resolve great issues involving one million displaced persons who did not know if they could or should return to their homeland. Eleanor performed superbly, so much so that John Foster Dulles, later to be a Secretary of State, apologized to her for his original doubts about her competence.

She went from one success to another. She became famous for exchanges with the Russians, with whom she won some notable verbal duels. Without her intervention UNICEF would probably have never come into existence. Then in 1948 came what she thought was her greatest work, chairing 85 meetings of the Committee creating the Universal Declaration of Human Rights.

The Assembly was meeting in Paris and Eleanor's excellent French was much appreciated by the French. But she did *not* appreciate the incredible slowness of the negotiations in her drafting committee. For instance the Russians, officially professing atheism, could not agree that Article 1 should read "All human beings are *created* free and equal." They pressed for and got, "All human beings are *born* free and equal."

At this time she lamented the excrutiatingly slow pace of negotiating texts at the U.N. and remarked that she thought she had reached the limits of which human patience is capable when she brought up a family. But since she had presided over the Commission on Human Rights, she had realized that an even greater measure of patience could be exacted from an individual.[2]

Eleanor Roosevelt demonstrated that it really is possible to be a public and a private person at the same time. Her grandchild, Nancy Roosevelt Ireland, told how her mother's mix of people at her picnics made them just like a small U.N. conference. At home at Val-Kill in the Hudson Valley, she kept a Christmas book in which she carefully recorded the likes and dislikes of 200 special friends. Someone gave her a present of a plaque with her name on it for her desk. On it was carved "Elanor." When friends remarked on the wrong spelling, she just said "Oh! leave it: it doesn't really matter."

When Eleanor was the President's wife, she used to hold press conferences for women journalists only. This forced all the leading newspapers to have at least one female journalist on their staffs. To get things done, she knew a touch of Machiavelli could come in useful every now and then.

Eleanor Roosevelt would certainly have enthusiastically agreed with the message of all the speakers at this special meeting in her honor. If the U.N. can become a model employer, that will influence nation states to give equal employment opportunities to women. It will not happen overnight. But it can and will happen. Hillary Clinton summed it all up exactly, "So, against all odds, the women inch forward."

Notes

1. Proclamation for International Women's Day. Group on Equal Rights for Women at the United Nations. March 14, 1995.
2. Lash, Joseph P. *Eleanor: The Years Alone.* Norton. 1972. P. 78.

7.   Gary Davis—World Citizen Number One

Not everyone who came to San Francisco in 1995 to celebrate the Fiftieth Anniversary of the U.N. was a good friend of the U.N. Some came as severe critics. And of those critics none was more disparaging and impatient of the U.N. as it is at present constituted than Gary Davis. But who is Gary Davis?

Gary Davis astonished the world in 1948 when he deliberately resigned his American citizenship and declared himself a world citizen. This was at the time of the Berlin airlift and he genuinely believed a Third World War was approaching. He had himself flown as a bomber pilot over Germany and his

316

brother had been killed at Salerno. He was determined it must not happen all over again.[1]

At the time of Gary's action the famous French writer Albert Camus wrote:

> Neither Davis, nor those who have welcomed him, pretend to be bearers of truth for the world. They have simply sounded an alarm as best they could, and it is quite possible this alarm was sounded in the desert. But before laughing at it, consider at least the ugly countenance of shame and calculation worn today by some realists . . . and that you, above all, do not throw the first stone.[2]

Over fifty years later, at the age of 76, Gary Davis is as unchanged and unrepentant as ever. He still believes that because the United Nations is a collection of nation-states it can never bring peace to the world. In 1961 he wrote:

> The nation-state is a whole-cloth myth, perpetuated by the slavery of tradition, unreasonable loyalties, and pieces of paper which at best only pretend to recognize rather than bestow existence upon an individual.[3]

Instead he believes that the only sovereignty worth having is that which resides in each individual. He believes individuals can get together without hierarchy and run the world. And in this age of cyberspace he believes individuals can communicate instantaneously and hold global referenda when required. The nation state, he argues, is horse and buggy politics and even if we were to achieve world government under the U.N., it would be rule by Big Brother.

The U.N., says Gary, has not brought peace to the world and the fact that there are twenty million refugees in the world today is a measure of its failure. The only part of the U.N. Gary approves of is the Declaration of Human Rights. And that is because it is essentially a document about the rights of individuals, not nations.[3]

Through the years, Gary has kept his faith. He has steered a course between those who believe he is Christ returned and those who have labeled him a crackpot. He has invented and perfected a passport which he issues under the rubric of World Services Authority. Thousands of these documents have been issued in seven languages and they have often helped people in remote places to establish an identity and sometimes to get them out of prison. He continues to proclaim and explain his creed of world government in his publication, *World Citizen's News*.

Gary himself has been in prison 34 times, but he continues to revel in the description of himself given to him in France back in 1948: "This guy is a nobody, yet he claims to be a world citizen."

Notes

1. Jacket, Ronald Clyne. *The World Is My Country.* Putnam. 1961.
2. Davis, Gary. *The World Is My Country.* Putnam 1961. P. 24.
3. From an interview. June 23, 1995.

8.   The Reformation of the U.N.

During the nineties there were at least three major reports about how best the U.N. could be reformed. One of the most interesting was "Renewing the United Nations" by Brian Urquhart and Erskine Childers. It was weighty, too, because both men — British and Irish — had served for a long time in the highest counsels of the U.N. Without Brian Urquhart's dedicated administrative skills, it is doubtful if the U.N. would have won a Nobel Prize for Peacekeeping in 1988.

The point these experts make is a simple and devastating one. The U.N. was originally meant to be a strong centralized organization in which all the parts are subordinate to control from Headquarters in New York. Instead the whole system became an uncoordinated mess! Too many barons rule independent realms, paying only lip-service to a distant king. For example, when peace was being negotiated in El Salvador in 1993, Urquhart and Childers report that both the U.N. Secretariat and the World Bank were working away more or less in separate compartments — "it was as if a patient lay on the operating table with the upper and lower parts of his body separated by a curtain, with unrelated surgery being performed on either side."[1]

Yet the founders made it absolutely clear what they had expected. It is all spelled out in Articles 57, 58, and 59 of the Charter. As Childers and Urquhart put it, "The imperative phrase in Article 57 was every part of the system 'shall be brought into relationship with the United Nations.'"

It was all quite simple. The General Assembly was to be the embryo world parliament and the keeper of the U.N.'s purse. The Security Council would take care of peace and collecting security. And the Economic and Social Council would be the tip of the spear in the complex battle against world poverty.

Nothing has turned out as planned, but it is especially regrettable that the Economic and Social Council has never become, as intended, a kind of economic Security Council. But it has become, with 54 members, large and unwieldy. It has no control over the U.N. agencies which sit awkwardly at the back during its meetings. Management of global economic affairs rests with the International Monetary Fund and investment priorities are largely determined by the World Bank.

318

The U.N. bureaucracy has rambled far more than ever intended. But the Charter has proved flexible enough for some unexpected, but positive things to happen that the founders never envisaged. The environment has become a center of attention and the vision of sustainable development now looms in front of the Economic and Social Council. Women's economic empowerment is getting far more attention than seemed possible in 1945. The human factor in economic development with a fresh and vigorous emphasis on health and education is also much better understood. These are all signs that even if the system has never yet been put in place as the founders intended, the U.N. can still produce results that build world community.

And nowadays there is, in fact, more cooperation at the highest level through the Administrative Coordination Committee (ACC), which relies on Gustave Speth, the Administrator of the United Nations Development Council (UNDP) to pull things together as best he can. The World Bank, for example, is a regular attender of the ACC.

The U.N. house that has been built has many imperfections, but it is still able to be the voice of the global community, as nothing else can be. The architect, Wallace Harrison, said he had tried to design "a workshop for peace." Anyone who has been attending the Preparatory Committee Meetings—the Prepcoms—for the World Summits in the U.N. basement, has seen the global mingling of peoples, and has felt the energy emanating from these international gatherings, will surely agree that Wallace Harrison's vision was the right one. Of course it is a clamorous workshop down there in the meeting rooms of the U.N. basement, but how could sorting out the politics of 5 billion people possibly be anything else?

Note

1. Childers, Erskine with Brian Urquhart. *Renewing the United Nations System.* Dag Hammarskjöld Foundation, Sweden. P. 187.

9.   Remembering Shirley Temple at the U.N.

Shirley Temple was the most famous child film star of the 1930s, known all over the world for her charm and talent. So what happened when she suddenly turned up at the U.N. in the 1960s? It was a huge surprise. Here she was as an American ambassador on behalf of a Republican administration. But that was the least of it. She was no longer the famous Hollywood film star, but a respected longstanding member of the Republican party. And she wasn't even just Shirley Temple any more: she was Shirley Temple Black.

But she also got a surprise! She discovered what all ambassadors have to learn. No one says anything at the U.N. without first checking it out with their home government; and for an American that means the State Department. In addition there are usually four or five people with ambassadorial rank at the annual General Assembly and the senior one has the last word before the text of a speech even goes for vetting to Washington.

When Shirley Temple Black was at the U.N., the Senior Ambassador was Ambassador Yost. He was not pleased when he saw the draft of a speech that she was about to give on refugees to the Third Committee. At the last minute he called her back to the U.S. Mission across the road from the U.N. This is how Shirley remembers what happened next.

" 'You can't give this speech,' said the Ambassador, shaking a copy provided him earlier. He said it nicely, but declared it was too radical. I had referred to the American Indians as being our original refugees. I used this analogy as the theme of my speech and Yost felt that I came on too strongly supportive of the Indians. Of course, my husband happens to be one-quarter Cherokee, so I had a personal reason for this. I got kind of exercised and I replied: 'What do you want? A puppet in the U.S. Chair? Theoretically, I'm representing the President. I'll bet he wouldn't buck at an expression of regret over past history, particularly when it's true and any schoolchild knows it's true.'

"Yost was taken aback by this argument. At last he said, 'Well, you can give the speech tomorrow, but we will have to launder it a bit.' And how they did!

"It still had the original thrust but it wasn't quite as fiery. It described how the Indians were rounded up in the nineteenth century and marched away for a thousand-mile death march from Tennessee to Oklahoma. Simmered down overnight, I gave it, still a strong speech which suggested U.S. regret over how our own behavior might be construed as an asset in our considering the refugee problems faced by Palestinians, Africans, and others displaced in the world.

"The day I made that refugee speech, Ambassador Baroody of Saudi Arabia came into the Third Committee with a stack of newspaper articles about the refugees, all uncomplimentary to the United States. When I got through my speech, he rose and said, 'I can't believe it, but I am agreeing with the United States. They've said it all.' It was a historical event. He just took his papers and left."[1]

That was in 1969. But in some ways little has changed. Nations seldom apologize for their conduct in the past and never for conduct in the present. Ambassadors still have to follow instructions from their national capitals and now in this age of faxes they are under stricter and more immediate surveillance than ever before.

Shirley Temple Black had struck a modest blow for freedom of speech for American diplomats. For speakers at the U.N. to use the language of apology gets no easier, but it is an approach that in this age of the Truth Commissions occurs increasingly in the language of diplomacy.

Note

1. Black, Shirley Temple. *Representing America*. Edited by Linda Fasulo. Facts on File Publications, 1985, New York, P. 157.

10. Where Are the Guardians of the U.N.'s History?

One person who surely was not rejoicing at the Fiftieth Anniversary was Clio, the Muse of History in ancient Greece. She must have been feeling that the U.N. should take her vocation to encourage and inspire historians of its activities much more seriously.

The reason is clear. The U.N. has never had in place a proper way to record its own history, as it is unfolding. And only an insider could hope to sort out the avalanche of documentation from the Secretariat.

Because diplomacy nowadays is being carried out by no less than 188 nations, the process is inevitably complex and overwhelming. A good example of an important subject where professional historians need to be on hand is the seemingly endless debate on the reform of the Security Council. But for the purposes of history, no one is charting the progress of the nations as they struggle through many contentious debates on their way to reach a consensus on this vital issue.

There are many other U.N. events where it is of the greatest importance to know what really happened. How was consensus reached for the Universal Declaration of Human Rights? Why did the Non-Aligned Movement nations eventually come around to signing the Nuclear Non-Proliferation Treaty when the nuclear powers remain so ambivalent about nuclear disarmament? When and where has the influence of NGO negotiators been important, even decisive? How has the U.N. evolved its method of relating to the American government in Washington?

321

It has never been adequate simply to interview people, especially only senior members of the international civil service who have retired from the U.N. In fact, that is already being done on a limited scale at Yale University. But it is a project almost entirely limited to senior retired people remembering the past. It will inevitably have limited value as a part of the historical record. The voices of those—and many were not "top people"—who were at the heart of critical diplomatic events will be lost. The historians will then have to subsist on a meager and unsatisfactory diet of speeches, press releases, and official Secretariat documents.[1]

The deposit of history is laid down as steadily as the tide brings in the sands of the ocean each day and night and it has to be sifted just as regularly and just as relentlessly. Only a properly-staffed unit based at the U.N. could hope to focus on telling moments in the U.N. calendar and record their significance for posterity.

Once the U.N. did indeed establish a body to do this work. It was called the United Nations Institute for Training and Research (UNITAR). The "Research" did begin, but when the results were ready for publication, nations who found themselves portrayed less than favorably, objected. This part of UNITAR's work was then quietly abandoned and in due course UNITAR itself became based away from U.N. Headquarters in Geneva.

The work of historians can directly benefit the present as well as explain the more distant past. When peacekeeping missions come to end, the key players at all levels need to be de-briefed so that the same mistakes are not simply repeated in the next operation. This de-briefing does happen to a limited extent, but so many of the personnel involved in a mission are on contract and they leave the U.N. immediately an assignment is over. So in all areas of U.N endeavor there is a constant danger of the old Roman saying being proved true yet again, "Those who do not learn from history are condemned to repeat it."

There will always be more than one key to unlock the history of the U.N. and nations will sooner or later have to realize that they cannot hold onto the keys to doors they do not wish to be open. The U.N. is too big for that and the issues are too important. Sooner or later all must submit themselves to the impartial bar of history.

Future generations will wish to know how the U.N. battled endlessly against the outdated limitations of national sovereignty and gradually gave birth to a global civilization based on a universally accepted Rule of Law. We must not disappoint them. No shortage of funds should be allowed to stop Clio beginning her reign at the U.N. as soon as possible.

Note

1. From an interview with Professor Harold Fruchtbaum. November 1997.

11.   Guyanese and Swedish Reflections on U.N. Reform

At its Fiftieth Anniversary, the U.N. was awash with advice about how best it can be reformed. Most of the reforms are about changing the structures. Enlarge the Security Council. Abolish the Economic and Social Council. Appoint a Deputy Secretary-General. The list is endless.

But at a deeper level there are vital questions to be probed—questions about identity, about belonging, about loyalty. If people and nations cannot answer these questions about their commitment to the U.N. in a positive way, then all the structural changes in the world will not make much difference. The public's attitude to the U.N. will continue to be what it always has been up to now. The U.N. is tolerated, respected at times, but seldom admired or loved.

One of the commissions on reform which is doing the most to sell its ideas on U.N. reform has produced a report: "Our Global Neighborhood." It was chaired by Ingvar Carlsson, a former Swedish Prime Minister and by Shridath Ramphal, a former Secretary-General of the Commonwealth and Foreign Minister of Guyana.

This commission has noted that the perception and feelings of the general public about the U.N. really matter and it has this blunt assessment of the situation:

"Save for rare glimpses of what might be possible—as during Dag Hammarskjöld's time as Secretary-General—the people of the world never developed a sense that the U.N. was theirs. It did not belong to them. It belonged if it did to anyone, to governments—and only to a few of those. It was the domain of high politics. It touched the lives of people in ultimate, not proximate, ways.

"A sense of ownership did emerge for a time as the many millions who were notionally part of 'We The People' in 1945 ceased to be subjects of European empires and became citizens of new states, who saw a seat in the United Nations as a seal of their independence. Yet even for them, as for most people of the founder nations, the U.N. remained a thing apart."[1] But the report does not give up. It continues.

"Yet the U.N. is 'us.' It is still made up of ambassadors put there by 'our' governments, and increasingly elected in a properly democratic way. It is 'us—at one remove.' "

When he came to speak at a Renaissance Seminar at Columbia University, Shridath Ramphal, the co-author of the report, spoke with passion about how he believed the U.N. could and would soon come to feel so much more like the people's organization than it ever has before. He stressed how history has moved on.

323

"Nineteen forty-five was a world of sovereign states. But now in nineteen ninety-five power is dispersed. 'People are on the move through international civil society.' And more than that. They are increasingly organized, as in the women's movement, and through the Internet. Sooner rather than later they will come to find a place in the U.N., through some sort of People's Assembly.

"There is a new awareness of our global neighborhood. And with it a fresh sense of interconnection between peoples, leading to a new awareness of injustice. When people have a sense of having been ravished, a new sense of urgency about the legitimacy of neighborhood action arises."

Shridath Ramphal said that the major plank of a new people's involvement in the U.N. should be the Right of Petition to the Security Council. So when people were being persecuted, or threatened with ethnic cleansing, they could appeal to a group of experts tied in with the Security Council. Minorities, of course, he noted, already have the right to appeal to the Commission on Human Rights, but that meets more seldom and does not carry the weight of immediate access to the Security Council.[2]

After this summary the audience could have no doubt that the reforms outlined in "Our Global Neighborhood" were not an optional extra for the U.N. If most of them did not come to life soon, then the whole legitimacy of the U.N. would be at stake. There was not much time to lose.[3]

Notes

1. Carlsson and Ramphal. *Our Global Neighborhood.* Oxford University Press, 1995. P. 226.
2. Ramphal, Shridath. Address at Creating a Civil Society in Our Global Neighborhood held at Columbia University, July 1995.
3. *Our Global Neighborhood,* P. 260.

Part Eleven

Religion

1. Remembering Hiroshima at the Cathedral for the U.N.

The Mayor of Hiroshima came to New York to mark the fiftieth anniversary of the dropping of the first atomic bomb on Japan. The Cathedral of St. John the Divine was chosen as the best place to hold this solemn event because it is so willing to involve all religions in planning its major events. The inspiration and the planning also came from both the Jewish and the Buddhist communities. The Cathedral is proud to call itself the Cathedral of the U.N. and time and again it can, and does, take hold of an important global issue being dealt with by the U.N., and put it on a higher plane of feeling, reflection, and resolve.

By holding this ceremony at this time, the Cathedral was adding its insistent voice to that of the millions, throughout the world, who are determined that a great wave of public opinion will build up to make nuclear testing and the abolition of nuclear weapons happen.

Jim Morton, the prophetic Dean of the Cathedral, struck the right note of remembrance, reconciliation, and warning.

"This is an occasion to celebrate life. We are not here to point fingers. Unless we recall with clarity and truth the awful events of the past, we cannot, as a people, 'have laughter, play, and love' in our future. God help us to remember."

Words alone, however eloquent, cannot by themselves evoke the prayerful response that such an occasion demands. So the drumming of the Soh Daiko Troupe stirred memories to their depths, while the Rushmore Orchestra, playing Bach and Camellia Johnson singing Handel, raised spirits of hope.

Dr. Robert Lifton recalled his experiences in Japan, meeting with those who had been there "on the day." One had said to him, "Such a weapon has the power to make everything into nothing." His plea was that both America and Japan must be still more open in examining the past and moving towards a point where on both sides responsibility, and guilt can be justly apportioned. Only then can everyone move on.

The Honorable Mayor of Hiroshima, The Honorable Takashi Hiraoka, said he believed blame for the disaster of world war could be established, but this was not the occasion to do that. This was an occasion to lament the folly of war. He said: "Let us transcend national security and think about global security. Let us end nuclear testing and bring about the total abolition of nuclear war."

The U.N. Secretariat building may be international territory but it does not exist in a vacuum. So much of the work it does depends on a favorable response from the people of New York. Sometimes it is Mayor Giuliani and his staff who help to carry things forward. Sometimes it is a march of youth from Harlem to the United Nations. Sometimes it is the Cathedral's musicians and actors. Sometimes it is the peoples of all faiths. On this occasion it was the Professional Network for Social Responsibility and the Temple for Understanding, a multifaith society, which, together rekindled at the Cathedral on this summer evening a new flame of international recognition and reconciliation.

2. Freedom of Religion at the U.N.

"There will be no peace between the nations until there is peace between the religions." This famous remark by Professor Hans Küng has every year since the end of the Cold War gained in strength and authority. In the newspapers nowadays we read of trouble threatening between Alevi and Sunni Moslems in Turkey, and in India, Hindus and Moslems manage only an uneasy coexistence. And hardly a day goes by without reports of the continuing dispute between Catholics and Protestants in Northern Ireland.

During the Cold War years it seemed that political rivalry was the real danger to peace. Nowadays, however, when conflict is *within* nations rather than between them, it is religion which is the critical force which so often triggers conflicts.

The question is asked, What can the U.N. do about it? The U.N. has always been cautious about dealing with religion and religious strife. It has always seen itself as more of a parliament than a church. But the framework that it has created to safeguard human rights does include some commitments to protect and enhance religious freedom.

But what about those who have beliefs which are not religions? Like humanists, for instance. In the United States there are four million of them. And what about indigenous religions? They often in a formal sense have no churches or priests. And what about those who believe in no belief—atheists for example? So it has been found necessary in promulgating this right always to use the expression "Freedom of Religion *or* Belief."

So, as is usually the case, the U.N. has moved along excruciatingly slowly to define this freedom. First came the landmark Universal Declaration of Human Rights in 1948. Then came its offspring, the Covenant of Civil and Political Rights, which spelled out in its famous Article 18 the fuller meaning of "the right to freedom of thought, conscience and religion." This convention did not actually enter into force until 1976 when 35 nations had ratified it. But this was *still* not enough to stop religious persecution.

328

Then in 1981 after some 20 years of effort, often driven forward by the NGO community and especially by the indefatigable Homer Jack, founder of the World Conference of Religion and Peace and the Father of the NGO Committee on Disarmament, the U.N. voted for a Declaration on the Elimination of all Forms of Religious Intolerance. This Declaration, of course, was simply repeating what was implicit in the Universal Declaration of 1948. But just to be "implicit" at the U.N. is never enough; it is essential to be "explicit." Nothing less will be good enough to have a chance of protecting victims of religious persecution by shaming their persecutors. The best words are the best weapons the U.N. can forge to fight the battle for this particular human right.

Freedom of religion, which is of course an essential component of freedom of speech, is still not yet well established throughout the world. The U.N. still has to go further. It is gradually getting more comfortable with the spiritual dimension to much of its work and more comfortable with introducing a religious perspective into its statements.

And so, pushed along by the NGOs, it may not be too long before the U.N. moves on to establish a Convention on Religious Freedom. Once a Convention exists, countries who sign it have to make its provisions part of their own domestic laws. Toleration of other religions is still difficult in some countries. But then who ever would have thought that in 1986 the Pope would host a meeting for all the world's major religions in the very heart of Italy at the shrine of St. Francis of Assisi?

In the meantime the U.N. has not left the subject alone. In 1996 the Third Committee, dealing with human rights issues, prepared yet another resolution on the elimination of all forms of religious intolerance to go forward for ratification by the General Assembly. It urged states to invite the Special Rapporteur on Religious Intolerance of the Human Rights Commission, Dr. Amor from Tunisia, to visit to their countries to clear their name of acts of religious intolerance. If he can afford to travel to the trouble spots—and regrettably the U.N. is still spending less than 2 percent of its regular budget on human rights—he surely will.[1]

Note

1. A/C.3/51/L. 47 November 21, 1996.

3. The Pope Visits the U.N.

As the climax of the Fiftieth Anniversary approached, the U.N. needed a visit from the Pope more than the Pope needed to visit the U.N. And this visit was never more timely because of the presnt inward-looking mood in America and the rest of the world. The American Senator Pell recently put it well when he said, "Instead of using reason and analysis to construct a foreign policy, we are using calculators."[1]

On this, his second visit to the U.N. in sixteen years, the Pope made two speeches—one to the diplomats and one to the staff and in both, with all the vigor he can still command, he proclaimed his conviction about the central importance of the U.N. Above all, he stressed that the U.N. is a universal organization with a universal moral manifesto to live by—The Universal Declaration of Human Rights.

Earlier on arrival in America he had said, "Nations, too, need a family: they cannot live alone as orphans."[2] In other words there can be no opting out from the United Nations. As if to underline his message about the universality of the U.N., the Pope composed his speech in all five official languages of the U.N.—Arabic, Chinese, English, French, and Russian.

Before he welcomed the Pope, the Secretary-General aptly reminded him that many in the U.N. family of workers could not be present in New York to hear him.

"They are not here because they are clearing land mines in Cambodia. They are disarming factions in Angola. They are digging wells in Central America. They are inoculating babies in Africa. They are comforting terrified elderly people in Bosnia. They are standing watch on the Golan Heights. . . . "[2]

The Pope praised the work of the staff and said to them, "You create harmony and stability. You see beyond your own cultures and traditions." And then after he finished, he suddenly spontaneously added a few more words to the staff, emphasizing they were of equal importance to the diplomats who had just met him in the same chamber: "You are an Assembly of U.N. representatives, no less important, no less important." Then he left slowly, threading his way through an enthusiastic crowd jammed into every corridor of the U.N. to catch a glimpse of him.

The Pope, of course, did much more than praise the U.N. and its staff. He gave all who heard him a reflection and a meditation on the world in which we live. He spoke of the key importance of the collapse of Communism and Totalitarianism in 1989 in Eastern Europe and how the ordinary person's longing for freedom had, in a uniquely nonviolent manner, won the day. As a citizen of Poland, he had himself experienced the long years of Communist repression firsthand. He summed up the sea change that had occurred.

"The revolutions of 1989 were made possible by the commitment of brave men and women inspired by a different and ultimately more profound and powerful vision: the vision of man as a creature of intelligence and free will, immersed in a mystery which transcends his own being and endowed with the ability to reflect and the ability to choose and thus capable of wisdom and virtue."[3]

The Pope was saddened that everything had not gone on smoothly. He continued.

"The world has yet to learn to live with diversity. Narrow nationalism can lead to a true nightmare of violence and terror."

He begged people to cultivate patriotism, not narrow nationalism. He said the fruit of the flowering of language and culture ought to be "spiritual sovereignty." He stressed that every people had a right to their own culture in which they could work out the meaning of personal existence. He added a cautionary note about the dangers of a people pressing for self-determination at any price:

"The fundamental right to existence does not necessarily call for sovereignty as a state, since various forms of juridical aggregation between different nations are possible—as for example occurs in federal states, in confederations, or in states characterized by broad regional autonomies."

Despite his age, the Pope is still alert, and always ready to add his own personal touch to a ceremony. To the children who sang to him, "Let there be peace on earth and let it begin with me," he remarked, "Do you know what Saint Augustine used to say about singing: 'It doubles the value of a prayer when it is sung,' and now you are adding even more: You pray as children and you have a special power over the Father. Your song will be fruitful."

This speech by the Pope was no mere collection of sentiments. It was a message from a master builder, who, under Communism, had himself endured the worst of times. He could and did speak with a special authority about how best to build a moral structure for the family of nations to create "a new springtime of the human spirit."

Notes

1. Pell, Senator Claiborne. *Washington Weekly Report.* October 2, 1995.
2. Secretary General speech of welcome to the Pope. October 5, 1995.
3. The Pope at the United Nations. October 5, 1995.

4. The Place of Women in the Theology of Islam

When the Commission on the States of Women holds one of its regular meetings, it has been remarked that this gathering is itself almost an alternative kind of U.N. General Assembly. Maybe it is even more useful than the General Assembly, because it meets for a shorter time, costs less, and has a narrower focus—the priorities for women.

The focus is in fact, both a broad and narrow one. The women of Asia, for example, have different priorities from the women of Europe and different cultural hurdles to jump over. So, for part of the day, the women often meet in caucuses which have a regional emphasis.

Moslem women—from Pakistan, Bangladesh, Yemen—are clearing the air about exactly what the Koran says about the relationship between the sexes. Dr. Riffat Hassan, an Egyptian scholar, explained to a group of NGOs that so often 'hadith,' or interpretation, has clouded the actual words of the Koran, and implied that woman has been created inferior to man from the dawn of creation. Thus popular prejudice has proclaimed—and it is a prejudice fed by the Bible as much as by Koranic interpretation—that woman was created from the rib of man, thus making her secondary to him. Eve tempted man, therefore woman is not to be trusted. Woman was created *for* man, because he was lonely.

All this interpretation, explained Dr. Hassan, is confusing and plain wrong. The Koran always speaks of the creation of "humanity." In thirty creation passages Eve is never mentioned! "Adam" refers not just to "man" only, but to the human species as a whole.

Dr. Hassan stressed the enormous advantages of getting rid of these misconceptions. For women who live mostly in villages, and who are still poor and illiterate, this clearing of the air is vital. It is this proper understanding of the equality of the sexes, based on a true understanding of scripture, that will liberate them from domination by men. Pronouncements on human rights, and women's rights in U.N. Charters, Declarations, and Conventions will simply not penetrate the deeply Islamic culture which regulates their daily lives.

Dr. Hassan emphasized that women in Islam have to be permitted to study and interpret the Koran themselves—a right which until recently has been denied them. This knowledge will also help them greatly to educate men on so many social traditions about such matters like divorce or the division of property which are based on custom, and not on religious authority.

A huge step forward was taken at the U.N. Population Conference in Cairo when the women of the entire world proclaimed that they were the owners of their bodies and no one, certainly no man and no government, could tell them what choice they would make about bearing children. Moslem women were a part of this unanimous decision and they will from now on be joining their sisters of all different religions in determining the shape of the family in the twenty-first century.

332

5. The Jains Celebrate a Day of Nonviolence at the U.N.

The U.N. is about nonviolence, because the U.N. is about peace. Nonviolence can never be prompted too much or too often in and around the activities of the U.N.

So it was heartening that the Jains—a 4,000-year-old religious group founded in India—took a day at the U.N. in 1995 to celebrate the life and message of their great modern prophet, His Holiness Acharyara Sushil Kumar Ji Maharaj, who died in 1994. Throughout the celebration in the multi-faith chapel in the Church Center close by the U.N., His Holiness was always referred to by all speakers simply as 'Guruji.' He died exactly one year ago. What was so special about him?

He was the first Jain in 4,000 years to venture overseas and to feel he had a special mission to relate the Jain message to the United Nations. From his base in New Jersey for twenty years, he focused on the central themes of his religion: Ahimsa (nonviolence) and Aparigraha (nonpossession). He spent his life showing how these two imperatives of his religion confront the two great scourges of our present times—the pursuit of war and the abuse of the environment.

Guruji always liked to use ancient Hindu stories to make a point about evils in the modern world. He used to tell this story about Vishwakarma, the architect of the world.

"When Vishwakarma created this world, he threw a feast and invited all the angels and the demons. At the feast delicious foods were served. However, he put a condition that everybody must eat the food without bending their elbows. The demons thought the Vishwakarma had gone crazy after creating the world. How could one eat without bending one's elbow? The demons walked off. The angels were also perplexed, but they thought there must be some logic to this request. They straightened their arms, took the food in their hands, and, without bending their elbows, they realized they could feed each other. They realized that Vishwakarma meant—in this world each one lives with the help of others. We are all interdependent."[1]

Guruji taught that anyone who practises Ahimsa can call himself a Jain. His generous attitude toward people of other faiths gave him the authority to persuade his fellow Indians that when the Pope first visited India, he should be greeted with respect and affection, not suspicion and fear.

Perhaps the highlight of Guruji's impact on the United Nations was his contribution to the work and spirit of the Rio Conference on Environment and Development in 1992. He sent his two representatives, Bawa P.N. Jain, and Shanti Jain Smith to attend the five-week preparatory committee at U.N. Headquarters and at the summit he himself was a main architect of the Declaration of the Sacred Earth Gathering. In his speech at Rio he said, "All Jain holy pilgrimage centers are on the top of hills, and Jain communities have now resolved to arrest erosion and deforestation and intensify the greenery all around."[2]

Bawa Jain is now a leading figure in the U.N. NGO Community and from his new base with the Interfaith Center of New York he is constantly meeting with Ambassadors and other U.N. officials. Jain's influence will undoubtedly be felt in U.N. work where the focus of their faith is especially relevant to such matters as the peaceful settlement of disputes and the work of the Commission on Sustainable Development.

Harold Stassen, the only living American to have signed the U.N. Charter at San Francisco in 1945, has recommended that in a revised U.N. Charter there should be a two-week Worldwide Conference of Religions to complement the work of the General Assembly. If and when this conference ever becomes a reality, the Jains, due to the pioneering work of Guruji, will surely be prominent in its work.

Notes

1. His Holiness Asharya Sushil Kumar Ji Maharaj. Crusader for Peace and Non Violence. International Mahavir Jain Mission. 1993. P. 39.
2. Ibid, P. 33.

6. The U.N. Year of Tolerance

After the fall of Communism with all its dogmatism about the way society works, it might have been expected that there would be a great outbreak of tolerance. But in fact the opposite has occurred. There is now much less tolerance. Racism and xenophobia—often more or less the same thing—are on the increase everywhere.

So the U.N. Year of Tolerance came just at the right time and UNESCO officially launched it in 1995. The NGO community was briefed by Ms. Gosner from UNESCO Headquarters in Paris about what the world could expect.

She painted a somber picture. Since the end of the Cold War, more than 100 conflicts have broken out, mostly different kinds of civil wars. It was particularly noticeable that in Europe things had been deteriorating. Apart from war in Bosnia, she noted that Gypsies had been attacked in Austria and in the past year there had been 120,000 racial incidents in Britain. She added that attacks against freedom of expression and against the marginal people—the victims of AIDS, the homeless was increasing. The main aim of UNESCO was, first to inform people and second to educate them. Simply deploring bad news could never be enough.

Ms. Gosner said that The Year of Tolerance was quite different from all other U.N. special years, as it promoted not a cause, but a *virtue*.

But even virtue can get diluted into a soup of a very weak brew. As Ogden Nash, the American satirist, once put it memorably:

Sometimes with secret pride I sigh
To think how tolerant am I;
Then wonder which is really mine:
Tolerance or a rubber spine?

It is generally agreed that 'People should tolerate each other' sounds much stronger than 'Toleration is good.' In other words the verb sounds so much more positive than the noun. Bawa Jain from India struck a right and positive note in discussion when he said we should strive for a culture of *harmony* and not just a culture of toleration.

Later in 1996, at the Third Committee, the Apostolic Nuncio Archbishop Martino, Permanent Observer of the Holy See to the United Nations, added his own reflections to the sense that there is nothing weak-kneed about toleration when it relates to religious belief:

"My Delegation wishes to affirm that tolerance does not demand that one shares the other's religious conviction or practices. In fact, it implies that one does not. What tolerance does demand is that the other's freedom of religious conviction and practices, provided that the just requirements of public order are observed, he respected and not impeded. Religious intolerance denies others the rights that one claims for oneself."[1]

Certainly UNESCO is not comfortable that the word *tolerance* fully conveys what they will be striving for, not just for a year, but for a decade or more. Federico Mayor, the Director General of UNESCO, came close to the heart of the matter when he explained, "Tolerance is not simply the acceptance of others with their differences, but a spontaneous movement towards others to know them better and to know ourselves better through them. . . ."[2]

In November 1995 the member states of UNESCO gathered in Paris and produced their thoughts on the full meaning of tolerance for the mid-nineties. In their Paris Declaration, they came up with a fresh, thought-provoking and positive definition for the rest of the decade:

"Tolerance is respect, acceptance, and appreciation of the rich diversity of our world's cultures, our forms of expression, and ways of being human. It is fostered by knowledge, openness, communication, and freedom of thought, conscience, and belief. Tolerance is harmony in difference. It is not only a moral duty, it is also a political and legal requirement. Tolerance, the virtue that makes peace possible, contributes to the replacement of the culture of war by a culture of peace."[3]

We are all invited by UNESCO to make the 16th of November every year a Day of Tolerance and on that day to think how we can make the Paris Declaration come alive in our own local community.

Notes

1. Archbishop Renato Martino. Before the Third Committee of the 51st Session of the General Assembly. November 19, 1996.
2. Dr. Federico Mayor. UNESCO NEWS. Vol. 2 No.1, January 1995.
3. UNESCO General Conference Resolution 28, C/5.6, A/51/201.

7. The Search for Values at the U.N.

Since the end of the Cold War, there has been an upsurge of interest in exploring and defining the values by which the U.N. lives. Diplomats continuously debate the role of values, often stemming from religions, in their ongoing political discourse. The NGOs have founded a multifaith Values Caucus. There is even talk of a Parliament of Religions which might offer regular advice on values to the General Assembly.

In a sense it was impossible to talk about values during the Cold War. But values were never absent from the U.N. They remained enshrined in the U.N. Charter which begins with a preamble that almost prayerfully expresses contrition for disastrously failing to live up to civilized values. The preamble goes on to call for dedicated determination in making progress towards affirming the dignity and worth of the human person.

The adoption of the Universal Declaration of Human Rights and its two International Covenants about Political and Economic Rights continued the U.N.'s affirmation of individual and collective values. But there has always been a difference of opinion about which of these values should have priority. Rich nations and individuals tend to give priority to political rights and poor nations and poor individuals give priority to economic rights.

During the Cold War, almost alone among the U.N. staff, Assistant Secretary-General Robert Muller spoke up prophetically about the spiritual vocation of the U.N. Growing up in Alsace Lorraine he had experienced the changing of his nationality from German to French and back again and he knew firsthand the curse of national chauvinism which had brought war to his homeland twice in his lifetime.

In 1978, the Pope spoke at the General Assembly and was a rare voice speaking about his Church's view of the spiritual vocation of mankind.

Nowadays, values come into the U.N. by the front door. But it is not easy to know which ones to highlight. A good place to begin is with issues that are absent from the Charter. Peacekeeping is one such issue. Even the Security Council has felt compelled to get involved with the humanitarian issues of peacebuilding after the end of the Gulf War.

Environment is another matter not touched on in the Charter. How far should we take reverence for life? Will creating an earth charter create a new global consensus about nature and our responsibilities towards the planet?

The Values Caucus has wrestled with some of these issues and senior officials have shown interest in its deliberations. Under-Secretary-General Nitin Desai has addressed the Caucus and even Ambassador Emilio Cárdenas of Argentina, who was at the time President of the Security Council, found time to come and speak about the personal strains on him and on the members of the Council. They were meeting, sometimes twice a day, to resolve the crises that arose in the aftermath of the Gulf War.

The U.N. is awash with large issues which demand strenuous thinking about their moral and religious dimensions. All the religious communities at the U.N.—and there are more than thirty Roman Catholic ones for a start—are getting involved, and together with their colleagues of different faiths, they are trying to insert the right values into the U.N.'s Agenda and into the U.N.'s lawmaking for the twenty-first century.

8. Balkan Prayer Vigil

Dag Hammarskjöld believed that the U.N. needed the spirit of prayer and meditation in all its deliberations. That is why, before he died in a plane crash in Zambia, he created a meditation room at the heart of the U.N. This room was deliberately set well apart from all the debating chambers in the rest of the building. This was to be a room, where all, regardless of church or creed, could come to reinforce the essential peacebuilding work of the U.N. on a spiritual plane.

The Meditation Room is a small rectangular space and the walls are plain and undecorated. Nowhere are there traditional religious symbols of any kind. The furnishings are simple, even austere, with low stools of the plainest wood, arranged in two rows with plenty of space between them. The light in this quiet oasis is soft and dim.

The eye is immediately drawn to, and almost transfixed by a big rectangular block of solid iron stone placed right at the center of this narrow room at the visitor's entrance. This iron block is solid, stark, and intimidating. In contrast to the brutal reality of this object, its whole surface is illuminated by the finest slither of light, and at its base, two avenues of sunlight create a more helpful mood. Looking up it is impossible to guess from where they come.

In his note on the design of the Meditation Room Hammarskjöld had this to say about this stone of iron: "The material of the stone leads our thoughts to the necessity for choice between destruction and construction, between war and peace. Of iron man has forged his swords, of iron he has made his plough-shares. Of iron he has constructed tanks, but of iron he has likewise built homes for man. The block of iron ore is part of the wealth we have inherited on this earth of ours. How are we to use it?"

At the far end of the room there stands, from floor to ceiling, an abstract painting. The shapes in this painting, circles, triangles, and squares, are all in soft blues, grays, and with touches of yellow and black. They all neatly intercon-nect with each other. In the picture there is a twisting symbol for a rope, which seems to stretch from earth to heaven. It is a warm, almost cheerful painting, which encourages aspirations of hope.

This room has over the years been sadly underused, but then suddenly in the nineties the continuing horror of the Bosnian War brought the room back to life. A global prayer vigil for peace in the Balkans was declared for thirty days in August and September 1996. Two imaginative and persistent U.N. women, Elvie Ruottinnen, a journalist at the U.N. from Finland and Maria Almeida from Goa and President of Pacem in Terris at the U.N. determined that the U.N. should join in this vigil. They had the idea of bringing together in this meditation room the three key Ambassadors involved in the conflict. They invited the Ambassadors of Croatia, Yugoslavia, and Bosnia-Herzegovina to meet there. And, to make it an even more solemn occasion they also invited the then current President of the Security Council and some of its members to join with them.

At first prospects looked unpromising. An aide to the Croatian Ambassador said that in view of the recent atrocities the Serb had no right to be on UN territory. The women responded that the U.N. Meditation Room was God's territory and God would welcome all. Then two days before the proposed

338

Meeting there was another bombing of Sarajevo and the Ambassador from Bosnia reacted strongly, "My people will never forgive me if I speak to the Serb." In response they pointed out that it was going to be a silent vigil. And so, in the end, against the odds the vigil took place.

After a while the Indonesian Ambassador Wishnamurti, President of the Security Council for that month, came out and said that all was well and that he, a Moslem, had led a prayer. As they all emerged, the two women presented each participant in this prayer for peace with a long-stemmed pink rose to mark this moment of reconciliation.

Hammarskjöld would surely have felt the room had come alive at this key moment and that this unique gathering had been a part of laying the groundwork for the end of the war and the start of peace.

The first ever summit-level meeting of the UN Security Council at the end
of the Cold War, 1992. Secretary-General Boutros Boutros-Ghali from Egypt
is addressing the council. (From left to right) Prime Minister Boris Yeltsin
(Russia); Prime Minister John Major (United Kingdom); President George
Bush (United States). (UN photo: John Isaac.)

Willliam Epstein, a Canadian, who has been
a leading advocate for disarmament at the
UN for more than fifty years. (UN photo.)

Carrying firewood in Rwanda, Central Africa. The World Bank estimates that in 1999 more than three billion people were living on less than two dollars a day. (UN photo.)

James Wolfensohn, President of the World Bank, visits a favela in Brazil to see the new clean water supply, funded by the bank. (Photo: World Bank.)

Brazil was host to the United Nations Conference on Environment and Development held in Rio de Janeiro in 1992. Bella Abzug, then President of the Women's Environment and Development Organization, addresses the conference. (UN photo: M. Tsoveras.)

In 1990 the United Nations successfully organized a general election in Namibia and a peaceful transition to independence for this new African nation.

Ambassador Julia Alvarez has represented the Dominican Republic at the United Nations since 1978. (UN photo.)

Children visit the United Nations and look at a mosaic of Norman Rockwell's painting inscribed with the words "Do Unto Others As You Would Have Them Do Unto You." (UN photo: J. Isaac.)

Conclusion

Six years have gone by since I began to put the *U.N. Jigsaw* together. And the puzzle is not finished yet. Events are always overtaking the U.N. and the whole system is rightfully in a constant state of change and reform. But here in my book is a collection of telling moments of the kind of work that goes on day and night at the U.N. I hope that its heartbeat can be felt in every chapter.

Most important of all I have tried to show how the U.N. fits together and interacts as one organization. There is no modern political organization where it is so clear that the whole is greater than the sum of its parts.

I have often despaired at the slow pace that things go forward. It is ironic that the faster more people want to strengthen the U.N. framework of law, the slower the process that it actually happens. But gradually I have come to believe that there is no other democratic way to move forward. Law—especially international law—cannot be created in a day. And at the U.N. no less than 185 member states are making the laws together. For example, it took fourteen years to complete the Law of the Sea. So much of the work of the U.N. lies on the frontiers of human experience, and this is what makes it so fascinating. Also nowadays the nations must take into account the views of a wide range of Non-Governmental Organizations whose numbers and effectiveness are increasing every year. Despite all the difficulties, an international framework for human and planetary security is slowly and steadily rising. It is unfortunate that too many nations are still reluctant to fulfill their legal obligations to pay for and to implement what they have so laboriously been putting in place.

Fortunately the U.N. can surprise even itself. In the early nineties a complete ban on landmines and the creation of an International Criminal Court seemed outside the realm of practical politics. Then suddenly in 1998, the impossible became a reality.

I began this book by recalling my childhood memories of a world at war. Those long years of fear and anxiety made me appreciate just what Dag Hammarskjöld meant when he said the U.N. is the product of a nightmare, not a dream. We have travelled a long way since that nightmare and as never before the rights of the individual have been carefully defined and protected. And as regards the practicalities of daily living, whether it is for trading or simply for our health and survival, it is so often U.N. laws that set them up in good order. The U.N., in fact, has become part of the DNA of the modern world.

I end my book with the hope that Member States, urged on by civil society, will do much more than they have so far to find the resources, both the people and the funding, to put the U.N. on a really secure footing for the future. In February 1999, the Member States owed the U.N. $2 billion, a figure which includes the cost of peacekeeping. Only if loyalty and commitment to the U.N. increase, then will it be possible to shape a U.N. that will safeguard the security and peace of our global community in the 21st century.

List of Abbreviations

ECA	Economic Commission for Africa
ECE	Economic Commission for Europe
ECLAC	Economic Commission for Latin America and the Caribbean
ESCAP	Economic and Social Commission for Asia and the Pacific
ESCWA	Economic and Social Commission for Western Asia
FAO	Food and Agriculture Organization of the United Nations
GATT	General Agreement on Tariffs and Trade
IAEA	International Atomic Energy Agency
IBRD	International Bank for Reconstruction and Development (World Bank)
ICAO	International Civil Aviation Organization
IDA	International Development Association
IFAD	International Fund for Agricultural Development
IFC	International Finance Corporation
ILO	International Labour Organisation
IMF	International Monetary Fund
IMO	International Maritime Organization
INSTRAW	International Research and Training Institute for the Advancement of Women
ITU	International Telecommunication Union
ONUVEN	United Nations Observer Mission for the Verification of the Elections in Nicaragua
UNAVEM	United Nations Angola Verification Mission
UNCHS	United Nations Centre for Human Settlements (Habitat)
UNCTAD	United Nations Conference on Trade and Development
UNDOF	United Nations Disengagement Observer Force
UNDP	United Nations Development Programme
UNDRO	Office of the United Nations Disaster Relief Co-ordinator
UNEP	United Nations Environment Programme
UNESCO	United Nations Educational, Scientific and Cultural Organization
UNFICYP	United Nations Peacekeeping Force in Cyprus
UNFPA	United Nations Population Fund
UNGOMAP	United Nations Good Offices Mission in Afghanistan and Pakistan
UNHCR	Office of the United Nations High Commissioner for Refugees
UNICEF	United Nations Children's Fund
UNIDIR	United Nations Institute for Disarmament Research

UNIDO	United Nations Industrial Development Organization
UNIFIL	United Nations Interim Force in Lebanon
UNIIMOG	United Nations Iran-Iraq Military Observer Group
UNITAR	United Nations Institute for Training and Research
UNMOGIP	United Nations Military Observer Group in India and Pakistan
UNRISD	United Nations Research Institute for Social Development
UNRWA	United Nations Relief and Works Agency for Palestine Refugees in the Near East
UNSO	United Nations Sudano-Sahelian Office
UNTAG	United Nations Transition Assistance Group
UNTSO	United Nations Truce Supervision Organization
UNU	United Nations University
UNV	United Nations Volunteers
UPU	Universal Postal Union
WFC	World Food Council
WFP	World Food Programme
WHO	World Health Organization
WIPO	World Intellectual Property Organization
WMO	World Maritime Organization

Index

362